Constitutional Reform in America

Constitutional Reform in America

ESSAYS ON THE SEPARATION OF POWERS

Charles M. Hardin

IOWA STATE UNIVERSITY PRESS / AMES

To Sallie and Julia

Charles M. Hardin is Professor Emeritus, Political Science Department,
University of California, Davis

© 1989 Iowa State University Press, Ames, Iowa 50010
All rights reserved

Manufactured in the United States of America

First edition, 1989

Library of Congress Cataloging-in-Publication Data

Hardin, Charles M. (Charles Meyer)
    Constitutional reform in America : essays on the separation of powers / Charles M. Hardin. — 1st ed.
      p. cm.
    Includes index.
    ISBN 0-8138-0118-4
    1. Separation of powers—United States. I. Title.
KF4565.A75H37 1989
342.73′044—dc19
[347.30244]   89–1736
                                                   CIP

Contents

Foreword

Since the earliest days of our existence as an independent nation, Americans have been taught and have believed that the principle of power divided between the executive and legislature is an important part of our constitutional system and essential to their freedom from oppression.

Professor Charles Hardin, a distinguished political scientist at the University of California, in this perceptive treatise on the constitution argues persuasively that in fragmenting the power of government the separation of powers undermines constitutional democracy and threatens the security and freedom of the people. Obviously this is a very controversial question and will surely arouse great interest in the question in view of the performance of our country during the past quarter of a century.

The performance of our government not only concerns Americans, but our best friends are perhaps even more alarmed than most Americans. Recently the *Wall Street Journal* printed a piece by a prominent official of a friendly allied government, which graphically describes this alarm. He wrote:

> Throughout most of the civilized world Americans are regarded with admiration, sometimes with envy and often with affection. That the U.S. government enjoys neither the confidence of its friends nor the respect of its opponents is due to the faltering performance of the institution of government. In foreign policy these institutions are uncertain and vacillating. Will the policy of the president or that of the Congress prevail. Or will we get a lame compromise between incompatibles.

Professor Hardin in clear and concise terms puts the responsibility for this faltering and uncertain performance upon the separation of powers. Not only does it lead to a stalemate in the operation of the decision-making procedure of the government, but the electoral system which results from the separation does not provide experienced people to guide and administer the complex affairs of the government. The electoral procedure presently followed often brings people to positions of vital importance to the country, people without any previous experience in the affairs of the nation especially in the vastly complicated field of foreign affairs, which now embrace practically every area of the planet.

Aside from the concern of our foreign friends, recent developments among members of the Senate illustrate a fundamental weakness resulting from the separation of power. A recent headline in the *Washington Post* reads: "Frustration without achievement in the Senate. For many weary lawmakers, Institution is losing its attraction."

The text of the article describes the recent decisions of some of the six Senators to retire from the Senate because of "the frustration with the Senate itself—with a life that demands all of one's time and energy without a compensating sense of achievement."

A system which is not attractive to men of judgment, ability, and integrity is not likely to provide the competent leadership which our nation requires to protect adequately the interests of our people.

The separation of power, says Professor Hardin, so fragments the power of the government that it cannot effectively compete with the myriad of special interests which have achieved the capacity to use the institutions of government for their own interests often in derogation of the public's interest. The fundamental question occurs: Is the interest of the people, of the nation as a whole, better served by people chosen by the citizens in popular elections or by the lobbyists employed by various private interests or by foreign governments?

This is a question all Americans should consider seriously, and for that purpose they should read Professor Hardin's superb treatise.

J. W. FULBRIGHT

Preface

In 1974, at the height of the Watergate crisis, I published a book on constitutional reform in the United States.[1] The product of seventeen years of oft-interrupted work, it still represents my systematic thoughts on the subject. In the 1980s, however, things changed. The question of fundamental constitutional reform seized a remarkably large group of experienced and knowledgeable people who became members of the Committee on the Constitutional System (CCS)— the name was suggested by James MacGregor Burns to embrace not only the Constitution but also the institutions and governmental processes that flesh it out and try to make it work, especially political parties.

Formed in a small meeting in Washington, D.C., in January 1981, convened to see whether men and women of affairs and political scientists could usefully confer on the subject, the CCS was incorporated in 1982, with a Washington office and a board of directors chaired by C. Douglas Dillon, Lloyd N. Cutler, and Senator Nancy Landon Kassebaum. Meeting biannually, the Committee produced a workbook based on the following assumptions and aims:[2]

> Government deficits, the spiraling imbalance of trade, inconsistencies in foreign policy, illegal immigration, unemployment, the decay of our cities, the abuse of the environment, the staggering cost of elections, and the piracy of special interest groups — these problems and a host of others have led thoughtful citizens to question whether our political system is capable of meeting the challenge of modern government. . . . [Such problems] demand a reassessment [that] is being undertaken by the Committee on the Constitutional System [whose membership includes] present and former members of the Senate and House, Cabinet and White House staff, governors, party officials, members of academia, journalists, lawyers, and labor, business, and

financial leaders [and whose purpose is to assess] the performance of our governing institutions and to stimulate a nationwide
debate about alternative structures and processes.

The CCS responded early to statements from Messrs. Dillon,
Cutler, former Senator J. William Fulbright, and Congressman
Henry S. Reuss. In addition there was the alluring hope of substantial funds from the McDonnell Foundation, just established in memory of the founder of McDonnell Douglas, who had reportedly become convinced that the United States could not safely continue with
the separation of powers. In the end, another generation saw things
differently and the CCS got no McDonnell funds. But "Mr. Mac's"
close relationship with an early head of the Brookings Institution
helped bring valuable support to the CCS; and he left another herit-
age: he had wanted "to see some action" instead of mere academic
talk; and that appealed to men and women of affairs. Five million
dollars from a single source, a major element in the armaments industry, might have become an embarrassment of riches to the CCS.
Nevertheless, the erstwhile "promise" was an important spur.

I organized the 1981 meeting from which the CCS emerged.
After 1974 and a flurry of activity respecting constitutional reform, I
had retired in 1976 and returned to research on agricultural policy. In
1979 a distinguished political scientist, Ferdinand A. Hermens,
wrote that he was using my 1974 book in seminars at the American
University in Washington, D.C. On December 23, 1979, James B.
Reston reported in the *New York Times* a speech by C. Douglas
Dillon that contained a strong criticism of the separation of powers
between the president and the Congress. Then on March 8, 1980,
Richard Strout reported in the TRB column of the *New Republic* that
Professor William Kreml was running in the South Carolina primary
against Senator Hollings on the platform that the United States
should adopt a parliamentary system and that three other political
scientists from Syracuse, American University, and the University of
North Carolina were supporting him. I wrote Mr. Dillon to ask if a
group of men and women of affairs might profitably meet to confer
with a few academicians on the subject. He agreed to finance and
attend such a meeting.

Since early in 1980, then, I have devoted myself to this subject.
I wrote a restatement of my earlier argument entitled "Constitutional

Reform in the United States: Renewing the Debate," that J. William Fulbright introduced into the hearings on *Political Economy and Constitutional Reform* held by the Joint Economic Committee chaired by Congressman Henry S. Reuss.[3] I also wrote a paper on Great Britain to anticipate the criticism of that country's difficulties because any constitutional alternative to the separation of powers will almost certainly embrace salient elements of the parliamentary system of which Britain is the classical example. I followed this with a review of Samuel H. Beer, *Britain Against Herself.* These three papers are included in this volume.

In 1983 I was invited to write a paper for a symposium of the American Enterprise Institute on the separation of powers.[4] In preparation, I turned to Charles H. McIlwain, *Constitutionalism: Ancient and Modern.*[5] It was a revelation to me. I was chagrined to have overlooked it so long. For McIlwain's conclusion to this ultimate flowering of his lifetime's research was that the separation of powers posed a threat to constitutional government itself.

This point is critical. It is not simply that the separation of powers leads to deadlock (or gridlock) and stalemate; or that it prevents finding a quick, legitimate, civil way of replacing a president who has failed politically; or that it condemns us to fixed calendar elections with their grievous faults rather than permitting elections on discretion of the government-of-the-day. It is rather, in keeping with Occam's razor, that the separation of powers poses a deadly danger to constitutional government itself.

Absurd! the critics will cry: The country has survived 200 years! It has, indeed, but after a shaky start this country was long blessed, endowed and insulated. Not only was there "enough and to spare in common for all" (John Locke) and "in America you have it better" (Goethe); there was the uniquely favorable isolation that Thomas A. Bailey wittily described as "a country bounded on the north and south by weak neighbors and on the east and west by fish." The Civil War, the one great test, brought forth worrisome flirtations with military coups. But our time of repeated peril, in relentlessly recurrent spasms, began only after the Second World War.

So, back to McIlwain. Why had I not invoked him sooner? In 1938–39 when he prepared and gave the Messenger lectures at Cornell that became *Constitutionalism: Ancient and Modern*, I had taken his celebrated course in English Constitutional History and audited his equally famous History of Political Thought. I had listened to him for six hours a week and had read him widely. But this vehement and categorical criticism of the separation of powers was not mentioned in either of his courses. Why not? Because each course ended before he reached the period in which the American constitution was written.

The first reason for this book then is to urge over and over again that McIlwain stated the essential problem of the separation of powers: that it undermines constitutional government itself. I found that McIlwain's indictment illuminated and gave point to the argument in one situation after another, on one issue after another, as I hope to have illustrated in the chapters on Belz, on the Friendly-Elliott book, on Price, on Sundquist, and on Wilson as well as in the chapter on Gramm-Rudman-Hollings, the *Synar* decision. I also invoked McIlwain in my paper for the American Enterprise Institute (AEI) symposium and only regret that I did not then perceive what I later understood to be his significance and insist that his stricture against the separation of powers become the central issue of the AEI conference!

There is a second reason for this book. Too often constitutional democracy is taken for granted. It is something with which we are endowed, like the temperate zone in which we live and the two great oceans that protect us. There is much glib talk about democracy (Secretary of State George Shultz: "Democracy is on a roll!") without enough evidence of awareness of the constant dangers to it, other than the threat from Soviet Communism. But the future of constitutional government is never guaranteed; it may be strong and resilient; it is always in danger.

My own conception of the danger was formed by my experience at Harvard from 1938 to 1945. Grave concern about constitutionalism was general, as people watched one after another European constitutional democracy succumb to fascism. My first university teaching experience was in Government 1 sections in 1940, the year that France fell. As I am at least half and maybe three-fourths German extraction, I became painfully conscious that it was only luck to have been twenty-five in 1933 in FDR's America rather than in Hitler's Germany. On Harvard's faculty, Elliott, Friedrich, Herring, Holcombe, Wright, Watkins, and Emerson all wrote on the subject; but none seem to me, in retrospect, as penetrating as McIlwain.

For McIlwain constitutional government was achieved through the uneasy cohabitation of *gubernaculum* (the political, administrative, institutionalized, sovereignty) with *jurisdictio* (the institutions and procedures that gave life to the rule of law). However uneasily, these two must coexist; each must be strengthened; each must accord the other its due. I know that there is resistance to McIlwain's Latin terminology. He was not an obscurantist. He was as lucid as he was scholarly. If he used Latin it was not only because the origin of the ideas was Roman. If we substitute "government" for gubernaculum and say that the separation of powers undermines government, what does government mean — the post office, the IRS, the INS, the FBI, the ubiquitous military, and maybe the county agricultural agent? None of these appears to founder; all flourish. To think about these things we need terminology with some precision. And, important as it is, we have to go beyond reverence for the document itself, the written Constitution. The text itself is no guarantee of its own viability any more than the marriage contract ensures a happy and enduring marriage; only living together, day in and day out, year in and year out, can do that.

So the second reason for this book is to insist again on the gravity of the problem. Constitutional democracy is arguably the greatest secular achievement of human beings, but it has an inherent vulnerability. And this leads to a third reason for publishing: to stress the need for an educational approach. I respect the desire of the political people on the CCS to press for something concrete. The most sense is made by the 4-8-4 proposal: elect all the House of Representatives, together with the president and half the Senate (with senatorial terms extended to eight years) every four years. Yet the roots of the problem are much deeper.

The relevance of these three arguments — that the constitutional problem roots in the separation of powers, that constitutional democracy is always at risk, and that the approach to the problem needs to be persistently, thoroughly, and enduringly educational — underly the significance of this collection.

Acknowledgments

Without implying that they agree with my analysis, I acknowledge an extraordinary debt to many professional colleagues. George Downs, now of Princeton, first suggested that I organize the meeting from which the Committee on the Constitutional System emerged. He and others at Davis, especially Larry Berman, John Freeman, Alexander Groth, John Owens, Randolph Siverson, Larry Wade, and Geoffrey Wandesforde-Smith gave valuable criticism and generous support. Elsewhere, Austin Ranney, of the University of California, Berkeley, was very important in encouraging this book. James Mac-Gregor Burns of Williams College; Ferdinand A. Hermens, American University; Dean McHenry, former Chancellor of the University of California, Santa Cruz; the late Robert E. Osgood, former Dean of S.A.I.S.; and Dwight Waldo formerly of Syracuse all were extremely helpful. A much longer list of political scientists, many of who are quoted in Chapter 11, gave valuable encouragement. All this strengthens my belief that my appeal to the profession to mount and sustain a profound inquiry into the viability of our separation of powers will not be in vain.

Constitutional Reform in America

1
Constitutional Reform in the United States

AS in 1973–74 so in 1980, concern has mounted over the adequacy of the United States Constitution. Congressmen Richard Bolling and Henry S. Reuss, Senator Patrick Moynihan, and Walter Cronkite have all made statements declaring their concern. TRB of the *New Republic* (Richard Strout) has repeatedly returned to the issue. For the first time a number of political scientists in major universities have publicly urged America to consider the parliamentary system as an alternative. A forthright statement by C. Douglas Dillon called into question the central institution of the American version of the separation of powers.

"What we are suffering from today is not incompetence in our Foreign Service, or in our intelligence services or in the office of the President. Unfortunately our problem gives every sign of being much more serious than that. It is, in my view, the beginning of a crisis in the operation of our basic system of government.

"We must learn to accustom ourselves to a new world, a world in which actions taken by others can have rapid and serious effects on our economy and on our standards of living, a world in which others have the military means to destroy our nation whenever they are prepared to accept the consequences. *I very much doubt that in such a world we can long continue to afford the luxury of the division of power and responsibility between our Executive and Legislative branches of government*" (italics added).[1]

Mr. Dillon has formidable credentials. He was undersecretary of state for economic affairs in the Eisenhower administration. John F. Kennedy appointed him secretary of the treasury, and he was a member of the famous ExCom or Executive Committee in the Cuban missile crisis.

If the separation of powers is questioned, it is logical to assume that the questioner has an alternative in mind. One alternative is the parliamentary system in which the executive is lodged in a committee representing the majority in the legislature. The United Kingdom provides the most common but not the only model. In his presidential address to the American Political Science Association convention in 1979, Professor Leon D. Epstein examined the British model of party government that after World War II had seemed to some American political scientists to provide an attractive alternative in the search for attaining more responsible government. Epstein's scholarly examination concluded: "What hopes we have (for a better political world) must evidently depend on using our own political institutions rather than trying to reshape them according to an operating model in some other country."[2]

Thus Professor Epstein, an eminent authority on comparative political parties as well as on British politics, seems to controvert the assumption that I have inferred from Mr. Dillon's criticism. But I shall offer a different view of the problems that compel a search for what Epstein calls a "better political world." The travail of the American political system transcends the one raised by Professor Epstein. I shall list several flaws that lead me to conclusions like those that Mr. Dillon has reached, arguing that the parliamentary system appears to provide either a cure for them or, at least, a promise that the effects of these flaws may be significantly lessened.

In invoking the parliamentary system, I am painfully conscious of the risk of going abroad to find solutions for problems that have risen at home. Louis Fisher has urged that the Framers of the 1787 Constitution heavily grounded their arguments "on what had been learned at home" rather than on the theoretical writings of Montesquieu or any other writer.[3] What I shall say about flaws in the American system will be largely based on what has been learned at home. But if the flaws are the outgrowth of the institutional arrangements that the Framers devised, then it is logical to look elsewhere for different arrangements. Indeed, even the perception of flaws in the working of institutional arrangements may require some comparison with other arrangements that seem to work better.

Professor Epstein's Argument

According to the professor, the chief explanation of the attraction of British parliamentary government for American political scientists of the "moderate left" lay in its ability to translate the presumed liberal, New Deal dispositions of the electoral majority into political programs and actions. In England parliamentary candidates compete in elections based on single-member constituencies, the winner of a plurality becoming the victor. That arrangement "helps mightily" to reduce the number of significant political parties and to produce a majority government even though the victorious party's plurality may be well under 50 percent of the total vote.[4] Members of Parliament (M.P.'s) then generally accept party discipline. They vote up or down as the government (or the Opposition front bench) has decided and as they are told to do by the whips. They are sustained in (or constrained to) this behavior by their ideological commitment to the party's platform, by their conception of the sanction given the platform by the voters, by their awareness of the enthusiastic loyalty to the government (or the Opposition) of the constituency party leaders to whom they owe their nominations and perhaps their elections, and/or by their fear that if, as a majority, they vote against the government they may cause its defeat and resignation with the odious consequence that the Opposition would receive the royal summons to govern — or (more likely) that the government would ask for a dissolution of Parliament, which would bring on an equally odious alternative, a new election.

Epstein suggests that this interpretation seemed vindicated by considerable evidence from 1945 to about 1968. But in the 1970s the British system could not be counted on to produce a "cohesive parliamentary democracy as it had during the previous three or four decades."[5] Whether Britain should join the European Economic Community provided the most significant policy choice in the decade and perhaps in the last forty years. British membership rested on a bipartisan parliamentary majority. Both major parties split. Moreover, a comparison of the 1950s with the 1970s shows a sharp fall in party cohesiveness in parliamentary voting on other matters. The Conservative government, 1970–1974, was defeated five times. In one whipped division, the government suffered a defection of two-thirds of its own members. These losses occurred even though the

Conservative majority was very thin, a circumstance usually considered conducive to stronger party discipline. The Labour government of 1976–79 finally resigned in April when it lost a vote of confidence wherein nearly all minority party members had voted with the Opposition. In the previous three years, however, "Prime Minister Callaghan remained in office . . . despite unreversed parliamentary defeats of several of his government's important policies." Thus, the system "had worked differently from the way in which many of us had told our students that it had worked in the postwar decades."[6]

Nevertheless, Epstein acknowledged a strong hankering among many American political scientists for more cohesive, more disciplined parties that would enable administrations in the United States to concert policies and carry them into effect more expeditiously. Moreover, he did say that American political scientists can "still appreciate that M.P.'s, while never as regularly docile as the most extreme pictures of party discipline might have implied, remained in the 1970s much more regularly loyal to their parties than American congressional representatives ever have been." And this: "Although Americans still have good reason to view each major British party as relatively cohesive and capable of responsible government, now as in the rest of the last century, we must qualify the sharper picture that we had a little earlier."[7]

What have we then? With all its problems of internal cohesion British party government may still properly seem attractive to American yearnings after stronger, more centralized, more disciplined— yes, more responsible— political parties. This would not only be true of the moderate left. Mrs. Thatcher's government may convince the moderate right of the same virtues.[8]

The grievous difficulties of adopting parliamentary government in the United States remain. There are profound risks and uncertainties. We have a continental system, plus Hawaii. It is markedly heterogeneous. It has a strikingly different political culture from Britain, West Germany, or Japan (but so do they all from each other; yet the parliamentary system works in each), and our system's pluralistic emphasis on group development has produced a flowering of interests each bent on achieving all it can, regardless of the consequences. All these distinctive features have long histories.

But we cannot stop there. The dangers that threaten our system are real: the politicization of every interest and issue, unremitting

campaigns and elections that settle very little, groupistic politics continually verging on anarchy and virtually achieving it in various localities, public opinion becoming more confused and disgruntled, and
the recent experience with inflation that nearly surged out of control.
In one form or another we may have drastic political change forced
on us.

What, then, are the flaws in the American system that the
parliamentary system appears able to cure or to ameliorate?

Replacing a Politically Disabled President

The first and primary weakness of the American system is its
inability to replace a president who has become *politically* (not necessarily physically or mentally) disabled. This is a weakness apparent in
one American institution that has been widely and rightly regarded
as having great virtues, the American presidency. Clinton Rossiter's
injunction, "Leave your presidency alone!" still rings in our ears. But
with all respect to his memory, we cannot safely do that. I shall give
only one example.

In 1940 it was probably crucial to Britain (and it may have been
equally so to the survival of the United States and to western constitutional democracy generally) that Neville Chamberlain be replaced.
This could not have happened in the United States. Hitler's panzers
and stukas would not have waited while the impeachment process,
assuming that it was relevant to the situation, rumbled into play.
This is expressed best by Winston Churchill, Chamberlain's successor. "The loyalties which center on number one are enormous. If he
trips he must be sustained. If he makes mistakes they must be covered. If he sleeps he must not be wantonly disturbed. If he is no
good he must be pole-axed."[9]

The inability quickly to replace the American president is a
constitutional flaw of first importance. It is separate and apart from
any disability that may have appeared in Britain in the 1970s to
maintain cohesive party discipline when confronted by extraordinarily difficult and divisive policy choices. The parliamentary system,
even though party discipline falters considerably, would still be able
to replace a prime minister who had become politically incompetent.
In Britain—but also in West Germany and Japan—it is standard (if,

fortunately, infrequent) operating procedure. Replacement is accepted by all parties in government, by "the constituent group," and
by the public. In order to operate effectively there must be well-
organized, responsible political parties—in the legislature, where the
action takes place. In 1940 Neville Chamberlain said, "I call upon
my friends." Most of them responded. But forty-one Conservatives
crossed the House of Commons to vote against him, and a considerable number abstained. His long-time friend L. S. Amery spoke the
words to him that Cromwell had used against the Long Parliament:
"You have sat too long here for any good you are doing. Depart, I say
and let us have done with you. In the name of God, go!"[10] Perhaps
even more important, the Labour party decided to oppose. Just as an
opposition party's natural function is to oppose in peacetime so in
war its natural place is in alliance with the government.[11] Hence
Labour's move into opposition showed that Chamberlain was now
insupportable.

Just as it is necessary for a great power to have a strong leader, so
is it necessary to have a known and settled way of getting rid of him
in an extremity. But there are also times when a leader who is per-
forming suitably, in general, may be prone to imperial mischief,
which calls not for removal but for chastening.

Government by Presidential Whim or Instinct

This second flaw in our Constitution also inheres in the presidency and produces government by presidential whim, idiosyncrasy,
or instinct. An excellent example, I think, was President Franklin
Roosevelt's scheme to enlarge (pack) the Supreme Court in 1937.
That possibility was first suggested to me in 1943 by Chester C.
Davis, then president of the Federal Reserve Bank of St. Louis. Mr.
Davis had just returned from Washington where he had served
briefly as the first war food administrator. He had resigned or been
fired or maybe it was a little of both. Still smarting, he suggested
that my current project, federal-state relations, although important,
paled in comparison to problems involving the accountability of the
president. His most compelling illustration was the meeting wherein
FDR disclosed his plan for the Supreme Court. As head of the Agricultural Adjustment Administration, Mr. Davis was included. At one

point President Roosevelt went around the table, calling for support. "Chester, you clear this with the farmers." Davis told the president that farmers would be very disturbed at any effort to change the Supreme Court. "And then FDR's eyes got glassy the way they always did when anyone disagreed with him."

That incident stuck in my mind where it was reinforced by others until I became convinced that it represented a serious problem. I was happy to find George E. Reedy discussing it under the heading, "The American Monarchy."[12] It is a characteristic of chief executives generally, but it is brought to its most significant and potentially dangerous pitch (within constitutional democracies) in the president of the United States.

At the same time one must quickly reassert that the virtues of the single president remain, as Alexander Hamilton laid them out in *Federalist* No. 70. Energy is essential in the executive. To have energy, the executive must be lodged in one person who must have a sufficient duration in office, and assurance of adequate support, and sufficient powers. Unity in the president, Hamilton considered axiomatic. "Decision, activity, secrecy, and despatch will generally characterize the proceedings of one man."

But if these are the virtues of a single presidency, each contains its peculiar dangers. Every president I have studied seems to provide examples of the undue exercise of presidential whim or mindsets.[13] Examples appear, I should argue, in the terms of every incumbent since Franklin D. Roosevelt, with his policies toward China and his idiosyncratic economics. Examples are most dramatic and disturbing in foreign and military policy, as the Pentagon Papers show, especially when supplemented by the Cambodian invasion of 1971 and the various military initiatives of President Nixon in 1972. Many significant examples occur in domestic policy, such as President Truman's support of an inflationary monetary policy in 1950–1951, President Eisenhower's persistence in a restrictive fiscal policy in 1959–60, and Lyndon B. Johnson's rejection of a surtax to finance Vietnam expenditures in 1966–67.[14] President Ford's precipitous pardon of Mr. Nixon and his action in the *Mayaguez* incident may be illustrative. So may President Carter's admission of the shah of Iran to the United States in 1979 as well as his effort to rescue the American hostages in Tehran in 1980. Western European allies were wracked by the fear of President Carter's unchecked and impulsive actions in the spring of 1980 (or, paradoxically, wracked alternatively by the fear of his impulse and the dread of his impotence).

What to do about government by presidential whim? James David Barber's analysis of presidential character may be relevant. He finds that persons with a certain character type that he calls active-negative are prone to commit themselves to disastrous courses of action.[15] Following his analysis, such persons should be diagnosed and eliminated during the process of selecting presidents (but how?); alternatively, the associates of presidents can counsel them against actions for which they show a dangerous proclivity.

But it is precisely this kind of chastening counsel that the close associates of the president are inherently incapable of providing. I find George E. Reedy more persuasive in that the office of the president in a sense demoralizes its occupants, whatever their character types. No one talks to the president "like a Dutch uncle." Rather, there is an "environment of deference, approaching sycophancy."[16]

The parliamentary system provides a specific antidote for the disease of government by presidential instinct or impulse. It offers a check to the expanding ego of the chief executive (prime minister) by requiring that he must face his counterpart, the leader of the opposition, in debate. For example, Samuel H. Beer, writing on the British "question period," said "it has been reported that a British Prime Minister, after referring sourly to the lofty unapproachability of President de Gaulle and of the effect on him of the deference of his 'court,' added that if the President of France had to come down to the House twice a week and stand up to a running fire of questions, this deferential attitude surely would be attenuated."[17]

Here we are again at the heart of the parliamentary system. It works not by separating the executive and the legislative but by bringing them together. W. Ivor Jennings wrote, "To find out whether a people is free it is necessary only to ask if there is an Opposition and, if there is, to ask where it is."[18] If the loser in the race for the presidency were given a seat in the House of Representatives along with certain powers and accessories, a constitutional convention or practice should develop that the president was regularly expected to defend himself and his government in that forum. This should also counter another defect in our present constitutional system, the tendency to endow the president with undue eminence as the recreation of the sovereign people.

The President: Legitimized but Not Deified

It has long been noted that the president tends to embody the American people.[19] Even before his election, George Washington was capable of personifying the "awful majesty of the American people" to an extent that unmanned at least one of his associates. Such a living symbol of national unity may have been essential to the young nation, but its continuation after two hundred years may become a threat because it deepens and strengthens the delusion of grandeur. Yet is has recently become almost a stereotype. "I and the American people have decided . . . " "I and the American people can no longer tolerate . . . " Unfortunately, the saving element of the ludicrous in such hyperboles diminishes to nothing as one approaches the throne.

But if the president is there because he is the leader of a winning party; if he has been nominated by party leaders, some of whom surround him and support him but who, in a grave emergency, might remove him and replace him with another; and if he must repeatedly face in debate the opponent he defeated in the last election but whose legitimacy rests on a pyramid of votes only a little less imposing than his own, *then* the presidency would be changed. The president would no longer embody the awful majesty of the American people. Rather, he would speak for the nation as leader of the victorious majority party. Certainly his credentials should be sufficiently impressive. But legitimation does not require deification.

Calendar Elections: Self-Inflicted Wounds

Still other weaknesses appear in calendar elections that compound a number of ills. First, in war they present enemies the tremendous advantage of acting when we are most vulnerable. Fortunately we have had presidential elections only twice during major wars since 1812, in 1864 and 1944. This point seems obvious. In Britain the Parliamentary Act of 1911 required elections every five years (reduced from seven). It was immediately breached during the First World War so that the first general election held in Britain after 1911 was in December 1918. Because of the Second World War, no general election was held between 1935 and 1945 (by-elections were held in both wars). A corollary holds when the country is not actually at war but (as now continually) is under grave threat. Presidential (and even off-year congressional) elections provide potential enemies with opportunities to harass the United States during peculiarly vulnerable periods.

A second unfortunate consequence of calendar elections is the endless protraction of campaigns. There is no need to devote an entire year (or more) to the nomination and election of a president or of other political office holders. British law stipulates that when Parliament is dissolved, an election must be postponed three weeks (to prevent the government's exploiting a sudden upsurge of public support by calling a snap election) and held within six weeks. Under calendar elections, by contrast, the "outs" are prompted to enter the field early; the "ins" cannot let them have this advantage, so the competitive stimulus to extend campaigns is irresistible. Moreover, calendar elections lend themselves to elaborate nominating procedures. Among political scientists there probably is no more unanimous agreement that that primary elections are unfortunate and that it would be preferable to charge party leaders with the task of nominating candidates — and at the same time to make them accept the responsibility for the quality of the nominees.

Nearly all knowledgeable people now want American political parties strengthened. To do so requires that control over nominations be restored to political parties. Primaries that all too often have proved a travesty on democracy should be ended. We should heed the counsel of the late E. E. Schattschneider, "Democracy exists *between*, not *within*, the parties." Party cohesiveness in legislatures would increase. They could then more easily concert policies. Responsible government (as Epstein defines it) would be enhanced.

Other advantages should also stem from ending calendar elections. The effect of money in campaigns would decline. One simply cannot spend as much in five weeks as in a year. Laws restricting campaign contributions by groups, corporations, associations, and individuals and constraining expenditures by parties, politicians, and others will be more enforceable and effective. The ability of organized groups to influence primary nominations and elections (I refer especially to the political action committees or PACS) will decline because it will be much harder to keep such organizations intact during long periods in the thought that an election *might* be called.

Moreover, the PACs would have less incentive to form because, with the disappearance of primary elections, they would lose much of their organized leverage to enforce commitments from candidates forced to enter sparsely patronized primaries.

As the role of money in campaigns would decline so would the incumbent president's use of spoils to ensure his renomination in presidential primaries. These would disappear. There would be no time for them. In 1980 Mr. Carter's use of spoils — exacerbated by the rise in state primaries from sixteen in 1968 to thirty-seven — was notorious. Some commentators congratulated him on his skill in the "great game of politics." But, in Neustadt's classic analysis of the president as educator, what kind of "lesson" did he "teach" the public already profoundly disillusioned with government and politicians?[20]

Finally, there is television's role in pumping up the image of candidates. The art of the demagogue is ancient as the origin of the term implies. But the consensus is strong that television has added its own inimitable perversions. The dangerous overdevelopment of "image" politics is one theme of James David Barber, in *The Pulse of Politics: Electing Presidents in the Media Age.* "Leader-mass politics is inherently unstable; given our Constitutional arrangements it is governmentally unworkable. There are grave risks in proceeding as at present." Reviewing Barber, Walter Dean Burnham says, "Just so . . . Barber's whole book leads to the core proposition quoted above . . . If Barber is serious about this, he must also conclude that these constitutional arrangements must be sweepingly — and soon — changed."[21] Thus, two well-known political scientists have recently proclaimed the need for fundamental constitutional reform. Their aims should be realized by the adaptation of parliamentary government.

The American Separation of Powers: Preliminary Summary

If the foregoing argument is persuasive, the reader will see that the fundamental flaw in the Constitution lies in the particular form that the separation of powers takes. To correct the flaws (or, at least, to mitigate their ill effects) one is prompted to turn to some version of the parliamentary system. If a president who fails in a dire emergency is to be replaced, it can be done by party leaders who, if they are responsible, must occupy central positions in a government that, if it is to be in some essential way a "government of laws," must form the law-making body. *Hence, the executive and legislative powers would be joined, not separated.* If a generally successful president still requires chastening, it can be done by subjecting him to debate with the one adversary who, in terms of his own electoral base, is the president's peer, namely, the major-party loser in the previous presidential campaign who would assume the leadership of the minority party in Congress. In the same way, providing the losing presidential candidate with a seat in the House of Representatives would encourage the development of an organized, centralized, and focused opposition that would logically evolve to create an alternative government. *The new separation of powers would replace the struggle of executive versus legislature with a struggle of government versus opposition.* Happily this may also remove the Olympian halo from the president as the embodiment of the people (whose voice is the voice of God) while leaving him with a sufficiently legitimizing cachet as leader of the governing majority.

The same is true if we are to escape the straightjacket of calendar elections. The alternative is election on dissolution. Dissolution is obtained by the leader of the government either after a loss of a vote of confidence in the legislature or, with a legislative majority behind him, because he feels that the time is ripe — or the need is great — for a renewal of his mandate to govern by the electorate. In any event, the legislature is intimately and unavoidably involved in the decision.

The Destructiveness of the Executive-Legislative Struggle

This by no means ends the bill of particulars against the separation of powers, American style. Presidential-congressional relations verge on an impasse. The Constitution divides and allocates power to create what has felicitously been described as "separated institutions sharing powers." The theory was elegantly stated by James Madison in *Federalist* No. 47. But the theory often obscures the fact of a struggle in which one side wins too much the victory. Consider the Japanese and Chinese Exclusion Act of 1924 and the Smoot-Hawley

Tariff of 1930. The first, A. N. Holcombe believed, helped put the Japanese on a road that led directly to Pearl Harbor. The second contributed to the worldwide depression that opened the path for Adolf Hitler. It is not simply that these were bad laws made by Congress. Presidents also make grave mistakes. But these congressional laws were classical expressions of the genius of Congress to act for domestic reasons without regard for the effects on foreign policy.

In a somewhat different way, this time in response to a public mood of revulsion following the Nye Committee Hearings on the "Merchants of Death," Congress passed the Neutrality Act of 1935; a "never again" club flourished in the 1930s just as one did in the early 1970s when the War Powers Act was written in 1974. The neutrality acts, revised and extended, did not inhibit Mussolini's conquest of Ethiopia nor Franco's victory in Spain (with the effective assistance of Mussolini and Hitler). In 1939 President Roosevelt tried to get Congress to repeal the act. Senator Borah, among others, checkmated him. In 1940 Congress did pass the first peacetime conscription act but only for one year; in the summer of 1941 it was reenacted, and it carried by one vote. Such were the signals imparted to Hitler's Germany.

In the 1970s, among other actions, Congress passed the Jackson Amendment that tied the Soviet-American Trade Agreements in 1974 to the freedom of Jews and others to emigrate from the USSR, even though Secretary Kissinger argued that the end could be achieved better by quiet diplomacy. The upshot was that the USSR called off the trade agreement in January 1975. Congress banned arms sales to Turkey pending a Cyprus settlement. In consequence Turkey closed down more than twenty common defense areas that the United States had used to monitor Russian material shipped to the Middle East, as well as the overflight of Soviet planes and Soviet troop movements—e.g., the troop movement in October 1973 that brought about a crisis with the United States in the Yom Kippur War. In the Trade Reform Act of 1975 Congress denied most-favored-nation preference to members of the Organization of Petroleum Exporting Countries (OPEC) in retaliation for the oil embargo; the act applied to Venezuela and Ecuador although they had not joined in the embargo. Years later the incident still rankled in Latin America. In 1980 Congressman Zablocki, chairman of the House Foreign Relations Committee, noted that Congress had passed seventy limiting

amendments on presidential conduct of foreign policy. Congressman
Satterfield said that any president who tests the War Powers Act may
find that he is no longer Commander in Chief, pending the resolution of the question by the courts.

Probably more important by far was the presidential withdrawal
of the SALT II treaty from consideration by the Senate in 1979. The
treaty had been under negotiation for eight years by three American
administrations. Craig R. Whitney, the *New York Times* bureau chief
in Moscow, called SALT II the "centerpiece of detente" that Brezhnev
and Carter signed in Vienna in June 1979. Prospects seemed to be
improving. Then the treaty went to the Senate. Reports multiplied
that it could not be approved. As TRB reported, out of a Congress
with 535 members, 34 Senators can kill a treaty: "The Senate just
delayed action. And the roof fell in." Professor Epstein argues that
when the margin of victory of British Governments falls to 40 percent
their mandate to govern is compromised. But the American Constitution vests the ability to veto a treaty in a handful of Senators who
may have been elected by 10–15 percent of those eligible to vote in
the United States. And we still call it Russian roulette!

Thus, one may explain the growing willingness to ask whether
the United States can still afford its classic version of the separation of
powers now that her isolation—and insulation—has ended. Rising
comprehension of the implications of the nuclear age has been com-
pounded by the growing dependence of the industrialized world on
Arabian oil, so far from the power of the United States, so close to
the Soviet Union, so wracked with the strangeness, the suspicion, the
financial dominance, and the military weakness of Islam. Mixed with
all this is the tension between Israel and the Arab states as well as the
fluctuating animosity between the United States and Russia—para-
noid (perhaps?) Russia has its new fear of revolutionary Islam to the
South, its consciousness of an inimical People's Republic of China to
the East, and its memories of devastating invasions from the West.

We need a foreign policy, a military policy, and an energy policy
that have some coherent relationship one to another and that recognize the mutual interrelationship between and among energy, military preparedness, the economic viability of the industrial West, and
continued coexistence with Russia in a situation in which neither
Russia nor the United States becomes so clearly dominant in the view
of the other that the ultimate war becomes a real alternative. We can

hardly hope to achieve the unity that Hamilton urged in *Federalist* No. 70 when our chief adversary has no surer knowledge of where power resides in the United States than the United States has in Iran.[22]

A parliamentary system, with a government resting on a clear majority, would not guarantee the survival of America in this incredibly dangerous period, but it would improve our chances of achieving the necessary cohesion in policy.[23] It would also provide an institutional basis for a "government of national union" if the tension mounts to the point in which one is clearly needed. But the vested interests in the institutional status quo will make the transition exceedingly difficult.

The "Special Interest State"

Pluralism, long the pride of America, has become a problem. The flowering of interests has intertwined with the rise of the managed economy, of promotional and regulatory government, and of the welfare state to produce a huge governmental apparatus.[24] The growth has been influenced by the nature of our institutions, shaped as these are to encourage decentralization and the proliferation of concentrations of semi-autonomous power. Generalizing broadly, the experience in Congress is indicative. The Progressive reforms of 1911 devolved power from the Speaker of the House into the hands of committees: the LaFollette-Monroney reforms of 1946 helped spread power further into the hands of subcommittees. In the 1970s the movement continued with power now disseminated into the hands of individual members, each with his lavish funds for staff so that he, in effect, would become an operator of a piece of the government.

In this way the triumph of "interest group liberalism" that Theodore W. Lowi deplored in 1969 has been accelerated.[25] The Bentleyian idea and ideal of "no interest without its group" has progressed into "no conceivable interest without its groups, its legislators, its laws, its agencies, and its budgetary entitlements."[26] In consequence, "iron-triangles" or what, following Richard Neustadt, I prefer to call simply "bureaucracies," have multiplied.[27] The result is a splintering of government that may find its rationale in ancient American political and religious beliefs, as Don K. Price has described under the suggestive title, "Irresponsibility as an Article of Faith."[28]

It is also argued by Lester Thurow that the result of the special interest state is inflation. His proposed solution, rare for an economist, is through strengthened political parties that would be able to resist the importunities of interest groups sufficiently to maintain a fiscal and monetary policy able to control inflation.[29]

As I have said repeatedly, a move toward a parliamentary system would (if we were lucky) help strengthen, centralize, and make more responsible our major political parties. Moreover, it could conceivably make for an improvement in public opinion.

The Changeability of Public Moods

Twenty years ago Richard E. Neustadt listed the emergent characteristics of the new politics, including, along with ticket-splitting and the weakening of political parties, the close approach of world events and the changeability of public moods. This is a theme that Walter Lippmann elaborated in his classic *Public Opinion* in 1922 and, again, in *The Public Philosophy* in 1954. Patrick Caddell rediscovered the phenomenon and reported it to President Carter who dwelt on it—uncharacteristically for a man given to the most extravagant praise of the American people—in a speech lamenting the "malaise" of the public in 1979.

One way of attacking the malaise of the public (or its "travail" as I wrote in 1974) is to embrace a theory of a sensible division of labor that would separate the act of creating governments (and oppositions) from the act of governing and then apply the theory in a proper system of government. As it is, we mistakenly endow the people with the sovereign capability of deciding all issues in their most minute detail; we overload them with a multiplication of elections and a proliferation of primaries to make sure that they not only elect but that they nominate as well; and on top of that we provide for direct government at the state and local level in which citizens are empowered to write laws and state constitutional provisions, to require that existing laws and constitutional provisions be referred to the public for reaffirmation or reversal, and, occasionally, to review the question whether existing elected officers should continue to serve their terms. The result, or at least, the concomitant occurrence has been a growing apathy not to say a demoralization of the people as citizens.

How much better it would be to simplify the citizens' formal task by limiting it to the one act that they and, in a democracy, *only* they can properly perform: the act of creating a government (and an opposition) by their vote.

Conclusion

The issue of the adequacy of American political institutions has been raised. The very fundamentals of the separation of powers between President and Congress have been questioned. I have asserted that a cure may be found if we embrace a different separation of powers, one between the government and the opposition, and that we may do so by adapting to American practices and conditions the principles of the parliamentary system.

2
Controversial Parliamentarism

SUGGEST that the United States consider adopting the parliamentary system, and face the query: "Do *that* when Britain, the Mother of Parliaments, is teetering on the edge of economic disaster?" In June 1980, Robert D. Hershey wrote "Britain's [economic] ills have become so visible and so seemingly immune to treatment that they have come to be regarded as a malady unique to these islands—the British 'disease.' "[1]

The problem has been apparent for some time. In March 1971, the British chancellor of the exchequer declared that, comparable to other countries, Britain, since World War II, had experienced "slow growth, recurring balance of payment weaknesses, faster-than-average inflation, a low rate of investment, a falling share of world exports, and increasingly bad industrial relations."[2]

Yet the problem arose fairly recently.[3] Eminently successful in both politics and economics during the nineteenth and early twentieth centuries, Britain had a per capita income in 1939 second only to that of the United States. In World War II, Britain had developed radar, the jet engine, and floating docks; and had attained a very high level of mobilization.

But after the war, British comparative performance fell. Why? Consider the severe economic straits Britain faced. In 1946 it had lost half of its foreign investments of 4 billion pounds and owed sterling accounts in London of 4 billion pounds. This occurred in spite of Britain's mighty wartime effort to pay half the war's costs of 27.4 billion pounds out of current revenue (42 percent of British income had gone to taxes and savings). Consider also the import/export needs. Although agriculture had become much more self-sufficient, Britain still had to import half of its food and all of its petroleum in 1946. Meanwhile the value of British exports had fallen from 470 million in 1938 to 257 million in 1944, and British shipping had shrunk from 40 million dead weight tons to 19 million. (Britain's need to export is still strong. In 1977 Britain's imports totaled 26 percent of its gross national product or GNP compared to 8.3 percent in the United States.)

Underlying these discouraging figures were basic economic disadvantages. "Britain, unlike the United States and some other industrial countries does not have a thick cushion of economic plenty to fall up on. Economic wealth (gross domestic product) per person in England is less than one-half that of the United States and less than three-fourths that of France."[4]

Nevertheless, during this century Britain survived two global wars and in 1940–41 stood alone against the concentrated strength of Hitler's Germany. After World War II, Britain maintained one of the highest expenditures for defense (in terms of GNP), retreated peacefully from empire into commonwealth, and preserved its political liberties at home while maintaining a moderately successful economic performance until the late 1960s.

In light of this record, the argument against the parliamentary system because of Britain's recent economic difficulties loses some force. Moreover, West Germany and Japan, the two most successful industrial nations in postwar years, both have parliamentary systems. That form of government is at least compatible with strong national economic performance under modern conditions.

Still the doubts persist. Britain's experience is critical to the evaluation of parliamentarism, so the question may remain: Can parliamentary government in its purest form be faulted for not coping effectively with economic ills (Britain's postwar rate of economic growth hovered at about half the rate of other industrialized nations); or even Does parliamentary government aggravate the tendency toward economic disaster?[5] To quote Hershey further: "The main cause [of Britain's seemingly intractable economic ills], depending upon whom one consults, is grasping, strike-happy unions, inept management, the class system, socialism, underinvestment, polarized major parties, the educational system, overtaxation, loss of empire, housing policy, government intervention, a phlegmatic national temper, egalitarianism, and even the highly developed retail distribution system that makes Britain a soft touch for other countries' exporters."

This list may, as Hershey implies, be a smorgasbord of separate "causes." But it might also be interpreted as a syndrome. It might then be argued that a number of Hershey's particular causes were fathered by the parliamentary system. Risking an exercise prone to scribblers that Joseph Schumpeter called *délire d'interpretation*, let us go through the list. Parliamentary government is party government. Between 1964 and 1970 and again in 1974–79 it was Labour party government; and that is when, according to S. E. Finer, party polarization occurred.[6] The Labour party (LP) and British trade unions are intimately linked. Ernest Bevin told the Labour Party Conference in 1935 that the party "has grown out of the bowels of the TUC"[7] In Britain, 46 percent of the workforce was unionized in 1976, up from 41 percent in 1951.[8] Forty-eight percent of the LP members of Parliament (M.P.'s) enjoyed trade union subventions.[9] The LP has professed socialism as its theory and goal since 1918. On coming to power in 1945, it began to enact a socialist program (here more of Hershey's particulars come into play)—a prime example of "government intervention," and a course pursued with varying persistence by subsequent Labour governments. Socialism and egalitarianism go hand in hand, leading to such programs as Britain's health and housing policies. Any remaining inequalities prompt increases in progressive taxation which, in turn, may diminish incentives to save and invest. Hence, production systems may obsolesce. Management appears inept. Businesses falter. Lord Ritchie-Calder complained that "in Britain, the losses are socialized while the profits are privatized."[10] Finer attributed the decline in political influence of British business generally (other than the financial interests of the City) to the enervating effects of subsidies to industries that were foundering or at least in economic trouble.[11]

Thus one might argue that the list of causes offered by Hershey actually contains a number that are interlocking, mutually reinforcing, and occasionally perhaps even synergistic. It can be asserted that they seem to stem from parliamentary government—that is, from party government. In 1973 Sam Beer wrote that "according to the concept of party government, parties are important instruments of social choice."[12] In this connection, note that one of Hershey's causes is "polarized major parties." In the clash between Labour and the Conservatives in the 1970s and in 1980, the English voter's choice seemed to be between polarized parties.

However, it was not long ago — as recently as 1972 — that Beer presented the interpretation that parliamentary government in England in the 1950s and 1960s led not to a *polarization* but to a *convergence* of the parties.[13]

Samuel H. Beer's Earlier View

Modern economic development in Britain produced collectivism, manifested in the managed economy and the welfare state. A managed economy was deemed necessary to prevent depressions, insure high employment, control inflation, and maintain a strong position for the pound in foreign exchange. The welfare state was required to provide social security, health benefits, housing, and education. Together, the managed economy and the welfare state led to mass political parties that, in turn, created a larger, more complex, and more powerful bureaucracy. As always, the expansion of government stimulates organization among the affected groups — the regulated, the employed, the facilitated, the financed, the promoted, the assisted, or whatever. Producer groups then formed and pressed their demands especially on the elite of the bureaucracy. Consumer groups also formed, but their demands were made primarily to political parties. The parties were prompted to bid against each other in their competitive appeal for the votes especially of the middle classes.

But this description is too mechanical to do Professor Beer's interpretation justice. Religious values, secular idealism, pride of class, self-love — these and other motivations were mixed in the pragmatic ideology that came to command something of a public consensus. World War II "strongly consolidated opinion behind the idea of dealing with the problems of peace as with those of war: by public planning, collective controls, and social guarantees to every individual of a 'fair share' of the national wealth. It is no exaggeration to say that Göring's Blitz was the force that coalesced all the converging strands of Christian humanitarianism, utilitarian pragmatism, idealistic statism, Fabian socialism, and aristocratic paternalism into the social program pursued since the War."[14]

Thus the Labour party's drive toward socialism was surrounded by the supportive sentiments of other groups; it was also tempered. Labour seemed to aim at socializing no more than a fifth of the economy. And it followed paths often previously charted by both the Liberal and the Conservative parties. The Conservatives, on their part, accepted the managed economy and the welfare state. What emerged was a consensus labeled "Butskellism" after Conservative and Labour chancellors of the exchequer, R. A. Butler and Hugh Gaitskell. Both accepted that the bulk of economic activity would remain privately owned, manned, financed, and directed; but both also held that the state should properly manipulate fiscal and monetary policy in order to maintain full employment, the control of inflation, and a healthy situation in foreign exchange.[15]

If Butskellism was generally benign, Beer came to believe that convergence might become complete enough to dampen political conflict and to threaten or even eliminate the opposition, which, in the parliamentary system, is the instrument by which power is checked by power. The end might then be pluralistic stagnation. To suggest that this was not solely a British phenomenon but rather a tendency in modern industrial states, Beer noted that the French and West Germans also had words for it — *immobilisme* and *Pluralistiche Stockung*. The idea is familiar to American political interpretation, e.g., Samuel Lubell's "stalemate" in the *Future of American Politics* (1951) and Theodore Lowi's "interest group liberalism" in *The End of Liberalism* (1969).

But Beer was careful to put his interpretation in a historical perspective. If the twenty years of convergence, not only in what the parties promised but in what they did in office, was so marked as to raise serious doubts about the parties as important instruments of social choice, one should remember that this period followed one of rather intense party strife. In the 1970s, the sharpening of the partisan struggle may be as characteristic of the parliamentary system as its amelioration and virtual disappearance was earlier.

I shall return to the promise and problems of socialism, but here I must confront a learned and vigorous recent critic of the British system of government.

The Strictures of S. E. Finer

In 1979, S. E. Finer, Gladstone Professor of Government at Oxford, saluted the earlier tradition of British parliamentarism. Elections had helped create governments based on durable, disciplined majorities in the House of Commons. Elections had brought forth distinct programs that gave voters a real choice, albeit one tempered by the necessity of both parties to compete for the shifting, centrist voters. Eventually, in a new election, the voters had known which party to reward or to punish.[16]

But this vaunted system, wrote Finer, has been undermined. First, governments have lost their claims to majority or even to impressive minority support. In 1970 the Heath government was elected by 46.4 percent of the electorate, but in 1974 the Labour government polled only 39.3 percent, and in 1979 the Thatcher Conservatives only 43.9 percent. Second, the system has recently produced governments with miniscule margins in Commons — in 1950, 1951, 1964, and in 1970; in 1974 the margin disappeared altogether. Third, whereas earlier, Conservative and Labour governments both seemed tacitly to accept the proposition that a successor government "would on the whole accept the legislation of its predecessor," such acceptance recently seems to crumble.[17]

Further, Finer called British parties unrepresentative.[18] He wrote, "A number of party activists, representing 0.15 percent of the electorate, selects 75 percent of the M.P.'s, and an even smaller number formulates national priorities (which are) often grossly unrepresentative of public opinion as a whole and even of party opinion as a whole. If elected, these activists carry out such policies, pleading the democratic right and duty to do so by virtue of their electoral victory, which, since 1935, has always proceeded from less than 50 percent of the votes cast."[19] Thus the Labour government elected in 1974, with only 39.3 percent of the votes cast, repealed the Heath government's Industrial Relations Act and passed a Fair Rents Act as well as an act establishing a National Enterprise Board to facilitate the nationalization of more industries, and nationalized the aerospace and shipbuilding industries. It also established a National Oil Corporation to control the exploration for oil by private companies, legalized the closed shop, and created the Advisory, Conciliation, and Arbitration

Service with the power to force private companies to recognize trade unions.[20]

In short, a government returned by only a very weak plurality acted as though it were the beneficiary of an electoral tidal wave. According to opinion polls, however, the voters generally and even Labour party identifiers specifically, disagreed with much LP policy. A "wide divergence" appeared between the views of LP members and the acts and manifestoes of the LP. For example, in 1974 on nine key Labour policies, an opinion poll reported majority support in the electorate for only two (renegotiating terms of entry into the Common Market—60 percent and raising pensions—94 percent). Even among Labour identifiers, some policies failed to secure a majority (more nationalization was supported by only 37 percent and the nationalization of land by only 44 percent).[21]

Finer indicates that the shift to the left both in the trade unions and in the Labour party leadership is paralleled by a growing public disenchantment with labor unions even among those who identify with them. Asserting a decline in the support of Labour party identifiers for LP politics toward trade unions and big business in 1964–1974, he suggests that it continued to May 1979, on the strength of a BBC-Gallup poll, which showed that 38 percent of the LP identifiers now supported "the very drastic proposal to stop social security payments to strikers' families; 63 percent . . . preferred trade union activities to be regulated by law rather than by voluntary self-regulation; and no less than 83.4 percent favored a legal ban on secondary picketing. All of these had been vigorously opposed by Labour in the 1979 campaign."[22]

Finer also criticizes British government as ritualistic.[23] That is, he denies that voters really choose between two different and distinct lines of policy as the classical theory holds. The policies of both major parties may be much the same as in the Butskellism period of the 1950s; or, again, as in the 1960s and 1970s when the parties winning elections formed governments only to make U-turns in policy. The parties broke faith with the electorate. He also denies that voters choose between rival leaders or groups of leaders. The public did not vote for MacMillan who succeeded Eden after the Suez crisis in 1957, nor had they voted for Callaghan who succeeded Wilson in 1977. He also uses the same argument in Britain that Americans employ to illustrate the confusion of politics in the United States: Democrats have to swallow Russell Long to get Ted Kennedy, or vice versa.[24] Moreover, Finer says that it is a myth that the House of Commons controls the government.

Finer recognizes the value of an accepted myth that the people have a real choice between conflicting parties and that the emergent government represents them. He would, however, "fine tune" the system's accountability by providing primary elections for nominations, by adopting proportional representation in order (he believes) to insure majority rule, and by introducing the popular initiative to make sure that voters get what they want.[25]

An Evaluation of Finer's Critique

I shall consider the critique from the standpoint of the question that this chapter addresses: Should recent British political-economic problems cause Americans to reject the parliamentary system as an alternative for the United States?

First, his proposal for direct democracy bears on the issue. The initiative is irrelevant to the central problems of government as expressed by Madison in *Federalist* No. 51: "In framing a government which is to be administered by men over men, the great difficulty lies in this: you must first enable the government to control the governed; and in the next place oblige it to control itself." When a country is threatened either by foreign enemies or by domestic violence, direct democracy is either meaningless or a dangerous delusion. Consider the British Peace Ballot of 1935 or the American proposal for a national referendum on war or peace (the Ludlow Amendment) of the same vintage. [26] Whether the popular initiative, properly emasculated (as, indeed, Finer proposes), would be a useful supplement to government need not be argued here: for Madison's critical functions of government the British parliamentary system has performed very well.

Indeed, Finer overlooks (or, more probably, takes for granted) the strengths of the British system in meeting the needs of national defense. Britain has properly and promptly produced coalition governments in wartime (in spite of her adversary tradition). It has been able to change leaders in midstream (Churchill for Chamberlain!). Britain has rallied the people to causes all but lost: recall the despair that permeated informed British circles in 1940–1941.[27]

Second, regarding primary elections, where Finer notes that his proposal is supported by recommendations of the Hansard Society, there is no consideration of the debilitating effect of primaries on political parties.[28] Primary elections undermine the ability of political parties to control the party label—to nominate candidates. Control of nomination is critical to the maintenance of discipline which, in turn, is essential to governmental cohesion. Only with a considerable degree of discipline and cohesion can party governments concert and support, enact and administer coherent policies. Curiously, Finer declares that the British parliamentary system, with all its faults, "is still arguably more [representative] than the governmental arrangements in, say, France or the United States." Apparently he would continue to maintain parliamentary sovereignty (except for the presumably rare use of popular initiatives and vetoes); he would still rely essentially on the House of Commons in which the government *must* have a majority; he would keep the vote of confidence and the dissolution—thus preserving both the freedom from fixed calendar elections and the invaluable facility of rapid turnover of power and the despatch in policy making and execution that are the hallmarks of parliamentary government.

Third, two of Finer's other criticisms may be linked. One is that when prime ministers are replaced but the government continues in office the people are cheated because they did not approve the successor. The electorate chose Sir Anthony Eden, not Harold MacMillan. But the voters *did* choose a party. The crucial thing (as I shall stress later) is for voters to have a choice. Another is that Finer complains that because 75 percent of the seats in the House of Commons rarely change parties, three-fourths of the voters lack a real choice. But Finer overlooks the virtue of continuity, experience in office, and stability that this situation has.[29] Moreover, from the national standpoint the fact remains that the losers not only have a choice, but that collectively they elect the Opposition, which is as essential to the well-being of the country as the government itself. This raises the question of proportional representation (PR).

Four, in recommending PR Finer leans toward the single-transferable vote. He wants the government to be composed either of one party that won a majority of votes or a coalition of parties that together make up a majority. Against the argument that governments then may well be composed of unstable coalitions, Finer cites the Dutch experience to show that PR is compatible with strong, moderate, representative, and effective government.[30]

I shall not attempt a full-scale analysis of PR which Professor Hermens has abundantly provided. I am dealing only with a parliamentary alternative for the United States as it is affected by recent British experience and shall simply cite W. Ivor Jennings, whom Finer invokes in his closing chapters. Jennings vehemently rejected PR, which, he wrote, "usually means not government by the people but government by groups. . . . It is important that every section of opinion should have . . . expression, but not that it should be proportionately represented in the House."[31] What PR has done is less to increase the individual's weight in politics than it is to add to the leverage of organized groups as staggered, multiple elections and primaries in the United States have played into the hands of single interest–single purpose groups.[32]

Jennings also rejected PR because it produced a multitude of parties. "In a world where strong and rapid government is necessary, only the two-party system works really well."[33]

Jennings was writing in 1941 when Britain, still a "great power," was engaged in a war of survival. The United States is now, as Holland is no longer, a "great power." Whatever holds true for Britain (and, following Bagehot, Hermens, Jennings, and Schumpeter, I should oppose PR), the United States must strive for a strong, stable government capable of firm, quick action. But Finer's invocation of Jennings raises even more profound questions that are involved in the consideration of parliamentary government in England as a possible (partial) model for the United States.

Finer and Jennings on the Democratic Essentials: *Fine-tuning vs. Dichotomous Choice*

Finer quotes from Jennings, *The British Constitution* (1941) that British democracy means that the people choose their rulers who govern according to the people's wishes. The choice is free, secret, and lies between parties of different principles. This, says Finer, is a myth, but so long as it is believed, even vaguely, it legitimizes government and provides invaluable social stability. Nevertheless, Finer faults British democracy because voters cannot discriminate between candidates according to their differing tendencies; voters can choose only between two parties; and they cannot pick and choose among policies offered by the parties but must accept or reject the whole bundle. "The elector [he writes] must acquire the power to fine-tune his choices."[34]

Finer conceives of citizens, or the bulk of citizens, as rational, discerning, anxious to be well informed, and reflective on their own interests. He sees them as desiring to clarify their opinions, as knowing which party (and what candidates) most nearly agree with their opinions and their interests, and as wanting to vote accordingly. Though he has occasional disclaimers, these statements indicate his conception of the citizen, of political man, indeed, of human nature. Jennings, I believe, would say that this conception is a myth.

Analyzing the British electorate as it had evolved in 1940, Jennings discerned a "floating vote" to which both major parties, after they had drawn on their natural and most loyal supporters, had to appeal. He located it in the lower–middle class of the suburbs and suburbanized county districts. This class was "politically timid," sensitive to their precarious social position, "very susceptible to rumour and panic. It has what may be called a *Daily Mail* and *Daily Express* type of mind. . . . It is thus a convenient soil for the cynical empiricism of the Conservative Central Office which the almost equal cynicism of Tranport House cannot offset."

Jennings enlarged on the tendency of marginal voters, those who made a choice, to be "swayed not by reason and knowledge but by emotion and propaganda. The parties are in fact vast propaganda machines. . . . The Conservative Party beats the mystical drum of patriotism . . . the Labour Party plays the shrill fife of social sympathy . . . " and he proposes something of a parallel to dictatorial regimes. But the difference was that "in a democracy the elector can choose between the drum and the fife[although] he has a good deal of suspicion of all the instruments of the political orchestra. He is apt to 'confound their politics' (in more Anglo-Saxon language) and turn to the racing results."[35]

Perhaps, with some oversimplification, let me say that Finer wants to perfect democracy by maximizing the influence of the maximum number of voters and by finetuning their choices so that they will more nearly and effectively reflect their informed preferences.

Jennings is trying to preserve democracy against the everpresent threat of dictatorship by maintaining (and improving) a system in which elections create both the government and the opposition (which is vital if "free government" is to be preserved).[36] All these unite in Jenning's theory: his conception of political man, his assertion of the importance of the vote in creating both government and opposition, and his stress on the comprehension by the voter of the significance of his vote. With respect, I do not think Jennings' conception is conveyed by Finer's word *legitimacy*.[37] An ancient and useful word, *legitimacy* is too facile to connote not only legality but also the sense of significance of the acts of the citizen in creating government and opposition (the need for this actions, their propriety, and his necessary awareness of both). It is this additional meaning that the parliamentary system, in what Robert Redslob once called its pure form, may provide. Jennings seems clear on this.[38]

A fundamental difference between Jennings and Finer turns on their views of human nature. Jennings' conception of political man calls for constitutional (limited) government. This raises the well-nigh insolvable problem of making a government that can govern while still incorporating institutions that control the government-of-the-day. Largely by improvisation, the British achieved a form of government that seemed to meet these profound and diverse needs.

But beware of rhapsody! Sometimes the British constitution, so haphazardly produced, seems as exquisite as it is sturdy and serviceable. One thinks of collegial responsibility, the development of the vote of confidence and of the power to dissolve, of the impartial speaker, of the convention that the prime minister must come from the House of Commons, and above all the role of Her Majesty's loyal Opposition with its corollaries, "through the usual channels" and "behind the speaker's chair." Not only the French can say, "It is the provisional which endures." But improvisation is not inevitably virtuous. Recently the mandate has been dangerously perverted.

To discuss fully the mandate would require an essay, if not a book. The problem arises from an overliteral application of the idea that elections not only create a government but provide a referendum on competing party platforms so that the winner has a mandate to fulfill exactly its platform promises and no others. The inapplicability of this principle in the United States has been considered sufficient to doom party government here. I have dealt at more length with the problem elsewhere.³⁹ But let me say that British parties while in opposition have had explosions of staff that have excessively elaborated party programs that, with victory, have become mandates endowed in all their fine print with the sacredness of covenants. To assume that with his vote the citizen not only returns a government but also endorses, verifies, justifies, and commands the performance of an infinitely detailed statement of policy invests him with a pre-science and an omniscience — not to mention a will — that he does not have. What is worse, such an assumption perverts the function of government, which must have sufficient time to formulate and carry out policies and enough flexibility to meet new problems and accom-modate for different perspectives on old ones. What is worst of all is that it distorts and even destroys the essential political myth: the simple meaning of the voter's function in creating a government and an opposition.

I suspect also that the abuse of the mandate theory has aggra-vated the difficulties encountered by "socialism on the march" to which I now return.

The Promise and the Problem of Socialism: The Promise

S. E. Finer's proposals and those of others — with one notable exception — to reform the British system would (if one overlooks PR) keep intact its essential features. The exception comes from the right. Finer quotes Lord Halisham's criticism of the present structure of British government as an "elective dictatorship" and says that his "view is widely held in . . . Conservative Party quarters. . . . There is little doubt that many Conservatives would happily introduce some version of the American system with a written constitution, . . . a separation of powers between the executive and the legislature, and possibly some form of federalism."⁴⁰ As Professor Finer himself notes, Lord Halisham's criticism is by no means universal among conservatives. The conventional hypothesis is defense of the status quo. "Many people see great strength and value in the present two-party system and do not want to change it. They include most Labour candidates and M.P.s, and a majority of the Conservative ones also."⁴¹

The significance of the British Conservatives who follow Lord

Halisham is that they may indicate the position of American conservatives on the issue of constitutional reform: rallying to the status quo
because it does divide power, because it pits president against Congress, because it increases the complexity of policymaking, and because it multiplies the points at which standpatters can rally to defeat
distasteful (i.e., liberal or radical) proposals. Conservatives may oppose the parliamentary system in principle on the same assumption
that rallies some liberals to its support: that party government will
empower the latent majority, which by hypothesis favors liberal, New
Deal, or even socialistic programs. A. Lawrence Lowell, the first ranking American political scientist to study British and American politics
in depth and to make comparisons, argued against the parliamentary
system for the United States on the ground that it would facilitate
the rise of socialism.[42] The bald fact that the English Tories ran their
government 60 percent of the time from 1885 to 1971 would not
impress American rightists who would condemn convergence as sur-
render.

When I say "socialism" I mean a broad use of the term to
include both Samuel Beer's "pragmatic-economic" and his "ethical"
or "ideological" varieties.[43] I mean to include the advanced managed
economy plus the welfare state in which the shift has been consummated from a guarantee to the citizen of only "certain formal rights
to the promise of a comprehensive social status," regardless of how
much or how little he produces. On both sides of the Atlantic, the
human tides demanding these ends were irresistible. In this sense,
the United States has shared in the socialist revolution, has enjoyed
notable social gains from it or along with it, and is now encountering
inherent problems. Before turning to Britain, a word on the United
States.

The 1930s were years of anxiety. After 1930, United States unemployment was never less than 14.3 percent of the work force
(1937) and for four years (1932-36) it was over 20 percent. During
these years, the idea of government's supplementing, complement-
ing, correcting, and, if necessary, replacing the private economy crystallized. Many Americans looked hopefully to socialist parties
abroad—especially to the Labour party in England—and lamented
that such parties did not seem to be able to get more than 40 percent
of the vote.[44] I remember Harvard professor C. J. Friedrich's remark,
circa 1939, "Socialism is on the march." Many of his students took

that as reassurance. In 1941 Harvard professor John D. Black traveled the country, studying New Deal agricultural programs at regional, state, and county levels. At last unemployment had dipped below 10 percent (9.9), but fear of it remained strong. Black made scores of impromptu speeches to audiences in land grant colleges or governmental agencies. Armed with Alvin Hansen's *Fiscal Policy and Business Cycles,* Black proclaimed: "We will never have another deep depression. The reason is that both political parties now know how to avoid it, and they will never let it happen again." Hansen was the leading American advocate of Keynesianism that dominated the parallel British development. I recall a visit to Harvard in 1943 or 1944 by Senator Robert A. Taft who came to do battle with Alvin Hansen in the name of free enterprise. Hansen was absent from the seminar, but he was well defended. At one point, Taft was asked: "Suppose your wish is granted. We roll back the New Deal and give private enterprise one more chance—and it fails again. What then?" "Then," said Senator Taft, "the American people will be ready for socialism, and I will lead them into it."

England witnessed a parallel mobilization of public opinion. In his *Parliamentary Government in England* (1935) Harold J. Laski predicted that the Tories, once concessions to the poor and the workers began to cut into their own level of living, would precipitate a civil war and, if necessary, impose a fascistic regime to protect their property. By contrast, W. Ivor Jennings compared the Conservative and Labour programs of 1935 to show that "there is far more in common between the two parties than is generally assumed" because "they were offering bait to the same fish"—namely, the 750,000 shifting, middle-class voters. Although differences remained wide enough to give voters "a real choice, and to give rise to acute controversy in the House of Commons," the question was reduced to one of "more or less." *"We are all collectivists now."*[45] (Italics added.)

In Britain (as I have already noted) and in many European countries, too, social democracy triumphed after World War II. The Atlee government, returned in 1945, nationalized the Bank of England, the coal mines, railways and long-distance road haulage, telecommunications, the importation and sale of raw cotton, electricity and gas, scheduled air services, and finally iron and steel; although the 1949 statute nationalizing the last two took effect only after the next election (1950).

In all this, a most important point is that when the Conservative party came into power in 1951, with the exception of iron and steel, it maintained Labour's socialization. And on the side of the welfare state, it went even farther, doubling the public outlays in 1951–59 for health care, the care of the elderly, public housing, education, and unemployment insurance. Beer wrote, "It was Labour's ambitious efforts in these areas that created the immense financial burden, the acceptance of which by the conservatives constituted so important a step in British political development."[46] This was part of the evidence of convergence between the two major British parties that impressed Sam Beer. The apparent result was to help produce and distribute, during the 1950s and 1960s, more creature comforts to more people (in Britain as well as in the United States and various European countries) than had ever been done before. Meanwhile, unemployment remained low and inflation was controlled. In any event, it was not the parliamentary system or any other particular governmental structure that produced this development. The force *majeure* was in the public demands and expectations. At the same time, the parliamentary system, a type of constitutional government with a strong element of majoritarianism in it, may have been a more effective instrument of the force *majeure* than the separation of powers of the United States.

Socialism: The Problem

Maybe it was still convergence, but when Labour returned to power and had again been replaced by the Conservatives, the latter found that there was a good deal more to converge with. Butskellism flourished more while Labour was in opposition than when it governed. During Harold Wilson's Labour regime, 1964–1970, British taxes rose from 32 to 42 percent of national income; and governmental expenditures jumped from 35 to 50 percent of the GNP.[47] Schumpeter had warned that the socialists would not be content with the "civilization of capitalism." Rather, they would kill the goose that laid the golden egg. Curiously, the geese gathered first were the stingiest egg producers. And, when the Conservatives got back in, they found the omelet decidedly difficult to unscramble: Who would buy back the nationalized industries? Meanwhile, other industrial nations were encountering economic difficulties.

In the 1970s, social democracy found itself in trouble that was exacerbated by OPEC but seemed inherent in its efforts to provide retirement security, assurance of employment or of income, health care, housing, and other amenities—and a progressive equalization of the access to the good things of life. Just as Hershey referred to the "British disease" so the Social Democrat, Professor Assar Lindbeck of the University of Stockholm, lamented the "Swedish sickness." The welfare state, it was said, with its burgeoning social benefits and high taxation, would in the end arrest the dynamics of the economic system.[48] Or, in the words of H. H. P. Starren, head of economic research at the Algemene Bank Nederland, it was the "Dutch disease."[49] S. E. Finer, however, found Britain's problems to be worse; they were aggravated by an excess of growth in white collar workers at the expense of industrial workers from 1961–1974, an upward jump "unparalleled in the western economies." Office workers' employment mushroomed. Producer employment lagged.[50]

In Britain the problem may have been exacerbated by the structure of industry. Full employment appeared to weaken national collective bargaining by shifting bargaining to the plant level. Power moved from national to local unions. Wildcat strikes increased. They undermined not only national collective bargaining but the "social contract" between the government and the TUC, which aimed to hold wage gains down so that they would be closer to gains in labor productivity. The tendency toward industrial anarchy was further increased by what Sam Beer called a "proletarian spirit," a dogged clinging to outmoded work practices to protect jobs (featherbedding). This was sometimes reinforced by paternalistic managerial impulses, as one employer expressed it, that "the first responsibility is to provide work for these chaps—to keep the shops occupied.[51]

The problems of the social welfare state may also be heightened by social norms. A sweeping characterization of the new coercion implicit in the social democratic dispensation was made by Ralf Dahrendorf, director of the London School of Economics, who described it as the "fundamental consensus of the world of the Organization for Economic Cooperation and Development (OECD). This consensus combines the desire for . . . economic growth . . . with the intention to extend the idea of citizenship from one entailing only certain formal rights to a comprehensive social status."[52]

The Function of Government

How much is parliamentary government responsible for the rise of the socialistic welfare state, the convergence on collectivism of political parties? How much is it to be credited with the amelioration of the human lot in, say, 1945-1968 and the social and economic problems that have emerged since then—the various national "diseases," marked by increasing inflation, rising unemployment, and the sharpening of tensions among and between various domestic ethnic groups and regions?

Surely many of the causes or the identifiable contingencies that seem to shape socio-economic development in the modern industrial countries transcend parties, conventions, voting, the formation of governments, and the political process generally. There was the imperative demand for equality, strengthened greatly by World War II and aggravated by the revolution of rising expectations—this drive recklessly enlarged the prerequisites of citizenship in a constitutional democracy from a guarantee of certain formal rights (presumably those encompassed in the phrase "due process of law") to a guarantee in Dahrendorf's terms, of a comprehensive status (presumably a good job, a decent house, equal access to education and health care, and, in general, fair shares of all good things for everyone).

In the United States, politicians, for a time at least, could ride these waves without losing their pragmatic aplomb. FDR could invoke "one third of a nation, ill-fed, ill-clad, ill-housed." And the Republicans, reading the election results, would soon learn to say, "me, too." Public wants, demands, and drives could all be included in a politics of interest. Politics and the political parties were interest-group machines, dispensing patronage; politicians rolled logs and dished out pork; labor had long before followed Gompers into "bread and butter unionism" (seniority, the heart of the union contract and control of the job) that undermined the socialist appeal by appearing to promise its benefits without requiring nationalization of industries. All this perfectly fitted American catchall political parties.

In Britain, by contrast, as on the continent, there was a socialist movement, informed with a body of theory, that seemed ready-made for implementation by British parties of principle. Edmund Burke had defined a political party as "a body of men united to advance the public interest on some particular principle in which they are all agreed." Even when major British parties converged, latent differences of principle remained.

When the time was ripe in the 1970s, the convergence that had marked British politics earlier on gave way once more to a confrontational politics of principle. Or perhaps one can say that the latent tendency toward a politics of principle quickened. The Heath government sought to assert conservative principles, but lost eventually in a struggle with inflation and with labor unions over wage increases. The Callaghan Labour government succeeded, pressed on toward socialism, encountered severe economic difficulties, sought a return to convergence, failed, and lost to Margaret Thatcher's Conservatives, who came in with a strong commitment to principle that, however precariously, has been maintained. The polarization of the major parties, that Hershey reports is lamented by some in Britain, is at least the cure offered by the parliamentary system to Britain's economic problems.

This conception of party government (parliamentarism) may repel Americans for whom ideology is anathema. A number of leading American intellectuals enthusiastically joined in announcing the death of ideology twenty-five years ago (the culminating meeting it later transpired, had been organized and financed by the CIA).[53] Many scholars have praised the pragmatism of American political parties. They have been hailed as parties of interest rather than of principle, although it has sometimes been said that occasions may arise when principles are needed.

The 1980s may indeed call for a politics of principle. We may learn that we cannot escape the need of ideology defined in accordance with the etymology of the word as a body of ideas that give a form or shape to what we know or think we know about the world in which we live. In view of the problems encountered by the managed economy/welfare state, the task of redefining modern government and of relating it to a workable theory of human nature is staggering. One of the virtues of parliamentary government may be that the governors it naturally trains are readier to assume this outrageous responsibility than those trained in the American system of the separation of powers.

British politicians and civil servants are educated in public schools and universities as well as throughout their careers by their experience in either government or politics to think and operate on national problems from national perspectives. By contrast, the bulk of American politicians and civil servants are trained to think in the politics of interests. They are steeped, saturated, imprinted, and conditioned by the wants and needs, the hopes and fears of business, labor, farms, schools, the bar, the army, the mines, the railroads. They tout the claims of wheat, cotton, corn, tobacco, beef, steel, coal, oil, Detroit, Boeing, . . . etc., etc. Even those politicians who are not only bitten with the presidential bug but do in fact manage to ride the crest into the oval office may find that the only way is to commit themselves unreservedly to a politics of interest.

This is not to say that a politics of interest lacks defenses or defenders. Professor Edward C. Banfield forcefully argued the virtues of "social choice" in which the ultimate criterion for making political decisions is the distribution of influence. But he noted certain qualifications. Some interests may not be asserted in the process of making choices or may be asserted only weakly, for example, interests in ends or results pertaining to the community as a whole.[54]

Banfield supported his conclusions by a study of political controversies in Chicago, "virtually . . . 100 percent of those . . . of city-wide or more than city-wide importance in . . . 1957–58." Chicago is a considerable political theatre. But it is not a nation. Despite the legends of Mayor Thompson in the 1920s, it does not have a foreign policy. It does not have to deal with other nations as allies or potential enemies in a world of force and counterforce that becomes increasingly complex, uncertain, and lethal. Worse, it does not have to deal with an international chessboard on which some of the pieces once though stoutly placed and highly dependable suddenly disintegrate. More and more the United States needs a government whose members think of the country as a nation, whose leaders have a national perspective. Yet the drift of American politics is toward greater articulation of more and more interests and an increasingly intensified schooling of politicians in finding and appealing to groups.

On many issues in many political theatres, social choice appears to have great virtue. In national politics, however, something more is often needed. Banfield labeled it "central decision." Monetary policy is an example. Without strong governments, monetary policy would repeat "the tragedy of the commons." A steadily growing money supply may be a paramount and universal interest; but what is politically articulated is the sharper, particularized interests of numerous groups in easy money (including the creation of various pools of credit at concessional rates), of other groups with an interest in tight money, and of still others clamoring for various and costly subsidies. A similar statement can be made about fiscal policy. Any government that seeks to resist pressures and merely to hold the line in defense of a conservative, stable monetary and fiscal policy requires formidable, centralized strength to maintain the necessary coherence. In military policy, the provision of armies and armaments loom large. It can hardly be argued that the amount of armaments a country needs, the various weapons systems, the mix, and the forward planning as different generations of missiles, aircraft, submarines, and tanks come in—that all of these are best evolved by the higgling of the numerous elements of the armaments industry in the political market place. Other issues—welfare, energy, immigration, for example—could be argued to call for considerable elements of central decision. The parliamentary system seems to have a superior capacity to train people for central decisions. Whether it will be sufficient is another question.

Conclusion

The question addressed—Do Britain's economic difficulties destroy the utility of the parliamentary model for the United States?—can be answered, "No!"

In contemplating fundamental constitutional change one may begin with Madison's two questions about the government's ability to control the governed and then to control itself. Both questions are contingent upon the government's ability to defend the country—especially when, as now, threats are manifold and extremely dangerous.

Constitutional governments (which are implied in Madison's second requirement that the government be obliged to control itself) are presently under stress because of demands for welfare, equality, and guaranteed status. Whether the result is nationalization of industry, the proliferation of entitlements, or the multiplication of pledges to citizens, the results may overwhelm economic production with demands for distribution and consumption.

Returning to Dahrendorf's comment on the shift from the assurance of civil rights to the commitment that all shall be guaranteed an affluent status, one may argue that even poor countries might attempt, with some success, to honor R. G. Collingwood's imperative that people should be treated in a manner to arouse their self respect.[55] But if a country insists on providing everyone equally with an abundance of creature comforts, then their production in the amount and variety that human idiosyncrasy and (often insatiable) appetite demands must be achieved and sustained.

Many behavioral studies tell us that the best stimulus to the production of mounting supplies of goods and services lies in increasing the economic incentive to producers.[56] Moreover, the myriads of decisions needed on what to produce (and how much) will be more promptly and efficiently made if entrepreneurs are free to respond to signals from the market just as consumers are often better off if they are free to go to the market to fulfill their wants. These observations suggest the wisdom of keeping a very large private sector in the economy.

Madison's principles then become more complex. Government must provide for the common defense, control the governed, and include some institutional means to assure self-control. In addition, the modern rise of mass democracy presses government to strive for economic abundance that is distributed with some attention to equity. A vigorous private sector seems essential if an economic abundance is to be attained. Is this sector compatible with Madison's principles?

Experience in numerous Western democracies shows that private business is compatible with constitutional government, whether it is realized in the form of separation of powers as in the United States or of separation of government from opposition as in parliamentary countries. True, private enterprise has sometimes been the supplier, the supporter, and the beneficiary of authoritarian states as the history of fascism shows. But it is also true that the greater the concentration of power in the state, the more difficult it becomes effectively to oppose it. Private business, even if highly concentrated in large corporations, may foster a decentralization in economic power that is compatible with and supportive of a system dividing political power between government and opposition.

This argument is anathema to Marxists, but Marxist governments have proven to be characteristically authoritarian. What of
democratic socialism? Pierre-Joseph Proudhon put it most strikingly.
"What is property? Property is theft." The contemporary battle in the
domestic economic politics of democracy may be ineluctably ideological. The socialist appeal to the politics of principle needs to be
answered by a principled appeal couched in political economic terms
that insist on a large role for the market. To be significant this
counter appeal must be made by leaders of a political party engaged,
like the socialists, in a competitive struggle for the people's vote. The
trumpet calls of utopian socialism ("love and produce! love and produce!") may not be answerable by appeals to pragmatism, incrementalism, and an apotheosized social choice.

How does Britain fit this analysis? Its majoritarian parliamentary
government implemented the managed economy and the welfare
state. It was responsive to the public demand for fair shares. The
success of the Labour party prompted Conservative imitation that led
to the congruence of 1950–1964. But shortly thereafter economic
adversity created tensions between and within the parties. The latent
commitment to socialism in Labour took shape and made a bid for
dominance even at the threat of splitting the party. The Conservatives drew apart, reasserting their own principles.

Both the welfare state and the interparty congruence are under-
standable in a government keenly sensitive to ground swells of public
opinion. But the government's tendency to fulfill the more aggres-
sive popular demands may have been aggravated by the perversion of
the mandate theory. At the same time, parliamentary government,
through its incorporation of the opposition, provided a structure
capable of producing not only a party but a countervailing ideology.
The political and economic choices have been excruciatingly hard,
and the outlook late in 1980 was bleak. But, at least, the parliamentary system was endeavoring to supply some answers.

But that is by no means all. Britain's parliamentary institutions
still provide for elections on dissolution, thus escaping the rigid dic-
tation of the calendar that is proving increasingly burdensome and
dangerous in the United States. Its governments are ordinarily returned for periods long enough for them to develop and test their
programs. The Opposition can perform its indispensable functions.
The government can act in defense of the realm with unity, vigor,

and despatch — while still remaining accountable to the House and to the Opposition. Finally, Britain continues to nurture strong and cohesive political parties that are widely held to be the most effective antibodies to fight off the "American disease" — a proliferation of interest groups that, although often benign in their early effect, have evolved enough now to show a cumulative ability to bankrupt the polity.

In view of these capabilities, even if Britain were to "go broke" tomorrow, its record over decades and even centuries, given its resources, might still make its governmental system an exemplary one. Obviously no governmental system provides a sufficient condition for a country's survival and success, but Britain's parliamentarism still comes as close as any to fulfilling the governmental function at the necessary level of performance.

3

More Problems with
Parliamentary Government

THE Committee on the Constitutional System (CCS) was formed by people who share a conviction that the venerable American Constitution may need basic reform. Cochairperson C. Douglas Dillon has observed a rather sudden accumulation of problems in the American polity: extreme divisiveness, voter apathy, a proliferation of interest groups, budgets out of control, an inability to place responsibility, and recurrent stalemate.[1] Cochairperson Lloyd N. Cutler has critically analyzed "the inability of our government to propose, legislate, and administer a balanced program for governing."[2]

At the heart of the American Constitution is the separation of powers, especially the executive and the legislative, which are divided in an effort to control political power. A contrast is provided by parliamentary government that fuses the executive and the legislative but seeks to achieve control by dividing power between the government and the opposition. The existence of parliamentary government may merely provide a useful vantage point and perspective from which the American system can be more effectively analyzed. But, beyond that, the parliamentary system may provide an adaptable alternative.

A leading authority on British parliamentary government, Samuel H. Beer, has provided an analysis that calls into question the viability of the parliamentary alternative. Despite eight hundred years of successful evolution and, in the twentieth century, its survival of two world wars, the great depression, and the loss of empire, Britain's mother of parliaments suddenly faltered in the 1970s. Beer finds its debility growing out of a decline in deference and in the acceptance of hierarchy as well as a weakening of the ties of class—all parts of a political culture that historically supported parliamentary government.[3]

By political culture Beer means the common beliefs and values of a given community (a tribe, a clan, a city, a nation) that permeate the community and are handed down from generation to generation—beliefs and values that establish the identity of the community and its peoples, how the community is organized and how it works, what are the do's and don'ts as well as the shoulds and should-nots, and how members communicate with each other. Political cultures tend to be disorderly, ambivalent, and confused; but they help explain why people accept authority—always and everywhere a primary political consideration.[4]

Until recently British political culture imprinted on its members (subjects) the idea that their community was properly and, indeed, naturally hierarchical. A few governed; the rest were governed. The governed deferred to the governors. There was a governing class that became the basis of the Conservative or Tory party. That party was balanced first by the Whigs or Liberals, later by the Labour party. Within the parties also deference obtained; members of Parliament deferred to their party leaders; members of parties in their constituencies deferred to the parliamentary parties (although with recurrent protests in the Labour party). But in the 1970s, these cultural pillars of parliamentary government crumbled.

These momentous changes in the political culture seemed to grow—or perhaps explode—out of collectivism. Collectivism, Beer wrote earlier, means "government intervention with the economic and social system *as a whole*."[5] It has been a recent development. Emphasizing the degree of convergence between the Conservative and Labour parties in 1941, W. Ivor Jennings wrote, "We are all collectivists now."[6] Beer found collectivism most sharply defined in the two major concepts that have seized all governments in modern industrial states: the Managed Economy and the Welfare State. It was natural for the Labour party to embrace these concepts. The Conservative party approved the managed economy in the interwar period and the welfare state after World War II.[7]

Collectivism meant that the government took on more and more of the tasks, obligations, and responsibilities that Britons had once done or met themselves or in their families or guilds. In order to produce and distribute the goods and services necessary to the welfare state, the economy had to be properly managed. People involved in production were already organized into groups or were given compelling incentives to become so. The recipients of welfare also became organized. Producer groups and consumer groups proliferated; the collectivist government had to galvanize, induce, and persuade producer groups into producing; the collectivist government had likewise to satisfy consumer groups in what and how much was delivered, when and to whom. Earlier, such groups had operated in a private economy; "their syndicalist power affected public choice only indirectly."[8] After the war these groups became both more organized and more engrafted into government itself. (Government became "the governmental process.")

As the groups became more and more insatiable, something of first importance was lost. The purpose of citizens and of political parties to preserve, protect, and defend the national community dissolved into an intense drive on the part of individuals and groups to prosper, to get ahead, and to use government as a means of doing so. Instead of a national shield, a structure in which the Leviathan is recognized but still controlled, and a common framework in which civility is to be sought, government became merely an instrument to personal and group advancement. Public activity lapsed into the "benefits scramble," the "pay scramble," and the "subsidy scramble."[9]

The efficacy of these groups, as it became stamped on the consciousness of their members, radically changed the political culture. A new system of power was created as the concept of class gave way and as deference disappeared or was seriously weakened. Rather suddenly, government became a means to advancement—to jobs, favors, subsidies, guarantees—not just for the happy few (princes had always had their favorites; before the Trevelyan-Northcote reforms Her Majesty's foreign service was called "the outdoor relief of the upper classes")—but for larger and larger groups until it became hypothetically all-inclusive.

This change in culture undermined parliamentary government. Parliamentary government had meant that the Parliament was the final authority and was efficacious. It ran the country. Control in Parliament became vested in the House of Commons wherein the majority produced a cabinet headed by a prime minister. Cabinet and prime minister were the effective rulers. But they could rise to power, and be sustained therein, only by a majority, a stable majority, hence by a party, a governing party, hence *Party Government*. What gave the party form, substance, durability, and the potential to provide the power base for the government were the class system and a pervasive sense of deference.

In the 1970s, however, parliamentary government in England suddenly weakened. Governments no longer seemed able to draft, enact into law, and administer their policies in the time between elections. A sharp increase occurred in defeats governments suffered in votes in the House of Commons—first of the Heath Conservatives, 1970–1974; then of the Wilson Labourites, 1974–79. This was a remarkable change from a situation in which the coherence of party voting, notable since the late–nineteenth century, had become extremely tight after World War II.[10]

At the same time, backbenchers in both parties, those members who did not belong to the cabinet or have an official part of the government or in its activities in the House of Commons, began to demand more active roles. No longer satisfied with expressing the sense of the House on policy formulated and presented by the government, they wanted a share in shaping policy. Under the Thatcher Conservatives fourteen committees were created, each shadowing a government department.[11]

Meanwhile, another major political development had happened: the rise of populism. Populism is an extreme version of democracy in which all decisions and actions (governmental, social, economic) are ideally decentralized, unraveled, or atomized until each individual shares in originating, formulating, and executing them in accordance with his ability and interest. In this view, everyone should eventually control the bits and pieces of public policy from which he profits or which directly affect him. Ideally, each day students in all classes will choose what to study and how (or whether to study at all); workers in every workplace will elect what to build, fix, process, assemble or whatever; and people everywhere will decide what laws or orders to obey and which to flout as well as what taxes to pay and which to ignore. The will-of-all conquers the general will. Benign anarchy smothers the war of every man against every man. Government does indeed wither away. We all become anticollectivists.

Admittedly, this is an imaginary and extreme view of the ultimate potential of the new populism, a parade of the horribles.[12]
Nevertheless, certain concrete populist policies appear to be real and
direct threats to parliamentary government. Such government, it will
be recalled, is party government. Majority parties give form, shape,
and discipline to the cabinet that, centering more and more in a
prime minister, concerts policies, formulates them as bills, gets these
passed into laws, and supervises their execution by the bureaucracy.
The governing party must permit and legitimize the choice of its
leaders by the party members in Parliament, the elected body of
people who, by British institutions, are strongly encouraged to have a
national point of view.

Meanwhile, the opposition, similarly organized, provides itself
with a leader and a "shadow" cabinet through which it unremittingly
subjects the government to scrutiny and challenge. *The relationship
between government and opposition is the essence of parliamentary
democracy.* This fact requires that the leaders of both be chosen by
partisan members of parliament itself. Parliamentary governments
can act, but they must explain what they do, subject to debate, cross
examination, and challenge in the legislature.

If the choice of leaders is elsewhere—for example, in the annual
party conference or in the constituency parties or in an electoral
college outside parliament—then the policies will be concerted elsewhere. Debate in Parliament will become meaningless. Parliamentary government is fatally wounded. By the same token, nominees
for parliament must agree to support their parties in that body; and,
during their nomination, their fellow members in Parliament must
collectively approve their qualities as loyal party members. This need
not mean that on every issue each M.P. must hew to the party line,
but it does mean that on the preponderance of important issues the
members will vote together. Parliamentary government, therefore, is
inherently hierarchical. It depends on and requires deference. If the
underlying political culture ceases to inculcate deference and the
recognition of the propriety of hierarchy, parliamentary government
may be like an ocean going vessel that has been rent from bow to
stern below the waterline.

Consider, then, the efforts of Anthony Benn, M.P., to reform
the Labour party. In 1979, he proposed annual election of the cabinet, relaxation of the fiction of cabinet responsibility, compulsory

reselection (renomination) by their constituency parties of M.P.'s for every election, the vesting of control of the manifesto (the party's program) in the National Executive Committee (that is, in a body whose center of power is *outside* of Parliament), and the election of the party leader by an electoral college representing various elements of the party; again the center of power would move outside of Parliament.[13] In 1979, the Labour party made reselection of M.P.'s mandatory. In 1980 the party adopted the principle of providing an electoral college to choose the leader and deputy leader of Labour. In 1981, the party vested the largest say in the electoral college in the trade unions and in the constituent parties, although it failed to give the National Executive Committee sole control of the manifesto.[14]

Comments on Beer's Analysis

The well-known economic and social problems of Britain since the late 1960s caution us against making sweeping claims for parliamentary government as a cure-all for the social, political, and economic ills of the United States. Professor Beer has forcefully argued that Britain's ills have not only proven too much for its government to cure but that recent events may have undermined parliamentary government itself by radically changing the political culture on which it has been based. At the same time, those aspects of the British political culture that seemed essential to parliamentary government but seem now to have been seriously weakened, if not virtually eliminated, (namely, deference and an acceptance of the principles of hierarchy as a proper rule in government and society) are not now and never have been effective parts of the rowdy, irreverent, and egalitarian American political culture.

What can be said in reply to Professor Beer? In the first place, he forcefully reminds us not to claim too much for any changes we may propose. "Government is one of the least perfectible of human institutions."[15] Granted. But World War I gave birth to the classic remark of the British Tommy: "If you know a better 'ole, go to it!" We may weigh and guess, misgive and doubt, and still decide that parliamentarism seems to be a "a better 'ole."

Second, if Britain's government failed in the 1970s, it failed in a task of unprecedented dimensions that it had attacked for the first time only very recently—and at first with dramatic, amazing success. The task was to take over the management of the economy in order to ensure the welfare of all. In 1962, Beer wrote that World War II "strongly consolidated opinion behind the idea of dealing with the problems of peace as with those of war: by public planning, collective controls, and social guarantees to every individual of a 'fair share' of the national wealth."[16]

After World War II, in Britain as well as in other industrial countries, an economic millennium seemed at hand. People lived longer and enjoyed more creature comforts than ever before—along with greater security in old age, improved health benefits, and practically full employment. Governments played big roles in these happy developments. A consensus emerged that governments could and should "build Jerusalem in England's green and pleasant land." The effect, however, was intoxicating. Beer called it "hubristic Keynesianism," an arrogant belief in the sovereign power of public spending and public management to create an economic and social heaven on earth. Public expenditure, 20.1 percent of the GNP in 1938, rose to 36.5 percent in 1958 and to 50.6 percent in 1968.[17]

But salvation proved elusive although the piper had to be paid. Soon, Beer wrote, "soaring [public] expenditures were absorbing resources that should have gone into exports" (on which Britain's economy was and remained heavily dependent). Meanwhile, the gratification of immediate wants stimulated other eventually insatiable) appetites.[18]

Not only did the British government fail. The parliamentary system itself seemed to facilitate failure. Under that system, the parties had converged (Butskellism), proving the unanimous acceptance of hubristic Keynesianism. If the governing party recognized the need for a new economic policy of reduced spending, of a rise in productivity, and of emphasis upon increasing exports, if necessary at the expense of expanding welfare programs, the opposition party would only have to proclaim its loyalty to the traditional course of taxing, spending, and ameliorating in order to win the election. Thus, the parliamentary system instead of promoting an effective alternative would work to perpetuate failed policies. Professor Beer also argued that the 1930s had demonstrated a similar weakness: the parties unfortunately bid against each other to embrace policies that, however popular, imperiled the polity. Facing the Nazi threat, the

Conservative government, in 1935, chose to accede to Labour's popular pacifism rather than to fight it by insisting on a strong, rearmed Britain.[19]

Granted that parliamentary government is not guaranteed against grievous political mistakes. Granted that it may even be prey to errors produced by its speed in perceiving and acceding to the public's desires (or what it mistakes for the public's desires). Is there still something to be said for parliamentary government?

There is. If Baldwin's Conservatives waffled on the "Peace Ballot" in 1935, Beer writes, "there is no doubt that they decided to rearm more quickly and more substantially than Labour would have done."[20] With some delay parliamentary government met the challenge. Moreover, after the Labour victory in the election of 1966 in which the virtues of public spending had been vigorously touted, the new chancellor of the exchequer, Roy Jenkins, "mustered the support of the Government for a drastic regime of increased taxation and real cuts in spending. Consumption, public and private, was held down, . . . thereby releasing resources for export. In crucial respectes the new policy achieved remarkable success." Again, parliamentary government seemed to meet the challenge. But in 1968 "a wage explosion erupted which sustained and heightened the cost-push inflation which continued to rage. . . . In 1970 Labour lost the election."[21]

The wage increase of 1968 prompts a further word about organized labor. Full employment enhanced the bargaining position of labor unions. It also was strongly centrifugal. The unions became decentralized. Union power shifted to the plant level. Leaders of national unions could no longer commit their followers. The "pluralism of this fragmented structure propelled British trade unionists . . . into the pay scramble that swept over the country in the late 1960s and continued, with mounting disorder, only briefly remitted, throughout the following decade." The Heath Conservatives (1970–1974) began with a well-prepared socio-economic program that failed as the government lost a number of battles in many of which trade union power was crucial. The second Wilson Labour government (1974–79) forged a "social contract" with the trade unions in order to reduce the inflationary effect of rising wages. Although the government fulfilled its side of the bargain, wage settlements in 1974 and 1975 exceeded the rate of inflation. Then came the wage-strike eruption of the winter of 1978-79, "the self-destructive bonanza."[22]

The intention is not to make a scapegoat of organized labor. Beer also stresses the "benefits scramble" and the "subsidy scramble." Still, organized labor's relationship to modern industrial democracies is often crucial. Wages, employment, the structure and role of unions, and labor-management relations are critical to economic policy. Inevitable in free societies and perhaps essential to modern industrial development, unions clearly present communities with extremely difficult problems of comprehension, assimilation, accommodation, and, in the last analysis, control. The word *control* may raise hackles; but in the end, the alternative to control is what Beer calls "pluralistic stagnation."[23] Similar analysis is applicable to giant corporations.

How do such institutional problems compare with cultural ones like the decline of deference as threats to industrial democracy? If the viability of industrial democracy is wholly dependent on a favorable culture, the decline of deference may be as fatal to it as the loss of innocence was to the Garden of Eden. But the influence of deference on political behavior may be amenable to changed institutional patterns. Surely deference and the acceptance of hierarchy flourished in the early and middle nineteenth century, when party discipline in the House of Commons was almost nonexistent. Between 1860 and 1890, however, party discipline in the House strikingly increased, apparently following the development of party organization that ensued after the extension of the suffrage.[24] Institutional changes appear to be the proximate causes of this rise in party cohesion. Again, it is difficult to reconcile the prevalence of deference in the England of 1941 with W. Ivor Jennings' description of the profound cyncism with which ordinary voters then regarded both major parties.[25] Yet party government was notably cohesive until the late-1960s.

It may be that leaders who boldly act as if the parliamentary system still works can carry the day despite an apparent decline in deference. The England that triumphed over vicissitudes for centuries may still cope with the Great Disillusion now that Beveridge's Full Employment in a Free Society has turned out to be just another mirage. But we must now note that Beer also cites some very disturbing institutional flaws in British parliamentarism during the Thatcher regime.

Mrs. Thatcher proposed to lower taxes, cut governmental spending, reduce the budget deficit, and withdraw from intervention in the economy. But in practice her government "spent countercyclically with greater munificence than any since the war, including Labour ones."[26]

Beer dwells on the institutional weaknesses of parliamentary government that produced these contradictions. Instead of a cabinet that concerts a policy and emerges with everyone saying (and doing) the same thing, we witness a "centrifugal pluralism of ministerial decision-making. . . . Typically, the individual minister is connected by a complex linkage with his department and its powerful dependents in the public and private sector. In the cabinet he confronts other ministers similarly urging their valid claims to public succor, not to say largess."[27]

When Professor Beer searches for a solution to the contradictions of collectivisim, however, he does so within the institutional framework of parliamentary government.[28] The emergent groups that have preempted so much of British politics have failed to unite behind a reasonable plan to reconstruct the polity. (Beer refers specifically to the failure of the trade unions.) So he turns from structural change, through reconstructed groups, to cultural change. He examines trust, a necessary ingredient of any community.[29] Public trust, I take it, results from a common perception of an identity or congruence between generally held ideals and the realities produced by the political process. When deference existed it "constituted a powerful bond of trust within the polity and it's decision-making components."[30]

Trust will come again, as I understand it, when some group of leaders articulates a program that will restore the "legitimacy and effectiveness of the mechanism of public choice." The apparent possibilities are Tories, socialists, neoliberals, neosocialists, and neoradicals. The task will not be just to win an election (although one must start with that) but to "mobilize lasting consent in the major sectors of society." This consent must be wide and deep enough to enable a government to embody its promises in institutions and programs sufficiently durable to protect them against a reversal by an opposition in a future election.[31]

Thus, Professor Beer's solutions are in the realm of ideas. He seems to assume that the parliamentary institutions described earlier ("the sovereign Parliament, the collectively responsible cabinet, the cohesive political party in and out of Parliament, the nationally organized functioning body"), which coped exceptionally well in the past, will continue to cope.[32]

The Divergence of the Committee on the Constitutional System

By contrast, the CCS is united in the belief that the United States seems compelled to start with institutional reform. In England the drift into pluralistic stagnation seems to follow the growth of the new producer and consumer groups as they distort parliamentary government. In the United States, a similar phenomenon (often called "the iron triangles") is not a distortion or an aberration but a natural consequence of the separation of powers; the principle of government itself is the enemy of cohesion.

The United States with its peculiar status and responsibilities must acknowledge the need for comprehensive policies, made from the perspective of the nation, in a number of fields. This seems clear in foreign and defense policy, in fiscal and monetary policy as well as in economic growth and in the attainment of some control over business cycles, and including welfare, retirement and social security. Another area calling for comprehensive policies touches race and ethnic groups. Relationships between the United States and Mexico seem bound to produce issues regarding immigration, trade, and the regulation of contiguous and overlapping markets and communities. One of the world's most difficult problem areas looms along with fifteen hundred mile border. It seems essential that these matters be addressed by a strong national government that can provide a comprehensive approach not only for its own agencies but also for the four border states plus a score of other only somewhat less directly affected. This is not a theater for broad decentralization inspired by the "new federalism" but rather one that calls for address by the united nation that Professor Beer has eloquently expounded.[33] Even though the principle of federalism is retained it is arguable that a parliamentary government will strengthen the sense of the nation among its citizens.

Not only can parliamentary government concert policies and inspire national sentiments; it has other virtues. Above all it can quickly, expeditiously, and legitimately replace leaders who have been found inadequate to the occasion. The prime example if Neville Chamberlain's replacement by Winston Churchill in 1940. Second, parliamentary government fulfills the ineluctable need for periodic elections while escaping the procrustean torment of fixed calendar elections that provide undue advantages to foreign enemies

and domestic mischief-makers while ensuring expensive, endless, un-
duly taxing, and boring campaigns. Third, like no other system,
parliamentary government (it can, I think, be argued) exalts the
virtues of citizenship related "to the skills involved in living a good
human life."[34] Citizens go to the polls to create a government and an
opposition; and for the good of the policy it doesn't matter which:
each is essential.

The act of creating a government can be fraught with meaning.
It can force on people—leaders, representatives, and citizens—the
realization that, if they are to be free, they will have to govern
themselves. It is the same for removing a government or a leader.
The challenge, repudiation, resignation, and replacement by an alternative leader—all are proper and fitting acts of government. They
can be done with gravity and civility but promptly and legitimately.
Not least is the creation and support of an opposition. "To find out
whether a people is free it is necessary only to ask if there is an
Opposition and, if there is, to ask where it is."[35] With the proper
political education people can be taught to see the connection between their action in voting and the emergence of the government
and the opposition. The lesson can be connected to the deed. "It was
the genius of Washington to recognize that the discipline required to
convert free men into soldiers could be strengthened rather than
diluted by an appeal to their memories of freedom."[36]

4

"We, the People . . ."

I am much impressed by the *Workbook* that was prepared for the March 1984 meeting of the Committee on the Constitutional System—by its intention, organization, and selections.[1] But I have some suggestions for the program of the CCS. First, we need further clarification of the central problem in order to form a fixed conception in our minds—always present in its implications for whatever aspect of the Constitution is under discussion. With respect I do not think that the emphasis on deadlock—important as it is—suffices. Rather, I propose a return to Charles H. McIlwain and his strictures against the separation of powers as an ill-advised assault upon government (*gubernaculum*) itself.

McIlwain spent most of his long life studying constitutional government.[2] He thought that gubernaculum preceded constitutionalism (*jurisdictio*). A community must be governed by some legitimate organization that provides protection from outside threats while laying down and enforcing the rules making for order at home. Within this government emerged the bundle of rights that were defined, codified, and applied to particular cases and controversies by official jurists: the process comprising *jurisdictio*. The reconciliation of *gubernaculum* and *jurisdictio* "remains probably our most serious practical problem."[3] McIlwain stressed "the same necessity now, as in past ages, to preserve these two sides of political institutions intact, *to maintain every institution instrumental to strengthening them both, and to guard against the overwhelming of one . . . by the other*"[4] (italics supplied).

After underlining the need for maintaining jurisdictio "against

arbitrary will," McIlwain strongly opposed the enfeebling of gubernaculum. "Among all the modern fallacies that have obscured the true
teachings of constitutional history, few are worse than the extreme
doctrine of the separation of powers and the indiscriminate use of the
phrase 'checks and balances.'" He could find little historical background for the theory of the separation of powers "except the fancies
of eighteenth-century doctrinaires and their followers. Political balances have no institutional background whatever except in the imagination of closet philosophers like Montesquieu."[5]

Nothing that I have said conflicts with the excellent statements
in the introduction to the *Workbook*. But McIlwain was considerably
more vehement. The more I reflect on it, the more I believe that his
vehemence was called for. I regret that I did not make a strong case
along this line at the American Enterprise Institute (AEI) conference
on the Separation of Powers in November 1983.

In any event, I now believe that we must articulate our major
premise so convincingly, so unmistakably, and so indelibly that it will
be everpresent in whatever deliberations we have, in the committee
of the whole or in panels, on the necessary details and aspects of
reform.

Second, growing out of the first point above, and considering
the need for an approach that is both comprehensive and radical in
the sense of going to the root of things, the CCS should attempt to
persuade the relevant academics, especially political scientists and
professors of constitutional law, to devote a significant part of their
curricula to the questions of fundamental constitutional change.

I applaud the effort by the CCS to draft a set of amendments to
accomplish its implicit purposes or, at least, to be a significant step
toward that end. This forthright aim may have attracted many of the
impressive list of notables who attend the CCS meetings. Absent a
cataclysmic crisis, however, the adoption of major changes is extremely doubtful. But if the CCS is right, and daily events grimly
endorse our analysis, the need for reform not only remains but intensifies.

Hence, the CCS might consider a second track: to try to get an
important part of the curricula certainly of political science departments and of law schools devoted to the question of fundamental
constitutional change. These curricula could use the rapid accumulation of excellent materials in the *Workbook*, supplemented by those

in the *Hearings* of the Joint Economic Committee under Henry Reuss's chairmanship on *Political Economy and Constitutional Reform*,[6] together with recent books by James MacGregor Burns, James L. Sundquist, and Don K. Price, and prospective books by F. A. Hermens, Don K. Robinson, and Sundquist. Much other relevant material is appearing. Reviewing Joseph S. Nye, Jr., editor, *The Making of American Foreign Policy*, William G. Hyland wrote that "all the authors point toward a central conclusion that the American policymaking process is flawed. As a nation, we are constitutionally not equipped for devising long-term policies. Our political system almost guarantees tension between the Congress and the White House, and foreign policy is not an exception. Public opinion exerts a growing influence. Shifts in opinion are becoming more frequent and the fluctuations are wider."[7]

By vigorously urging that the examination of constitutional reform be given a prominent position in the curricula of political science, we might seize the imaginations of many movers and shakers in the profession. I say this because of the response I had two years ago when I wrote to ask political scientists if they would "join" us in the CCS. I do not have a similar impression about law schools but Lloyd N. Cutler, Gerhard Casper, and Professor A. E. Dick Howard may. Moreover, the teaching and research approach should appeal to foundations that are leery about supporting "action" programs. Finally, the same approach would be much needed if my third suggestion is adopted.

Third, in addition to present CCS panels, I suggest one on defining and providing a proper role for the people.

On "the People"

The present focus of the CCS on the deadlock that often results from the unwieldy and obstructive relationships between the president and the Congress continues to vindicate the original statements of the problem that first galvanized the Committee. But I am becoming more and more convinced that the CCS should explicitly add an additional focus on the constitutional role of the people. The CCS is, after all, the Committee on the Constitutional *System*. The emphasis on system includes the conventions and institutions that supplement the original document of 1787, as amended: above all else, the political parties. On the most monumental failure in past American politics, James MacGregor Burns wrote: "The immediate cause of the Civil War lay in the derangement of the nation's two political systems—the constitutional system of the 1780's and the party system of the 1830's— and in their interaction with each other."[8]

Government of and by the people means government by political parties. Joseph Schumpeter defined democracy (or the democratic method) as "that institutional arrangement for arriving at political decisions in which individuals acquire the power to decide by means of a competitive struggle for the people's vote."[9] The struggle inevitably has come to be organized by political parties that aim at controlling the personnel and policies of the government. Parties name candidates for political offices; in democracies, voters choose among or, preferably, between them. I shall return to political parties.

"We, the People of the United States . . ." in the Constitution of 1787

The role of the people was highly significant in the Constitution. But its significance then differed markedly from what it has become. In the 1787 Convention the people were spoken for (and sometimes against); they were invoked as the necessary source of legitimacy, especially by and for the benefit of the lawyers whose interpretations were often determinative. Sometimes the people seemed to hover like "a brooding omnipresence in the sky." But they did not seem to have the almost palpable sense that they have now. Their collective presence was not so apparently concrete; their collective wisdom was not so regularly perceived (or, at least, trumpeted) as providential.

The role of the people can surely never be settled for all time. But present exigencies call for redefinition and for appropriate new institutions and procedures that will not only facilitate the proper expression of the public will but also provide a collective experience that will reinforce the popular grasp of and belief in constitutional government.

In the 1787 Convention the role of the people was broached early respecting the manner of election to the first branch, the House of Representatives. Should it be elected by state legislatures or by the people? On May 31, 1787, the issue was resolved in favor of the people, six states voting aye, two no, and two divided.[10] The next issue concerning the people rose out of the manner of ratification of the new Constitution: should it be by state legislatures or by conventions in the states, elected for the purpose by the people? On July 23, a lively debate resulted in the defeat of Oliver Ellsworth's motion to vest the power in state legislatures, seven states to three.[11] Near the convention's end, on September 15, Governor Randolph and George Mason urged that the state ratifying conventions be instructed to propose amendments that would be submitted to a second general or national convention. Mason lamented: "This Constitution has been formed without the knowledge or idea of the people." To this General Pinckney replied, "Nothing but confusion and contrariety would spring from the experiment." And the motion lost. All states voted against it.[12]

Turn now to the way the famous words "We, The People of the United States" came into the preamble. The phrase was in neither the Virginia nor the New Jersey plan: but Charles C. Pinckney introduced a plan that began "We, the People of the State of New Hampshire, (etc.) do ordain and establish, . . ." and on July 24, when the committee of detail was created, his plan, along with the other proceedings of the convention, was turned over to it. In the committee's report, August 6, Pinckney's language was included. It was accepted without debate on August 7 and remained in the penultimate draft given to the committee of style on September 10.[13]

Two days later, the committee of style reported with a draft containing a number of significant changes. The preamble no longer invoked "the people of New Hampshire, Massachusetts, etc." Rather, it began with capitals: "WE, the People of the United States," and it went on, "in order to form a more perfect union, to establish justice, insure domestic tranquility, provide for the common defense, promote the general welfare" (all new words, before it picked up Pinckney's language) "and secure the blessings of liberty to ourselves and our posterity, do ordain and establish this constitution of the United States of America."

No debate on the remarkable change from we, *the people of the*

several states to *we, the people of the United States* was reported; nor
was there debate on the new statement of the ends of government in
the preamble.[14]

Moving to the state ratifying conventions, we find that only in
Virginia was debate on the preamble reported. Patrick Henry referred to the members of the Philadelphia Convention and asked:
"What right had they to say, *We, the People?* My political curiosity as
well as my anxious solicitude for the public welfare leads me to ask,
Who authorized them to speak the language of *We, the People* instead of *We, the States?*" Governor Randolph, who had changed his
mind, replied, "I ask, Why not? The government is for the people;
and the misfortune was, that the people had no agency in the government before . . . I take this to be one of the least and most trivial
objections that will be made to the Constitution . . . "[15]

The Founders and the People

Thus the people—the whole people—was an essential concept
of the Founders. The people were vital to the social contract, a necessity of political theory once the doctrine of the divine right of kings
was beheaded. An appeal to the people seems integral to human
gropings for legitimizing symbols. It tapped an ancient myth.
Charles H. McIlwain wrote the Roman constitutionalism found its
essence in "the older, deeper principle that the *populus,* and none
but the whole *populus,* can be the ultimate source of legal authority."
First, centuries of Roman jurists and, later, centuries of English jurists
asserted the same principle in support of their perilous stands against
the claims of princes.[16]

The Founders of the American Constitution were in this tradition. "That 'the people' should govern themselves was a doctrine
living not so much in the written Constitution as in the American
spirit."[17] But there was ambivalence. James MacGregor Burns writes:
"Loving liberty, the Founders hated Tyranny in any and every form—
religious, kingly, mob, economic, governmental . . . Of the need of
government, they had no doubt . . . Still . . . government itself
could be the most tyrannical force of all. The Founders were not so
simplistic as to think that some autonomous mechanism called 'gov-

ernment' itself was the source of tyranny; it was *people*—majorities, minorities, factions—working in and through government that were the threat."[18]

In part, at least, "We, the People of the United States . . ." was written into the Constitution to help ensure a check on the extremes of democracy. The authors were the committee of style—James Madison, Alexander Hamilton, Gouverneur Morris, Rufus King, and William Johnson. In Madison's famous analysis, they sought to neutralize the threat of factions by "extending the sphere" of government, that is, by creating a national government whose laws would prevail over those of the states. They perceived a threat especially in the popularly elected state legislatures, wielding an authority delegated to them by the people. The legislatures could be overridden by a superior body, the government of the United States. This end could be facilitated, as subsequent judicial decisions showed, by clearly and unmistakably asserting that the authorship of the federal Constitution had been and its ratification would be by the people, the whole people, acting directly, and not just by the people filtered indirectly through state governments. The national or federal government, empowered by the people, could act directly on, for, and with the people.

With this robust legal argument Hamilton anticipated the doctrine of judicial review in *Federalist* No. 78. Superior laws prevail over inferior laws. Deriving from the whole people, the Constitution as superior law prevails over laws merely emanating from representatives of the people. The duty of the court to apply the law requires it to give precedence to superior law. This logic informed *Marbury v. Madison* in which Chief Justice Marshall cited the "original right" of the people "to establish for their future government such principles as . . . shall most conduce to their own happiness." In *Martin v. Hunter's Lessee* Justice Story reaffirmed that "the constitution of the United States was ordained and established not by the states in their sovereign capacities, but emphatically, as the preamble of the constitution declares, by 'the People of the United States.'" Shortly thereafter came *McCulloch v. Maryland*.[19] Arguing that the state could tax the branch of the Bank of the United States, Maryland's counsel urged that the Constitution came not from the people but was "the act of sovereign and independent states." But Chief Justice Marshall held that the Constitution, although framed by a convention composed of delegates from state legislatures and chosen by state legislatures, was only a proposal, reported to the Congress with the recommendation that it be submitted to the people in conventions called in each state. The Constitution was "submitted to the *people*." They acted on it in the only manner that they can act "safely, effectively, and wisely, on such a subject, by assembling in a convention. True, they acted in their several states. How else could they act? But the measures they adopt do not, on that account, cease to be measures of the people themselves, or become the measures of the state governments."

"We, the People . . ." then was necessary if the federal Constitution was to prevail. First, however, it had to be ratified; and in that difficult struggle, when success often hung by a thread, there was no national electorate but rather a series of thirteen separate and distinct arenas of combat.[20] Even after New Hampshire (despite its general apathy throughout the campaign) provided the ninth ratification that enabled the federal government to organize, Virginia, New York, North Carolina, and Rhode Island had still to act. "Their ratification was essential . . . , if only because their exclusion would divide the nation's territory into three non-contiguous parts."[21] In the five most populous states, Virginia, Pennsylvania, North Carolina, Massachusetts, and New York, the issue was either in some doubt or was desperately close. To win ratification the crucial grasp of political divisions, personalities, interests, and procedures had to be intensely local.

Thus, "We, the People . . ." was a stroke of genius, an expression of a thread of democratic thought that had been present in such forums even in ancient Rome, a stratagem essential to the salient legal fiction of the Constitution, and (almost certainly unconsciously) the seed of a political myth of towering proportions.

The Founders could evoke the people at the same time that they insulated their Convention from the press, prescribing and maintaining the tightest security that lasted for decades. The people were denied the flow of news necessary to their guidance of the Convention of 1787. What an outrage such policy would now create! Moreover, the Founders could fashion a constitution in which the impulse of the people's power was exquisitely separated, checked, and balanced. Indeed, they arranged to have the president, who has become the tribune of the people, elected, not by the people themselves, but by a college of electors, popularly chosen, but supposedly enjoying virtually complete discretion in their choice.

The People — 200 Years Later

For the Founders "the people" was a necessary abstraction. For us the abstraction has achieved some reality. There is a national electorate. Even if the president must accumulate his majority by states, he stands alone on his unique pyramid of, say, fifty million votes.

But "the people," in addition to the degree of reality it has acquired, has also been monstrously reified. The American people, collectively personified, have become the universal solver of issues. Relentlessly, the media reports the pollsters' findings on the public's attitudes and preferences on a multitude of issues (the sample is "scientific" and a miniscule margin of error is scrupulously acknowledged). The reification of the public purports to fulfill a need for a final seat of power where the buck really stops — for an institution where perplexing issues are finally and authoritatively resolved. The reification is all the more poignant because it tacitly acknowledges how well the separation of powers has undermined gubernaculum.

In 1951 President Truman fired General Douglas MacArthur for insubordination. The general's homecoming was greeted by huge welcoming crowds. An avalanche of mail, much of it abusive of President Truman, piled into the White House. A Senate subcommittee published hearings on MacArthur's discharge that paraded the country's military secrets, including its grand strategy, its estimates of its own capacities, and the details of what it knew and did not know of the strength of the enemy. "Before God," declared Senator Charles W. Tobey, "the picture makes me stand aghast." Why was all the information published? "These were the facts that would be needed for judgment, not only by the Senators but by the public — from whom, in reality, both sides were asking a verdict." Meanwhile, the public had lost interest.[22]

Similarly twenty years later in Watergate, Americans were repeatedly told that they were the jury, that the Senators were only bringing out the facts on which they would have to judge. But how could the public judge such things as use immunity, constructive knowledge of criminal events, the nature and limitations of subpoenas, executive privilege, the exigencies of national security, its use in justifying presidential secrecy, and, indeed, the separation of powers the meaning of which has been eruditely argued for two hundred years?

Presidents and public figures vie in attributing omniscience and omnipotence to the public. "The American People want the Germans to live . . . but do not want them to have a higher standard of living than other states, such as the Soviet Republic" (Franklin D. Roosevelt). The American public "would probably support a . . . credit of three billion dollars [to Britain] if a satisfactory . . . commercial policy could be reached" (Undersecretary of State Will Clayton). And this from Thomas B. Watson, Jr., president of IBM, who was discoursing on the priorities between civil rights and national security:

I honestly believe . . . that the people of the United States are sensible enough so that they in their own minds will put one above the other in the correct order and will devote their attentions to the most important.[23]

A recent example was provided by Robert C. MacFarlane, President Reagan's national security adviser. Asked about the role of the CIA in Central America, he responded that the American people "will have to wrestle with the question of should we or should we not have some immediate action of policy—covert action."[24] Or consider Ronald M. Peters, Jr., director of the Carl Albert Congressional Research and Policy Center, on the present trends of the Speakership in the House of Representatives: "We've created a situation whereby . . . you drive the legislative process . . . by influencing public opinion rather than by trading for votes."[25]

This reification of the people as the universal solvers of all political problems recommends itself to some opponents of proposals of constitutional reform. Arthur M. Schlesinger, Jr., turns to Lord Bryce who a century ago recorded the foreign view that the separation of powers made it nearly impossible for the American political system to solve major problems. American leaders, Bryce noted, retorted that the failure was not attributable to defects in the institutional structure. Rather, "the division of opinion in the country . . . has been faithfully reflected in Congress. The majority has not been strong enough to get its way" not only because of institutional obstacles to the concerting of policies "but still more because no distinct . . . mandate toward any particular settlement . . . has been received from the country. It is not for Congress to go faster than the people. When the country knows and speaks its mind, Congress will not fail to act."[26]

A sounder view was set forth by James Madison in the Constitutional convention of 1787. Delegates were discussing the frequency of elections of members of the House of Representatives, should it be for one, two, or three years? Elbridge Gerry said that "the people of New England will never give up . . . annual elections." Arguing for the longer term, James Madison said "that if the opinions of the people were to be our guide, it wd. be difficult to say what course we ought to take. No member of the Convention could say what the opinions of his Constituents were at this time; much less could he say what they would think if possessed by the information and lights of the members here; and still less what would be their way of thinking 6 or 12 months hence. We ought to consider what was right and necessary in itself for the attainment of a proper Government."[27]

Were it not for the habitual forthrightness on the issue shared by Madison and his colleagues, one might attribute this frankness to faith in the confidentality of the convention.[28] Few public persons would make such a statement today. But the widespread public ignorance on the essential details of many public policy questions is not only well known to common sense but is unquestionably established by social science.[29] Public ignorance should not be read as public stupidity. Many busy people wisely refuse to acquaint themselves with a host of public policy issues over the resolution of which they have neither responsibility nor influence.[30]

And yet the public can and should have a role that far exceeds anything it possessed in 1787 or even in 1987. That role is not to be the unfailing solver of political problems and resolver of public issues. Rather, it is periodically to decide whether the government-of-the-day shall continue for another term and at the same time to confer legitimacy on both the elected government and the opposition. Before stating the implications of this conclusion, however, another aspect of the people in our governmental system demands attention.

The People, the Constitution, and Political Parties

An immediate problem with the people emerges out of the main concern of the CCS with the frequent inability of the political system in the United States to produce a government that can concert and carry out effective, coherent policies, economic and otherwise (energy, the environment, immigration). For the political structure to generate such governments it must be conducive to the formation of fairly stable popular majorities. To repeat, the only known means for organizing such majorities are political parties that aim at controlling the policies and personnel of government by organizing the competitive struggle for the people's vote. Yet the Founders mentioned political parties only to decry them. None of the Founders set forth a theory of political parties "that rivaled their theory of checks and balances." One little-known Anti-Federalist in Maryland did say: "the object of a free and wise people should be to so balance parties that *from the weakness of all you may be governed by the combined judgments of the whole,* not tyrannized over by the blind passions of a few individuals." No one could have said it better, wrote James MacGregor Burns, "but nobody of importance seemed to be listening."[31]

The CCS should seek to strengthen parties to help ensure stable congressional majorities that will support cohesive and effective governments. In a timely effort to discover what induces party discipline in legislative bodies that will be conducive to stable majorities, Lloyd N. Cutler surveyed the governments of the United Kingdom, France, West Germany, and Ireland.[32] Two explanations appeared. First, parties in these countries exerted much more control over nominations than American parties do. Second, the rewards for following the party line and the punishment for flouting it were much clearer and more immediate in Europe.

Actually, everything turns on the first explanation. Without control of nominations, as E. E. Schattschneider pointed out (confirmed, by implication, by Pendleton Herring)[33] political parties cannot develop a system of rewards and punishments. In America, however, control over nominations has essentially been taken away from parties and settled on the people, but the people fragmented by the effects of the separation of powers and federalism. The results are clear even in the presidency. Not since 1952 has a major party convention required more than one ballot to select a candidate. Democratization has surged. Between 1960 and 1980 the number of states with presidential preference primaries jumped from sixteen to thirty-one. Yet the apparent strengthening of popular choice has been perverted by the effective presumption of the experience: that candidates for the nomination to run for president of the United States must compete in a myriad of localities on the basis of their promise to deal with localized issues. Aspirants for the nomination (usually, other than the incumbent) are forced to seek popular votes in caucuses or primaries not by addressing the people as a whole but by appealing to the people splintered into, and encouraged to think of themselves as members of, their sectional, local, and peculiar interests.

The popularly elected president is our strongest institutional force in favor of limiting the major political parties to two. For one prize there will usually be only two contenders. (Exceptions in 1912, 1924, and 1980 were soon superseded; the major exception in 1860 was part of the Civil War derangement noted by Burns.) Having two major parties is good. It encourages majority government. Under this regimen people should learn by their actions (their voting) that they are creating a government or, equally important for the good of the country, an opposition. The people can thus have a share, however diluted, in making the difficult and wrenching choices that are the lot of all governments. But this share tends to be lost because of the present nomination process in which people are encouraged to press for their immediate interests to the ultimate degree, as though each candidate's excuse for being was his willingness to carry out their hearts' desires. Thus gubernaculum is weakened.

It is further debilitated by the requirement of the separation of powers that elections of the executive and the legislative must be insulated from the significant influence of the other. Crucial to this end are fixed calendar elections. The alternative to calendar elections are elections at the discretion of the government. And that step, however much it may be in the national interest — indeed, the time may come when it will be important to national survival itself — would mark the end of the separation of powers.

In the present way of doing things, gubernaculum is destroyed. Inexorably, the people are drawn into, or are said to be drawn into, the nominating process where they are out of place. A vital part of government, or gubernaculum, is the selection, training, and promotion of leaders. Like any other activity that requires great skill and art, government works best when the responsibility for advancement is clearly fixed in the peers of aspirants to higher office. How is this to be reconciled with the demands of democracy? Democracy requires choice. But the choice had better be between teams of contenders, teams that propose to make up a government, but teams that make their own choices of candidates. To say that the electorate must get *inside* the team and nominate the candidates will destroy the team; it would be like the football fans choosing the quarterback for today's game, or the baseball fans selecting the battery.

Yet this is what we have. Our institutions require every candidate for the state legislature and every candidate for United States senatorial or congressional seats to build his or her own party. These individual ends are accomplished at the cost of the destruction of government itself.

Majority Rule, the Opposition, the Mandate, Accountability

The CCS must therefore address itself to fundamentals. Especially when the CCS breaks down into panels to look at aspects of the governmental process, it must keep the fundamentals in mind. As John Marshall wrote in *McCulloch v. Maryland,* "we must never forget that it is a *constitution* we are expounding."

The present constitutional system has a strong component of majority government. Presidents are essentially elected by a popular majority. So are Senators and Members of Congress in their states and districts. Both branches of Congress organize themselves by majorities. So do committee and caucuses. The Supreme Court votes by majorities. Despite all the provisions for extraordinary majorities in the Constitution, it is the observance of the principle of majority rule that gives the government what efficacy it has.

But this does not mean that the majority is necessarily right. It signifies only that a majority vote is a natural and effective way of settling disputes (James Madison, Walter Lippmann and Lindsay Rogers). Hence the vital importance of the opposition, without which constitutional government cannot exist.

The people need to learn as part of their "operative political ideals"[34] that when they go to the polls their right and duty is to select, first, a government that can govern, even though its decisions may prove faulty and, second, an opposition whose function it is to criticize the government even when its decisions prove relatively satisfactory. The procedure of government should be suffused with an air of contingency: events call for actions that may prove insufficient or even counterproductive. Very well; government must try again, always subject to the vocal scrutiny of its critics in the opposition. The whole system testifies to the idea that government is necessary, that it must act even though imperfectly, but that it must also be subjected to continuous criticism — and that the public, no longer invested with the wisdom of Jehovah, is in a real sense involved: it is *its* governing party that is acting — and it is *its* opposition that is cavilling and complaining, "we could do it better."

What is meant by the mandate that is frequently invoked with great specificity? With perhaps very rare exceptions, the mandate should be simply to govern — and to oppose. The public is saying by its vote: "We recognize that government is necessary; that government must act on a multitude of issues, even though its action may sometimes be ill-advised. Like life itself, government must proceed largely by trial and error. We create a government that can govern for a limited term, and we also create an opposition whose function it is not only to offer reasoned alternatives but to jeer and hoot. We identify with both; we suffer and exult with both; both are ours."

Likewise accountability; it ceases to be for specific performance. Governments should not be elected to make good on discrete campaign promises to various groups or even to the public at large. They should be elected to govern (and a large part of them to oppose); and it should be for this that they should be accountable to the voting public. What they would really be accountable for is maintaining both gubernaculum and jurisdictio intact during their period in office. Just as this should be the essential test of the accountability of the government to the people, so the people should be accountable, too. They should be accountable to their forebears and to future generations. They are the present members of, and the contemporary participants in, as Edmund Burke put it, "the partnership not only between those who are living, but between those who are living and those who are dead, and those who are yet to be born."

This does not mean an absolute repudiation of "interest group liberalism." A politically ingenious people with free elections will always produce activists who will find their way to the candy store. But the search of the CCS should be for arrangements that will provide a durable, resilient, and overriding set of institutions that, to amend Roland Young's arresting phrase, will compel not only the Congress but the citizens to have a national point of view.

Nor does it mean that politicians will cease to bid against each other in the struggle for the peoples' votes. Nevertheless, in drastically shortened campaigns followed by general elections in which the entire government is returned or the opposition is voted in, the people will be able to put campaign promises in a proper perspective. Party platforms can then become useful exercises in which the parties show their ability to analyze present problems and suggest remedies rather than lists of detailed promises in the specific performance of which governmental "accountability" is measured.

Conclusion

Whatever happens to the package of constitutional amendments the CCS is formulating, if the foregoing analysis is correct the long-range educational task of constitutional reformers is formidable. We may get a hint of how to proceed by referring once more to James Madison who worried not only about factions but also about the increase in population in future years that would swell the ranks of those who would "labour under all the hardships of life, and secretly sigh for a more equal distribution of its blessings." Viewing the ends to be served by government, he postulated, first, protecting the people against their rulers, but, second, protecting the people also "agst. the transient impressions into which they themselves might be led."

At the same time, he argued that the people under favorable circumstances are capable of comprehending the basic realities of constitution making. "A people deliberating in a temperate moment . . . on the plant of Govt. most likely to secure their happiness, would first be aware that those charged with the public happiness, might betray their trust." This, Madison argued, could be corrected by dividing the trust between different bodies of men who would check on each other. But then the people would also foresee "that they themselves were liable to temporary errors, thro' want of information as to their true interest . . . Another reflection equally becoming a people on such an occasion, wd. be that they themselves, were liable to err also, from fickleness and passion."[35]

Unfortunately the remedial separation of powers that Madison recommended (the division of trust) contained a lethal attack on gubernaculum. But he had a heartening belief in the educability of the people. To exploit this we might refer to Kurt Reizler's analysis of the great numbers of human beings characteristic of modern societies as masses, crowds, herds, and the people. The masses are large conglomerates without interconnections other than temporary proximity through chance. Crowds are masses united suddenly by fear, hatred or other deep emotions; stampede may be imminent. Herds are crowds under the hypnotic sway of leaders. The people, by contrast, in "all their various groups and associations, responding to one another and being responded to by one another, form together a universe of mutual response." But the universe of response may be sundered if "workers are listening only to workers, manufacturers only to manufacturers." Then "the people will soon see the last day of their relative freedom."

In maintaining the people and in preparing them to accept the idea and then the possibility of fundamental constitutional change, Reizler's theory of political education may be in point. He would rely on a relatively few (but actually on several million in so large a nation) anonymous leaders "whose voices count, they are asked their opinion by the many."[36]

Consider also the conception of the "third cadre" by James MacGregor Burns, less numerous than Riezler's anonymous leaders (but one can well imagine the reciprocation between the two groups). According to Burns they served the country well in 1787–88:

> "And so the issue was put to the American people in the late fall of 1787—put not to a great mass public, though large numbers of voters would turn out to elect state convention delegates, put not to small national or state elites, though established leaders would exercise heavy influence in many of the contests, but put to about 1,200 delegates who would be elected to the state conventions . . . A first cadre in Philadelphia had written a charter, a second cadre of state leadership was quick to join the battle; now the issue would depend on a third cadre, composed largely of local politicians . . . The future of the republic would turn on the perspicacity and vision of country politicians, circuit-riding lawyers, money-minded men of commerce, and cracker-barrel philosophers—on a critical mass of men who would have to lift their sights above gables and chimney pots and see their way into the possibilities of nationhood."[37]

As the twentieth century lurches toward its close the people may be informed by Riezler's "aristocracy in overalls" and eventually represented by a contemporary version of Burns' third cadre, but the entire process, in the presence of a fractured (if not a shattered) gubernaculum, needs the kind of analysis provided their ancestors of 1787 by both Federalists and Anti-Federalists: a serious discussion of the roots of government and of the possibilities of constitutionalism in modern mass societies. The CCS ought to make sure that its side of the argument is fully stated and vigorously presented. Then the CCS should call on the universities of the nation, and, within them especially the departments of political science and the schools of law, to mount an appropriate and durable teaching program on the questions of fundamental constitutional reform.

5

Herman Belz
Constitutionalism and Bureaucracy

THE spring 1984 issue of APSA's *NEWS for Teachers of Political Science* contains Herman Belz's provocative piece on "Constitutionalism and Bureaucracy in the 1980s." His definitions of both terms are unsatisfactory. His concept of constitutionalism is anemic. It fails to recognize that governments must have some characteristics of Leviathan: they must be large and formidable. To constitutionalize such governments is proportionately difficult. In the United States the difficulty is greatly aggravated by the bureaucracies, which the separation of powers fosters, that tend to fragment government into quasi-independent power blocks. Nor are these bureaucracies mere aggregations of civil servants. They typically include political administrators, veteran legislators, and experienced group leaders. Let me turn first to Professor Belz's argument.

Belz says that the "basic purpose of constitutionalism [is] to limit government in the interest of individual liberty while assuring effective government for the accomplishment of collective social ends." If peaceful methods of political change obtain and violence is eschewed, a "minimal" constitutionalism exists, "but there is much to demand of a constitutional state beyond keeping the peace."

Some claim, Belz writes, that our government is too weak to control the excesses of private power. Some lament the decline of confidence in our government. More often complaints are that our

First published in the *NEWS for Teachers of Political Science,* American Political Science Association, Washington, D.C. Republished by permission.

government's efforts on behalf of national security or of equalization appear to threaten "constitutional liberty." Although these complaints cite the executive, Congress, and the courts, "the principal danger to liberty . . . is thought to come from administrative institutions," from a "remote and irresponsible bureaucracy."

Tracing the rise of bureaucracy, Belz finds the progressive movement pressing for governmental authority to regulate a rapidly changing economy. "Rejecting popularly elected, if corrupt and inefficient, legislatures reformers favored . . . delegation of legislative power to independent administrative agencies." The reformers believed that this "would lead to nonpolitical yet democratically legitimate policymaking by trained and knowledgeable administrative experts, acting in accordance with a broad statutory mandate to promote the public good."

With respect to bureaucracy-out-of-control, Belz says that the critics of bureaucracy have expressed "mere disagreement with an administrative decision, or dissatisfaction that an agency has not followed a congressional directive or allowed the fullest participation in decision making." Then he says: "If by control one means accountability of administrators to elected officials, citizen and interest group involvement in policymaking, and effective implementation of programs, then the bureaucratic state can be shown to operate under a system of flexible controls and in accordance with check-and-balance limitations."

He adds that in the United States "the bureaucratic state has been adapted to the political culture. It has been democratized, politicized, and fragmented sometimes at the expense of general, prospective and clearly defined rule making that characterizes the rule of law. Yet the rule of law is not the sum and substance of constitutionalism." Since its origin at the turn of the century, he says, the administrative state has conjured up the bugabear of unified and concentrated power. But political reality dispels the threat. "Diffusion of authority and reciprocal restraints have remained the constitutional norm. The administrative state has become constitutionalized as the fourth branch of government."

In his concluding paragraph, Belz repeats that the bureaucratic state, though powerful, has generally followed public policies determined by the political branches "in accordance with public opinion organized and expressed through party competition." But a possible threat emerges. Political parties and legislatures have weakened. While administrators, the executive, and the courts have become more powerful, Congress has often been odd man out. With a conservative instead of an activist president, the executive branch may also weaken. Then a "permanent government" of courts and the bureaucracy may "thwart executive policymaking in response to public opinion." The courts and the bureaucracy would apply "standards of substantive rationality and correct morality that are intended to end political debate."

Belz might assuage his concern by recalling his own "strong argument . . . that the bureaucratic civil service, in its social, economic, and cultural diversity is more representative of the American people than the assembled members of Congress." May not the weakening of Congress, the potential weakening of the president, and the decline of political parties be simply more manifestations of the evolution of the political culture to which, he says, the bureaucratic state has adapted? Will not the faithfulness with which the bureaucracy represents the people nullify the mischief of the courts?

I shall undertake a fuller answer.

Critique

I shall begin with an appeal to Charles H. McIlwain's conception of constitutionalism and to his strictures against the separation of powers for its assault on government itself. The mischief done by the separation of powers is manifest in bureaucracy, conceived differently from Belz.[1]

Professor Belz would probably agree that a weakening of *gubernaculum* is apparent in the scorn heaped on the Congress and in a detached and inactive president (if the latter, in fact, impends), but I shall argue that bureaucracy, developing out of the separation of powers, often poses a major threat to gubernaculum.

Neustadt wrote that "in the decade of the 1940s an extraordinary element was added to the government of the United States: an executive establishment, a body of officials, which for size, scale, and corporate survival was a new creation, unlike anything our governmental system knew before."[2]

In an effort to control the bureaucracy (to simplify Neustadt's complex and sophisticated argument) the president acts according to his genius, which is to run or manage things by coordinating, synthesizing, and integrating them and by designing his administration so that issues are flushed up to him. The Executive Office of the President, "established not only an organization but a doctrine; the rightness of a 'President's Department.'" This was done "in the nick of time"; without it the presidency "would by now [1965] have been a hollow shell."[3]

Meanwhile, Congress, following its own genius to run or manage things by dividing them up and parcelling them out, creates quasi-independent bureaucracies—this was Neustadt's term for what others have called "whirlpools," "iron triangles," or "subgovernments." "The gainers, ordinarily, are of two sorts: on the one hand, effective agency careerists; on the other hand, well-placed committee members, especially seniority leaders (or their staff)." Later Neustadt added: "If clients and constituents are brought into the combine to the satisfaction of all sides, so much the better."[4]

In their contrasting efforts to control, the president and the Congress clash with each other. ("But phrases twist the fact into a conflict between president and congress.")[5] Bureaucracy escapes control. But bureaucracy is not composed merely of quasi-independent administrative agencies; it has an indispensable legislative component. This fact must be kept in mind even when one reads Neustadt's conclusion. "Bureaucracy has brought a new contestant into play: the great prospective struggle is between entrenched officialdom and politicians everywhere." And, later: "The moral is plain. To paraphrase Karl Marx: Politicians at the two ends of the Avenue unite! You have nothing to lose but your pieces of power—and even now these may be slipping out of reach."

So far I have offered only a counter assertion to Professor Belz's pronouncement that the "the administrative state has become constitutionalized." He may mean that so long as concentration camps have not appeared and organized political opposition has not been outlawed, constitutional government survives. I argue that by the time these drastic events take place it is too late and that we can already discern unfortunate developments in public policy that justify our concern about the working of the constitutional system.

An argument based on public policy developments may be dismissed by Belz as unscientific. Thus, he rejects critics or bureaucracy for expressing "mere disagreements with an administrative decision" and his conclusion criticizes "substantive rationality." Political scientists should eschew judgments on policy; they should not make judgments appropriate to physicists, chemists, engineers, economists — or politicians; rather, they should confine themselves to the examination of governmental processes in order to discern uniformities of behavior that other independent observers can verify.

By contrast, I think that the nature of the subject matter often requires political scientists to include in their analyses an evaluation of the policies that political systems produce — or, better, an evaluation of political systems based on an appraisal of the policies they produce. (One must recognize that sometimes the best or even the better alternative is not clear.)

Here, again, Neustadt's conclusions about bureaucracy appear to reflect his adverse judgments on the kind of policies that the present system is prone to produce, e.g., his citation (drawing on Douglass Cater) of "the subgovernment" in the nation's sugar program or his statement that "the most critical of government decisions, the war-or-peace decision, have been snatched away from Congress by technology."[6]

As I understand Neustadt, his call for politicians to unite to produce a better-regulated, better-run polity is as much policy-oriented as James Madison's call for a national government that would "extend the sphere and . . . take in a greater variety of parties and interests." "A rage for paper money, for an abolition of debts, for an equal division of property, or for any other improper or wicked project, will be less likely to pervade the whole body of the Union."[7] I shall offer two illustrations: one from the price support/production control program in agriculture, the other from military policy, exemplified by the nuclear arms race.

Agricultural Price Support/Production Control Policy

A classical example of the kind of bureaucracy posited here was provided by the chairman of the House Committee on Agriculture, Congressman Flannagan (D., Va.), in 1945, when he said on the floor of the House: "The tobacco program has been the most successful agricultural program ever inaugurated in the country. It works. If this House will continue to leave the tobacco problems to the growers and their Representatives in Congress it will continue to work." Congressman Hope, the ranking Republican member of the committee, retorted: tobacco growers "already have what amounts to a monopoly . . . If you do not have a quota you cannot produce unless you pay a very heavy penalty. It is not only a closed shop proposition but it is a closed union with a closed shop."[8]

On its face, the agricultural price support/production control program did sometimes pose a threat to liberty. But I shall dwell on other unfortunate effects or consequences of the policy over time.[9] Begun in 1933 with the first Agricultural Adjustment Act, the price support/production control program has been continuous and widespread, covering especially the "basic crops," cotton, corn, wheat, rice, and tobacco, and acquiring a large bureaucracy with a unique "farmer committee system" at its core. But it has enjoyed numerous ties to members of Congress and has accounted regularly for at least two-thirds of the agricultural budget.

A significant early illustration of the unfortunate influence on policy of the agricultural bureaucracy, motivated by its intense fear of surpluses, was its impediment to increasing farm production and to shifting among crops produced as called for by the war effort — "it was 1944, two full production years after Pearl Harbor (wrote Walter Wilcox), before the Agricultural Adjustment Administration and [its] congressional supporters . . . became convinced that they could take the 'brakes' off the agricultural production machine."

The level of agricultural price supports also became a critical issue. In 1938 the Agricultural Adjustment Act provided a sliding scale for support of the "basic crops" at 52–75 percent of parity. With the economy improved by the military crunch, and prodded vigorously by the American Farm Bureau Federation as well as by the Farmer Committee System, Congress raised supports to 90 percent of parity to be maintained for two full calendar years after hostilities had been officially declared to have ceased. Hence, January 1, 1949, became the critical date.

Economists in and out of government agreed on the wisdom of returning to a flexible price support system but at a higher range than enacted in 1938. Accordingly, the Hope-Aiken Bill set price supports at 70 to 90 percent of parity (to be adjusted reversely to the size of the carryover). The American Farm Bureau Federation, after a bitter fight, accepted flexible price supports (but some southern state Farm Bureaus were adamant: "they'll lick us in Chicago, but we'll lick them in Congress"). The Grange and even the Farmers Union agreed to flexible supports. So did both political parties, the United States Department of Agriculture (formally, at least), a committee of the Association of Land Grant Colleges and Universities, and nearly all agricultural economists. Only the Production and Marketing Administration (as the old AAA was now called) and its farmer committees insisted on 90 percent of parity. Congress passed the Hope-Aiken Bill but postponed its application for one year. Successive annual postponements followed and, in 1952 (in anticipation of a Republican victory), a two-year postponement assured the retention of 90 percent supports until 1955. Even then the departure from that level was very modest.

The agricultural price-support bureaucracy was a significant factor to overriding what seemed in 1947 and 1948 to be a promising effort to bring the numerous political actors into agreement behind flexible price supports. The retention of higher supports probably pushed up land values, encouraged production increases that undermined the soil bank program, and helped (along with important technological improvements) to produce mountainous surpluses, especially in feed grains. These surpluses fueled the movement to turn Public Law 480, the Agricultural Trade and Development Act of 1954 (later, Food for Peace) into a gigantic effort to push American farm surpluses abroad, often in a manner difficult to distinguish from dumping.

The domestic farm price support/production control program conflicted with foreign policy. In 1949, President Truman's inaugural address announced a "bold new program for making the benefits of our scientific advances in industrial progress available for the improvement and growth of underdeveloped areas." Truman's "Point four" survived subsequent changed in administrations. But its effects were repeatedly undermined by the defenders of American agriculture. In 1967, the President's Scientific Advisory Committee declared that "domestic political constraints have so eroded the [foreign assistance] program and the agency responsible for it that there remains virtually no possibility of commitments to . . . the systematic solution of . . . problems."

A final word about equity and effectiveness. The price support/

production control program has by no means been egalitarian. It could work only by giving larger farmers incentives to comply. In 1964, of 3,573,000 census farms, some 384,000 or 10.7 percent with incomes from farm sales of $10,000 and over, received 54.5 percent of the government's payments to agriculture. At the other end of the scale of farmers whose chief source of income was from farming, the 463,000 with income from farm sales of $2,500 to $4,999 constituted 13 percent of the farmers and got 4.7 percent of the governmental payments.

It might be added that 42.7 percent of the farms that received less than $2,500 from farm sales, all 1,823,000 of them, received only 4.6 percent of the total payments. This large group earned three times as much income from off-farm employment as they did from agriculture. But they gave the farm program the public image of having a mass base. They averaged $51 in governmental payments annually against $2,391 for the farms selling $10,000 or more. Given the aims of the program and the means of operation, it cannot be faulted for failing to achieve an egalitarian objective. But it is proper to point out that the windfalls of the well-to-do were supported politically by the pittances to the poor.

Nor is this quite all. How well did the program succeed in attaining the goal maintained since 1933 — parity for farmers? The USDA calculated in 1964 that to increase the incomes of the top 10.7 percent to parity would require only an additional 2 percent. But that calculation failed to include the net gain in the value of farm real estate, which was increasing during the 1940s, 1950s, and 1960s at least three times as fast as the increases in the consumer price index. The top farmers were getting real returns much larger than parity. But the USDA also found that the 13 percent earning from $2,500 to $4,999 from farm sales would need a 74 percent rise in incomes to achieve parity; and the department offered no calculation whatsoever for the 42.7 percent of the farmers with less than $2,500 income from farming.

After thirty years and the expenditure of scores of billions of dollars, these were the results of "the farm program."[10] Was this the "accomplishment of a collective social end," according to Professor Belz? Was the program vindicated by being "accountable to elective officials," by involving "citizens and interest groups in policymaking" — was this an example of "the bureaucratic state" operating "under a system of flexible controls and in accordance with check-and-balance limitations"? Had the farm program with its persistent overrewarding of the few and its repeated failure remotely to approach parity for the many become "the administrative state constitutionalized as the fourth branch of government"?

The Military Bureaucracy and the Nuclear Arms Race

In *Presidential Power and Accountability,* I dwelt at some length on the growth and effect of bureaucracy as productive of malworking of our governmental institutions sufficiently severe to warrant fundamental constitutional change. Here I shall offer only one example of this influence: the early effect on the nuclear arms race, especially on the number of deliverable Intercontinental Ballistic Missiles (ICBM) deployed by the United States and by the USSR. The 1960 electoral debate resounded with Kennedy's forebodings about the impending "missile gap" when the number of Soviet missiles would dangerously exceed ours. In retrospect, Charles L. Schultze said that the missile gap was promoted by the military bureaucracy "at a time when there was not a single ICBM . . . deployed." Only later did we learn that the Russians "actually built only three percent of the missiles predicted by 1963."

In 1961, Secretary of Defense Robert S. McNamara joined the government determined above all else to reduce the world's capacity to make nuclear war. But once in office he became acutely aware of the direct relationship between the number of warheads he requested and the degree of his support among the flag officers and their congressional allies. After the hyperboles of doom had reverberated away, the new White House staff had reached a consensus that 450 ICBM's—the number that the United States already had—were enough. McNamara agreed. But he was adamant that the administration must request 950. The Joint Chiefs of Staff were asking for 3,000. Therefore, 950 was "the smallest number we can take up on the hill without getting murdered."[11]

About eighteen months later the United States and the USSR were "eyeball to eyeball" in the Cuban missile crisis. At the time, the American strategists (according to a recent report) knew that they had four hundred deliverable ICBMs. They believed the Russians to have one hundred. The United States learned later that the Russians probably had only ten deliverable ICBMs at the time.[12] In 1969, William C. Foster, the former director of the Arms Control and Disarmament Agency wrote that the Soviets had only a small ICBM force in 1961; but the United States, assuming that they would build a large number, began a sizeable expansion. "We thus ended up with a considerably larger arsenal of missiles and warheads than we actually required. But then the Soviets also began extensive deployment—probably in response to our efforts." In confirmation, Robert McNamara said that Soviet fears of the power of the United States' nuclear missiles probably triggered the massive buildup of the Soviet ICBMs in the 1960s and set off the nuclear arms race.[13]

War is too important to be left to the generals even when linked with their associates in the Congress, in the armament industries, and in whatever other cadres make up the military bureaucracy. The same criticism that Madison applied in *Federalist* No. 10 is relevant, together with the same cure—"extend the sphere." The extended sphere must then be provided with a government that will concentrate the power and the responsibility, both now and historically, for decisions of this magnitude.

Conclusion

My argument with Professor Belz is grounded on different conceptions of constitutionalism and of bureaucracy. Rather than defining constitutional government as a means of ensuring liberty and achieving agreed social ends, I follow McIlwain in placing the initial emphasis on government itself for defense against foreign foes and against domestic subversion and disorder. I shall reinforce McIlwain by quoting from R. G. Collingwood.

> Our favourite nightmare in the twentieth century is about our powerlessness in the giant grip of economic and social and political structures; the nightmare which Professor Arnold Toynbee calls "The Intractableness of Institutions."
>
> The founders of modern political science made it clear once for all that these Leviathans are "Artificial Animals," creatures formed by the art of man, "for whose protection and defence" they were intended.

This is the ground of the nightmare. Oppression and ex-
ploitation, persecution and war, the torturing to death of human beings in vast helpless masses, are not new things on the
face of the earth, and nobody thinks they are; nor are they done
in the world on a greater scale or with more refinement of
cruelty than they have been done in the past; nor have we grown
more sensitive, to shrink as men once did not, from blood.

But Hobbes (and others, but especially Hobbes) has for the
first time in history held up a hope that there would be "protection and defence" against these things; and by now the hope has
sunk into our common consciousness; so that when we find it to
be precisely the agents of this longed-for safety that are the chief
authors of the evils for whose ending we have made them, hope
turns to despair and we are ridden by another Frankenstein-
nightmare, like Samuel Butler's nightmare of humanity
enslaved to its own machines, only worse . . .

To strengthen the hope until it overcomes the nightmare,
what must be done is to carry on the work, sadly neglected since
Hobbes and a handful of successors began it, of constructing a
science of politics appropriate for the modern world.[14]

Against McIlwain and Collingwood, Professor Belz's conception
of constitutional government seems inadequate. It is too genteel, too
trusting of the uniquely favorable historical conditions of the United
States. Norman Malia's comment on the abortive Polish constitutionalism, circa 1450–1650, comes to mind: "This 'republic of no-
bles' was able to establish its power because, until very late, Poland
lacked neighbors dangerous enough to make royal absolutism a
necessity for national survival."[15]

Once gubernaculum is established, freedom from its abuse is
achieved not as an abstraction but by the official assertion of concrete
limits to power and of specific rights against the state by judges and
lawyers who may rise to heroism in the process. It is thus that the
great writ of habeas corpus and the noble proscriptions in the Bill of
Rights become established. The civilizing mission of the keepers of
jurisdictio continues: witness the "Unlikely Heroes" of the old Fifth
Circuit Court of Appeals in the 1960s and 1970s.[16]

Bureaucracy as described in this paper is not Belz's administrative state nor his constitutionalized fourth branch of government.
Rather it consists of the quasi-independent whirlpools or triangles of

power that emerge from government, itself fragmented by the vaunted separation of powers. To evaluate the effects of such bureaucracies requires us to break through our methodological shells and examine their influence on policy. If we do, I think that we will conclude that the distortions and malworkings caused by, e.g., the agricultural bureaucracy, while perhaps supportable by themselves, are, when added to others, cumulatively dangerous to gubernaculum. Some of the effects of the military bureaucracy are vastly more threatening. Even though it takes major institutional change, we should seriously consider reconstructing our institutions so that these momentous decisions are no longer systematically hived off into obscurity but are clearly made the inexorable responsibilities of gubernaculum. There is no guarantee against "the march of folly," but the best insurance against it must lie in the injunction of *Federalist* No. 51: "The interests of the man must be connected with the constitutional rights of the place."[17]

To this end power should be consolidated rather than divided, so that those who govern are accountable for their acts not only to the electorate but to history. Power, thus concentrated, should be held pending the next election and subject to the unremitting and official opposition organized in a shadow government that will not only help prepare its members for their putative assumption of power but also teach all, voters and politicos alike, that if the great pillars of constitutional government should be timeless, the policies of the government-of-the-day should be acknowledged as contingent and experimental however logical and even necessary they seem at the time.

6

The Disruptive Separation
of Powers

I N a recent book and subsequent public television series, Fred
W. Friendly and Martha J. H. Elliott provided a lucid, scholarly, and impressive background for and understanding of
pivotal issues concerning the Constitution of United States.
However, there is a problem in that, although they do purport that
their work is all-inclusive, they do not provide an adequate analysis
of the separation of powers between the president and Congress.[1]
This separation, one that institutionalizes a continuing struggle over
who shall rule, can hardly be described as a delicate balance.

Moreover, the authors perceive the Constitution to be highly
adaptable. "It turns out that the 1787 version of the Constitution was
only the first draft of what we now call the law of the land. A parade
of disparate claims brought by citizens and noncitizens demanding
their day in court has made all the difference." Their Epilogue returns
to the theme of extreme adaptability—"The Constitution has been
described as magnificently ambiguous."[2]

The aim of the book is "not to change but to open minds, to
provide insights into how Supreme Court justices, presidents, journalists, and others have faced up to . . . decisions . . . We hope this
book, along with the television series, will provide a way for all
citizens—not just lawyers and judges—to take part in the great constitutional debates of our time."[3]

Constitutional Rigidities and the Institutionalized
Struggle for Power

But crucial parts of the Constitution, notably those that this book does not attempt to cover, are categorically rigid. The doctrine of the separation of powers is set in concrete. The president and the Congress are established (with all their "sharing of powers") essentially independent of each other. There is nothing ambiguous about the four-year term for the president, the two-year term for representatives, and the six-year term for senators. Elections are riveted to the calendar. The Government could acquire discretion over the date of elections if the legislature were enabled to replace the executive by a vote of no confidence and if the executive were reciprocally empowered to dissolve the legislature (and his own position) and to call for new elections. These moves would end the separation of powers, but they might create a balance (although probably not a delicate one) between the president and the Congress and between the government and the opposition.

The book appears to devote only one paragraph to the separation of power.[4] Here it is implied that the separation plus "checks and balances" result in a sharing of powers that provides not only a sufficiently strong but also an adequately controlled government. Appropriately, this paragraph occurs in the final chapter that deals with the power to make war. The book ends with a clear recognition that the main question before American governments now is: Who shall leash and unleash, control and direct, the dogs of war? War, cold, lukewarm, or hot, but always teetering on the brink of an unprecedented catastrophe, is now the unremitting lot of this country. The final words of the book are "struggle between the president and the Congress over the power to make war."[5]

I do not mean to diminish the book's explication of the Bill of Rights. As Justice Potter Stewart says in stating the theme: "these great constitutional rights came from the judges of this country."[6] Amen, especially if the *judges* is a generic term to include courts, lawyers, law schools, and, indeed, the legal estate. All but two chapters focus on the rights of individuals under the constitution, especially on the Bill of Rights as they apply to the exercise of government power over individuals. The authors deal with freedom of speech, of religion, of the press, and of assembly; with freedom from arbitrary arrest, search, and seizure; with the exclusionary rule; with the death penalty and the insanity plea; and with the right of privacy.

They also discuss the rights of immigrants; the application of the Bill of Rights to the states under the Fourteenth Amendment, and the right to equal treatment under law and the relationship thereto of affirmative action. One differing chapter is on federalism — states rights versus national sovereignty (15); the other is on the power to make war (16).

In its main argument the book often weighs the rights of individuals against the interests of the community (as expressed by its government). Examples include the establishing and nourishing of political parties; the exercise of a degree of authority over immigration (the control of the nation's borders); and the surveillance and perhaps sometimes the outright quashing of groups aimed at overthrowing the government. The authority of the government to mount covert action may activate rights of individuals and inspire appeals to the rights of the public — thus, the Bay of Pigs is discussed eventually as a question of the right of the public to be informed and of the press to inform the public. "The rationale was that we should have government in the sunshine, open and well-aired, responsible to an informed electorate."[7]

This venerable approach to the Constitution commands great respect. It deals with what (following Charles H. McIlwain) I shall call *jurisdictio*. It assumes that a durable, resilient, and potent government exists so that due process of law has a secure framework in which to function. Then there is a delicate balance — or a series of delicate balances — to be sought: the continual arbitration in the clash of right and wrong (or right and right) "between whose endless jar justice resides." The balance will be sought by the legal community whose personnel has the requisite learning, intelligence, passion, courage, stamina, and integrity to serve as the guardians of jurisdictio. For jurisdictio to exist, however, a strong government is necessary. (McIlwain's word for it is gubernaculum.)

Charles H. McIlwain: Jurisdictio and Gubernaculum

For the theoretical basis of my argument I turn to Charles H. McIlwain.[8] He dwelt heavily on the seminal role of the Roman Republic (hence the Latin terms, *jurisdictio* and *gubernaculum*) and on the emergence of constitutionalism in Britain, particularly as influenced by English justices.

McIlwain professed his inability to offer a "strict definition of constitutionalism" based on his quick survey. But he made some observations. Referring to Bodin (1576), McIlwain noted the European stress on "the need of strong and efficient national rule" with emphasis on the government's rights rather than on its duties, all fostered by memories of the excesses of local lords and the disintegrating effects of religious differences.[9]

"Constitutional history is usually the record of a series of oscillations." Now private right is stressed; now order. The sixteenth century witnessed order elevated over anarchy. In England, the seventeenth century witnessed a swing back toward private rights, the eighteenth century a return to strong government, "but now, as never before, a power vested in the national assembly instead of the king."[10]

"The constitution was held to be a thing of balanced power and right, and the modern theory of sovereignty is the result of a belated recognition . . . that . . . the perfect balance can never long be maintained."[11] As Hobbes saw, the struggle could never be ended without a complete victory of order over rights. (Note that one cannot add "or vice versa" because rights without order would be meaningless.)

From this a novel and monumental question emerged. Earlier the control of power meant merely controlling the monarch. Can the power of the people, the successor to the monarch, be contained? In the early nineteenth century the tendency was to narrow the powers of government, to exalt laissez faire. "This often lead to a callous disregard of those who had few inherited rights to be protected." Then came the swing in the opposite direction, noted by Dicey in *Law and Opinion in England*, the trend toward collectivism. McIlwain noted similar trends in the United States with some current indications (1940) that the country might be leaving the phase of collectivism and of regimentation for a return, perhaps an extreme one, to laissez faire.[12] (Writing in 1985: perhaps he was forty years too soon.)

What, then, might be derived from history? McIlwain thought that the reconciliation of gubernaculum and jurisdictio "remains probably our most serious practical problem." He would go further to stress *"the same necessity now, as in past ages, to preserve these two sides of political institutions intact, to maintain every institution instrumental to strengthening them both, and to guard against the overwhelming of one . . . by the other."*[13] (italics added). "Never in recorded history, I believe, has the individual been in greater danger from government than now." "If *Jurisdictio* is essential to liberty, and *Jurisdictio* is a thing of the law, it is the law that must be maintained against arbitrary will." Essential to this is an "honest, able, learned, and independent judiciary."[14]

McIlwain's Attack on the Separation of Powers

But what of gubernaculum? McIlwain opposed the enfeebling of government. "Among all the modern fallacies that have obscured the true teaching of constitutional history, few are worse than the extreme doctrine of the separation of powers and the indiscriminate use of the phrase 'checks and balances.' " So far as McIlwain could see there was little historical background for the theory of the separation of powers "except the fancies of eighteenth-century doctrinaires and their followers. Political balances have no institutional background whatever except in the imaginations of closet philosophers like Montesquieu."[15]

When representative assemblies took over from kings, "they assumed a power and a responsibility that had always been concentrated and undivided." McIlwain rejected the *separation* of powers in favor of the *limitation* of powers. "The true safeguards of liberty against arbitrary government are the ancient legal limitation and the modern political responsibility." The latter is "utterly incompatible with any extended system of checks and balances."[16]

Checks and balances, McIlwain thought, originated in Rome where, based on class antagonism, plebian tribunes could block actions of the patrician consul. Denouncing the institutional encouragement of class and group antagonisms, McIlwain called for "full political responsibility to the . . . whole people." But power must be concentrated to be held accountable. With us the inability to fix responsibility has been the main stimulant of "pressure groups," and has "led to 'log-rolling' and every other form of crooked politics." The result is government for private interests or groups instead of for the whole people. Irresponsibility breeds corruption.[17]

McIlwain could find no "good precedents" in history for "this dissipation of government" that has "worked disaster ever since it was adopted." "Unlike the legal limitations in our Bill of Rights, it is not the matured result of centuries of trial and error." The separation of powers "is a figment of the imagination of eighteenth century doctrinaires who found it in our earlier history because they were ignorant of the true nature of that history. These political balances were unknown before the eighteenth century, were almost untried before the nineteenth, and have been disastrous wherever they have been tried since." McIlwain feared that if the dissipation of government developed much further it would precipitate a reaction that might sweep away "every protection of any sort, legal as well as political, to leave the individual naked and unprotected against the ever-present danger of arbitrary government."[18]

Unfortunate Effects of the Separation of Powers

McIlwain's attack on the separation of powers would be disputed by some. Commenting on a recent critique of foreign policy making, political scientist Kenneth N. Waltz writes: "The process is messy . . . But conflict may sharpen issues, define possibilities, encourage consideration of different views and interests and help to build consensus. Policy is not necessarily confused, incoherent, and erratic just because it is messily made."[19] And he concludes that, "despite all the thrashing about, the main features of the President's program still become the policy of the land if the President works hard enough for them. And for better or worse, policy continues to point in the same direction."

It is not just a question of messiness. Rather, the separation of powers tends to *distort*, to *undermine*, and to *disrupt* government (gubernaculum) itself. It distorts, for example, by greatly extending the process of selection while shrinking the period of effective government. It also distorts by assiduously nursing special interests until the only recourse is to magnify dangerously the president as the sole representative of the public interest. The president is then encouraged to improve on and to emphasize his resonance with the public in a way that reifies and caricatures the public so that its true and essential role under the Constitution is obscured.

At the same time, the separation of powers undermines confidence in the legislature; the old saw that if the voters despise the Congress they still love their own representative ignores the harm done by the vilification of the legislature as an institution.

The separation of powers leads to the disruption of government by fostering the conditions of deadlock or stalemate, often observed when the control of the executive and the legislature is divided between two parties. Accountability is compromised when the voters cannot hold one party responsible. In 1874–1896, the same party controlled the president, the House, and the Senate in only four years. In 1952-1984 unified control was realized in only twelve years. When the Democrats have had nominal control the situation is further complicated by the tendency of many Southern Democrats to retain their party label but to vote with Republicans (Dixiecrats, or later, Boll weevils).

The Iron Triangles

But the disruption of disintegration of the Congress has another dimension. The classic outcome of the separation of powers has been the emergence of quasi-independent configurations of power that typically include a governmental agency or bureau, a cadre of influential legislators, and an organized interest group (commonly the agency's clientele). The striking label for this phenomenon is "the iron triangle" but it has also been called a "whirlpool," a "subgovernment," or a "bureaucracy."

The iron triangles are fostered by the same tendencies, rooted in the separation of powers, for the Congress progressively to decentralize, even to disintegrate. Woodrow Wilson described the government of the 1880s as congressional or committee government. This was followed by an interlude of strong Speakers (the "czars") that ended in the Progressive Revolt of 1910–1911, after which the committees flourished again. The LaFollette-Monroney reform of 1946 was frustrated when decentralizing and fragmentizing tendencies reappeared in the proliferation of subcommittees. Shortly thereafter centrifugal forces inherent in the separation of powers spurred the rapid growth of the influence of individual legislators who were aided by their mushrooming staffs, and by improved modes of traveling (and fatter expense accounts) so that members could multiply visits to their districts. I dwell on this disruptive tendency partly because it reflects a much more deep-seated problem than that caused by "divided government."

Now Professor Waltz may say that none of this matters because the policy outcomes remain benign or, at least, bearable. He may also argue that policy is more or less stable and that, in any event, it reflects the president's (and, therefore, the people's) will. Some may also argue that it is improper to evaluate policies because that means to substitute the mere preferences of the analyst for his proper function, which is to disclose uniformities of behavior. On the contrary, I shall argue that some flawed policies owe their defects to our peculiar political process, the salient characteristics of which are forged by the separation of powers.

Domestic Economic Policy

Agricultural price policy exemplifies the growth of the iron triangles in government. Moreover, the triangle became intrenched when one party, the Democrats, nominally controlled the presidency and both congressional houses; it was not the outcome of divided government.[20]

But the size of the agricultural budget, however large in proportion to its dwindling prime beneficiaries, is dwarfed by other economic policy developments, the growth of which may have been aggravated by divided government, although its central stimulant still seems rooted in the iron triangles. Reference is to health care, social security, and governmental retirement programs. An argument can also be based on the vagaries of monetary and fiscal policy. Especially foreboding is the recent rapid rise in the public debt, fueled by the horrendous deficits since 1981. These developments suggest deep flaws in our gubernaculum. Contemplating the separation of powers, Pendleton Herring was reminded of a loving cup that was passed around lest one of the company get drunk. He failed to consider that our exceedingly liquid and affluent society permitted a staggering number of folks to get drunk at once.

If there is anything more dangerous than general intoxication, it occurs when the revelers are all armed with loaded pistols, so we turn to foreign and military policy. But, first, a word is needed on the malevolent effects of the separation of powers on the president.

The Separation of Powers and the Executive

The gravamen of the charge that the separation of powers disrupts government rests heavily on the Congress, a national scapegoat at least since Mark Twain (e.g., "Once there was a Congressman, I mean there was a son-of-a-bitch, but why do I repeat myself? or Henry Adams, "A Congressman is like a hog. You have to kick him in the snout"). One thinks at once of the failure to ratify the Versailles Treaty after World War I or of the passage of the Immigration Act of 1924, excluding Japanese immigrants. E. S. Corwin called the latter an extremely deplorable romp of the legislative bull in the diplomatic china shop. A. N. Holcombe discerned a direct line from it to Pearl Harbor.

The concentration of criticism on the Congress leads to an unhealthy benevolence toward the president. He becomes the "magic helper." He alone towers over the disreputable and selfish "scuffle of local interests" in the Congress. We need (it is said) only to strip his last vestige of corrupting vanity by limiting him to one six-year term and then give him the item veto.

Insulated, elevated, the constant focus of sycophancy, the president may be all but canonized. The danger inherent in his eminence does not derive merely from personal vanity; rather, it is produced by his image (in his own mind's eye as well as in that of the populace) as the embodiment of the people. At the same time, the president is handicapped within his administration by the effects of the same forces, stemming from the separation of powers, that tend to fracture and fragment the Congress. The agencies or bureaus that make up an indispensable apex in each of the iron triangles are parts of the president's administration. Charles G. Dawes said that cabinet secretaries are the natural enemies of presidents. To lead their departments the secretaries need to work closely and amicably with those bureaus and agencies that willy-nilly must develop political bases of their own, in the Congress and in the country. An administrator's influence and effectiveness is in direct proportion to his independence vis-a-vis the president.

In consequence the president turns more and more to his unique source of strength—half-real, half-mythical—the people. Overtly there is every effort to burnish the president's image as a popular leader. Covertly, the tendency is toward a convoluted and arcane administration to protect the presidency from the disintegrating effects of the power-hungry iron triangulators.

A recent book by U. Alexis Johnson supplies an illustration, offered in a review by Robert Manning, who served as an assistant secretary of state during the period concerned.[21] Mr. Johnson told of his experience in Washington's intelligence community as the State Department's member of several secret groups that dealt with major intelligence initiatives against foreign governments or persons, including a group set up in 1961 that reflected the determination of the John F. Kennedy and Robert Kennedy to remove Fidel Castro from power. Mr. Johnson reported that the special group never discussed assassinating Castro. He also wrote: "All programs originated by the CIA or proposed by other agencies were carefully staffed and considered by the committee."

Mr. Manning comments:

> How does one account for these statements from such a high-ranking official in the light of the disclosures from hearings before Senator Frank Church's Select Committee on Intelligence and other inquiries into the Government's efforts to rid this planet of Fidel Castro? What do they betray about communication within the high levels of government?
>
> Perhaps Mr. Johnson was absent from the special group's meeting on August 10, 1962 when the Cuban missile crisis was brewing and Secretary of Defense Robert McNamara raised, albeit ever so hypothetically the notion that the Castro problem might be solved by having the fellow killed. Did the C.I.A. not make him privy to the Aug. 13, 1962 memorandum by Edward Lansdale, who ran Mongoose, requesting from a subordinate proposals for "liquidation of [Cuban] leaders"? Was he not told of, or has he forgotten, the many cockamamie schemes, beginning in the Eisenhower Administration and continuing well into Kennedy's, for eliminating Castro—a poisoned diving suit, an

exploding sea shell, a box of cigars impregnated with some death-dealing agent, not to mention the C.I.A.'s enlistment of Mafia figures to take the contract?

Since "The Right Hand of Power" is exceedingly—I would say excessively—respectful of the roles of the C.I.A. and the Pentagon in American foreign policy, the book's treatment of the Castro case may reveal more about the darker side of government than the author intended. It would not be the first time—and very likely not the last—that the intelligence community made mockery of the liaison function and the so-called "oversight" process.

Manning's comments recall McIlwain: "The true safeguards of liberty against arbitrary government are the ancient legal limitation and the modern political responsibility." Power must be consolidated to be held accountable. The goal is "full responsibility to the . . . whole people."

I have some inquiry into the meanings of "accountability" and the "people" elsewhere. Here let us look once more at the magnitude of the problem in the delusions of power that beset the imperial presidency from time to time.

Delusions of Grandeur

There are times when nothing but a cliche will do. The presidency seems to lead its modern holders into imprudent undertakings. One is reminded of President Roosevelt's effort to enlarge the Supreme Court after his sweeping victory in 1936. President Truman succeeded to power, flushed by global victory and self-evident supremacy. In response to Soviet adventurism in Greece and Turkey, following Britain's explicit withdrawal from providing their support, Truman asked Congress for funds to help them resist Soviet aggression. His policy pronouncement that became known as the Truman Doctrine proclaimed unlimited hegemony. "It must be the policy of the United States to support free peoples who are resisting attempted subjugation by armed minorities or by outside pressures." Prudence was flung to the winds. Since then we have had many examples of excessive presidential policy commitments. As Walter Lippmann said of President Dwight D. Eisenhower's Secretary of State in 1958:

"Dulles has gone around the world promising every nation that would accept . . . an American military guarantee. In this Dulles has shown himself not to be a prudent and calculating diplomat but a gambler who is more lavish than any other secretary of state ever dreamed of being with promissory notes engaging the blood, the treasure, and the honor of this country."

"For man holds in his mortal hands the power to abolish all forms of poverty and all forms of human life," John F. Kennedy proclaimed in his inaugural, thus confusing the real power of catastrophic destruction with the elusive ability to manage the world's economy. Nor have his successors shrunk in their proclamations of omnipotence and omniscience. A current manifestation is President Reagan's Strategic Defense Initiative (SDI) or "Star Wars." Philip Geyelin wrote:

> The awful truth—the commentary on the presidential style—is that he had no proposal worked out when he first floated the idea almost casually in a speech devoted to other, known quantities of is military program. He had only a fatuous vision of a nuclear free world.

"My fellow Americans [President Reagan had said on March 23, 1983][22] tonight we are launching an effort which holds the purpose of changing the course of human history." After listing a number of questions about the SDI—including whether it is reversible, whether it is workable, and whether it will ultimately become an offensive weapon, Leslie H. Gelb stressed that the hard questions got little attention in the administration's inner circles. "By almost all accounts, support for the program has become the touchstone of loyalty to the President."[23]

A salient weakness of our gubernaculum may be that it tends to inhibit raising the hard questions in the right circles and on time.

Presidential Hubris, The Iron Triangle, and the Nuclear Arms Race

Once the atomic bomb was created, the nuclear arms race may have been unavoidable. But it seems to have been given an unfortunate fillip in the early 1960s. In the presidential election of that year Kennedy exploited the predicted missile gap. The Russians, it was said, were about to enjoy a superiority in nuclear weapons that would tempt them to launch a nuclear war against us (compare Ronald Reagan's fulminations about a "window of vulnerability" twenty years later).

But when the Kennedy administration came in, his staff learned that the missile gap was a chimera, that the United States did not need to "catch up," rather, an arsenal of 450 ICBMs would suffice — conveniently, the number we already had. But Defense Secretary Robert S. McNamara had quickly acquired an insight into the military triangle. He told his colleagues that they must ask for 950 ICBMs. If they did not, the admirals and generals were prepared to ask their friends in Congress for 3,000!

Recently, more light was thrown on the situation by a discussion of the Cuban missile crisis in October 1962.[24] At the time the United States counted on a four to one superiority in ICBMs over the Russians — about four hundred to one hundred. Later it was learned that the Soviets probably had only about ten deliverable ICBMs at the time.

> In one of the most famous remarks of the era of brinksman-ship, Dean Rusk . . . said, as Soviet ships steamed home with the rockets on their decks, "We were eyeball to eyeball, and the other guy just blinked." To the Soviets, that interpretation of the outcome rankled. "You Americans will never be able to do this to us again," Gromyko's deputy, Vasily Kuznetozov, had said sternly to his American counterpart, John McCloy. The episode clearly stimulated the Soviet Union's decision to undertake its twenty-year military buildup, of which the SS-20 program was one of the most visible and troublesome manifestations.[25]

To point up the argument of these paragraphs: Begin with the unprecedented rise of two superpowers armed with the ultimate superweapons. Witness then the presidential hubris of the 1950s manifest in "massive retaliation," the "roll back" theory (which, together with semiofficial encouragement to revolt may have prompted the disastrous Hungarian attempt of 1956), flavor with "brinkmanship," and crown with "pactomania." Mark also the effort to push American military power as close to the USSR as possible, including the egregious placing of Jupiter missiles in Italy and Turkey — "practically forced" on these countries "by an administration unable to find any worthwhile use for them."[26]

Then recall 1960 and the inflated presidential debate about the missile gap that, on JFK's ascendance to power, proved to be inverted! But the military triangle frustrated the administration's efforts to back off. Shortly afterwards came the Soviet effort to place missiles in Cuba, very likely equated by them with American missiles in Italy and Turkey. Ensued the escalating confrontation, the looming nuclear holocaust, the peaceful denouement, the Soviet retreat, and the agreement with its hidden clause confirming the removal of American missiles in Italy and Turkey—and its masked Soviet commitment "never again" to confront such overwhelming nuclear odds.

Without diminishing the danger of the Soviet adversary, the subsequent arms race, much against the interests of the United States, seems attributable, in part, to American mistakes fashioned by our policymaking process, shaped by the separation of powers.

Would a differently structured government have performed better? There can be no guarantee. But the concentrated enormity of the problem seems to call for a strong and coherent national government with a degree of control vested in an equally concentrated opposition rather than with its control derived from its own division and fragmentation, surmounted only spasmodically by a perilously inflated president, empowered by his embodiment of the people, grotesquely reified.

Conclusion

Our system of government displays flaws that *The Constitution: That Delicate Balance*, with all its merits, does not address. The book deals excellently with jurisdictio. But to address the distortion, the undermining, and the disruption of gubernaculum by the separation of powers requires something other than a search for more subtle, sensitive, and imaginative juridicial analysis to explicate the Bill of Rights. It demands a fundamental reexamination of the structure and process of government.

The flaws in the system—in gubernaculum—all caused by or growing out of the separation of powers, are:

1. The inability quickly and legitimately to replace a failed or discredited president

2. Increasingly grievous ills caused by fixed calendar elections

3. The distortion of the presidency arising out of the alternative excesses of acclaim and denigration

4. The disruption of the legislative process; its progressive fragmentation; the fostering of quasi-independent iron triangles

5. The unremitting vilification of the legislature

6. The impossible conception of the people as the omniscient, omnipotent, and infallibly correct arbiter of all questions — at the expense of trivializing the one practical and necessary function of the people to create by its vote a government and an opposition

7. The progressive weakening of political parties, the only known instruments capable of organizing the parts of government into a working whole

8. The failure sufficiently to examine the essential concepts of democratic government, including majority rule, the loyal opposition, accountability and responsibility, and the mandate.

In addition, the approach, both analytical and educational, would appear to require something different from the approach to jurisdictio in *The Constitution: That Delicate Balance*. The latter assumed a sufficient general knowledge of the underlying system (which was postulated as generally adequate and also quite flexible) and concentrated on the refinement of the juridicial applications of the constitution. But when the sufficiency of gubernaculum is called into question, something more is needed.

The analysis of gubernaculum calls for the articulation of a model of constitutional government as an organic whole — or, rather, of two models: what it is and what it might be. The second model might well be informed by generous adaptations from the parliamentary system. In this endeavor both models would be kept in mind throughout the analysis. Gubernaculum would always be in the mind's eye: fully panoplied — in its executive and legislative aspects, in its judicial and administrative manifestations, in its diplomatic engagements, in its political parties, in its involvement with organized interests, and in its response to the people. Even more than this gubernaculum would have to be conceived as dynamic:

continuously subject to the influence of its surrounding society and culture, and constantly buffeted by mutlifaceted outside forces.

The urgency of the task is heightened by the recurrent drive, so often disillusioned, of human beings to improve their management of economic and social affairs — and by the inexorably escalating ability of humanity to self-destruct.

7
Don K. Price
America's Unwritten Constitution

THERE is a fairly widespread sense that something is seriously wrong about the way the federal government oper-
ates in the United States. A Committee on the Constitutional System, chaired by Lloyd N. Cutler, C. Douglas
Dillon, and Senator Nancy Landon Kassebaum, has been meeting
biannually for four years on the subject. A significant debate on it
may take place—that is, a debate involving a considerable number of
people for an extended period of time—a sustained debate that,
although it ebbs and flows, becomes implanted in the curricula of
institutions of higher education and eventually in the secondary
schools and through this educational osmosis begins to inform
American opinion on government.

In this debate (if it comes about) a major question will be: How
deep, how profound is the problem? Does it require major changes
in our governmental institutions? Or is it amenable to adjustments
born of improved perceptions of politics as the art of the possible,
perhaps abetted by some statutory changes?

The issue arises most clearly over the separation of powers. "We,
the People" created a government in which the president and the
Congress are separately ordained, empowered, and provided for.
Each is to be separately elected. Although the powers granted to each
overlap somewhat (the presidential veto on legislation as well as the
senatorial approval of treaties and appointments both make for a
"government of separated institutions sharing powers"), the fact of
separation remains the most salient feature of the constitution. Ex-

cept for brief presidential honeymoons, three somewhat longer periods of congressional preeminence in the nineteenth century and the surges of presidential freewheeling during wars and in foreign and military affairs especially (but not exclusively) in this century, relations between the executive and the legislature have been repeatedly marked by conflict.

In light of this history, and in view of the immense and dynamic changes since World War II, C. Douglas Dillon wrote in 1979, "The future will be a world in which the United States will be faced with recurring crises of kinds that cannot possibly be foreseen, crises that will test our will and our fortitude and which will require prompt and united response from our nation. I very much doubt that in such a world we can long continue to afford the luxury of the division of power and responsibility between our executive and legislative branches of government."

Don K. Price on America's Unwritten Constitution

A formidable critic of proposals for fundamental changes in the written Constitution of 1787 is Don K. Price. In *America's Unwritten Consitution,* he agrees that the American government needs much more coherence and responsibility in policymaking but argues that fundamental constitutional changes toward that end are virtually impossible.[1] Like many analysts, whether they are explicit or not, Price assumes that the alternative model to the American separation of powers would be the parliamentary system. But he believes that it is unattainable not only because of difficulties of amendment but also because of an underlying intransigence toward authority imbedded in the political beliefs of Americans. Price ends his Introduction, "The Confused Sources of Authority," as follows: "Finally, how more effective leadership and a tighter system of accountability might be developed in America if we were to recognize that we cannot deal with such fundamental problems by legalistic changes in the formal constitution but only by a political consensus to amend our unwritten constitution."[2] And in his concluding chapter he says, "The first step in the right direction would be to quit talking about the separation of powers." But then, while still warning Americans not to try to incorporate the parliamentary system by formal amendment, he nevertheless advises the United States "to imitate the parliamentary system's essence — at least to some extent — by changes in our unwritten constitution."[3]

By contrast, I think that the written Constitution sharply constrains what the unwritten constitution may contain. The American Constitution stipulates separate elections for the president and the Congress. Elections are thus bound to the calendar. They shall be on a fixed date, set by statute, to be sure, but necessarily a fixed date. This means that aspirants for House seats, for example, are invited to campaign immediately after the election to unseat the incumbent two years hence. The incumbent feels constrained to meet his challenger — hence, the continuous campaigns. Fixed dates also invite primary elections, which Price, along with many political scientists, decries. Primaries deprive the parties of control over nominations (not always, but generally, and progressively more and more). The eventual result of interminable campaigns and primary elections is that each legislator (and each serious candidate for election as a legislator) must organize his own party and arrange for his own finances. To the extent that he succeeds and is continually reelected, the legislator becomes more and more independent from his nominal party.

The alternative to fixed calendar elections is elections at the discretion of the government (in England essentially of the Prime Minister). In effect, the Constitution forbids the president to dissolve the Congress and call for new elections. To provide this power would require a radical change in the written Constitution. But without it, the unwritten constitution's inexorable evolution progressively fragments and weakens political parties. At the same time, if the power of dissolution was granted to the president (presumably with the requirement that he also dissolve his own office), his potential power would be greatly increased. He would be able to end the life of the Congress. But the Congress would have no reciprocal power to end his occupancy of the presidency unless it were granted the right to oust the president by passing a vote of no confidence. If both powers were granted, both the right of dissolution and the vote of confidence, the written Constitution would have to be changed radically. Nor is this all: with change of this magnitude and this intent, the Senate as it now exists, with its six-year tenure and its imposing powers, would be anomalous. Something would have to be done about the power of the Senate: another radical constitutional change.

Such changes are, indeed, intimidating. But without them the United States *cannot* achieve "the essence of the British system" by changes in the unwritten constitution. There are other items that might be cited. Senatorial courtesy, a salient part of the unwritten American constitution, and a convention that further undermines party discipline by empowering individual senators, grows directly out of the separation of powers. So does the congressional seniority principle. But these unwritten constitutional customs are trivial compared to the great questions of dissolution/vote of confidence.

This chapter endeavors to restate Price's analysis, to examine it, and to answer it. In doing so it will also inevitably be drawn into the question of accountability: to whom? for what?

Price's Interpretation in General

Price's adjuration "to quit talking about the separation of powers" comes in his concluding chapter, "Accountability under the Unwritten Constitution." Examining British government, Price finds that the parliamentary system unifies power in the king (or queen) in Parliament, a union based most importantly on a "complex relationship of mutual support" between the Privy Council and His Majesty's Civil Service, which has succeeded the established church as the "institutional prop of the monarchy." It is this mutual support that empowers the prime minister to define the problems, to propose solutions, and (assuming that we can win a vote of confidence or, failing that, an election), to get them enacted into law, and to see that the laws are applied.

What of the vote of confidence? "The act of demanding a vote of confidence in the House of Commons on a crucial issue is a dramatic and impressive ritual, but its drama obscures the essence of the parliamentary system."[4] The essence lies in the mutual support. Bernard Crick wrote in 1965: "A British Government whose party was elected with a majority of seats in the House of Commons has not been defeated on a vote of confidence since . . . 1886."[5] Price warns against the vote of confidence in the United States. If the president's "tenure were at stake in every decision, including decisions on the appointment of his principal subordinates, his position would be hopeless."[6] This is no idle warning. Experience in the

French Third Republic and under the Weimar Constitution for Germany in the 1920s shows how hapless government can be with an unrestrained vote of confidence.

So Price rejects the "one big test" of the vote of confidence and recommends instead that the Congress move to ensure "a somewhat higher degree of executive accountability by changes in the unwritten constitution."[7] The essential means to this end is to increase and improve the delegation of powers from Congress to the president and from the president to his subordinates.

"More coherent and effective leadership within each house of Congress, with stronger party discipline, would let the Congress as a whole (even if the two houses were not controlled by the President's party) bargain on equal or more than equal terms with the President on issues of sufficient importance to warrant the attention of the voters."[8] Price argues that American experience with congressional delegation to the president (e.g., the executive budget) given time and goodwill, will suffice.

But there should not be too much coherence. "Greater coherence is the ideal of those who would . . . imitate the British parliamentary system [by moving] toward a single big check on the tenure of the executive. . . . But either the calculation of aggregate costs and benefits or the choice between the programs of two disciplined political parties may ignore two crucial political values."[9]

These values are laid out in three paragraphs that require quotation in full:

> The first is the value of justice with respect both to fundamental rights and to the distribution of benefits and costs among the various regions and groups of the population. The Congress and the President will not want the secretary of defense, for example, to be able in his calculation of our military needs to ignore the civil rights of minority groups or even to allocate contracts without regard to the impact on various regions or segments of the economy. Nor will they want to let the administrator responsible for the protection of the environment ignore the special impact of particular regulations on particular industries or on employment opportunities.
>
> The second is the value of freedom from arbitrary political power: a free people will prefer less bread and fewer circuses if the sacrifice will let them maintain more popular control over their own affairs.

Especially in a large federal system, with a diverse population, it is inevitable that the electorate will want to draw back from the idea of a tightly unified system in which the only check on the power that it delegates is by its choice between two political parties. It is not only inevitable but desirable, in recognition of what history may teach us of the temptation of any political elite or any tightly organized bureaucracy to distort its perception of national policy in order to maintain its own profit and power. In a unitary state in an era of restricted governmental functions, a tightly unified and disciplined parliamentary system produced an admirably coherent policy. But it did so on a completely unscientific basis. In order to bring various groups together in teamwork, there is no way to calculate precisely, on a systematic utilitarian basis, just what choices will most fairly distribute benefits among them. A somewhat looser system, in which parts of the majority may open issues up for public debate and independent voting in the legislature, may have its advantages.[10]

Government must deal with the great issues—but with due regard for distributive justice and for freedom from arbitrary government (still paraphrasing). Government must deal with the threat of war, with the social trauma inherent in the abrupt decline of available fossil fuels, and with the deterioration of the environment. But government must do so while maintaining the preeminence of our moral and political values over the means of protection from our enemies, achieving new fuel supplies, and managing the environment. "To this end we must pay at least as much attention to insuring the accountability of our executive institutions as to improving their efficiency and economy. Indeed, we need to give prior attention to accountability, for it is the fear of irresponsible power that leads us to hobble our executives and destroy their effectiveness."[11]

A Bow to Accountability but with the Accent on Delegation

If the initial stress is on accountability, Price also emphasizes delegation. Government must be effective. Effectiveness requires a strong executive who must have much freedom, much discretion. "In order to be held truly accountable, an executive—especially the President—needs to be given a greater degree of freedom in the formulation of policy."[12] To the extent that policies are carved out and handed over to independent regulatory commissions, to the federal reserve, or to governmental bureaus that are linked with congressional committees, the president cannot be held accountable—and no one else can either.

Price is more explicit. Major issues, other than the conduct of diplomacy or of military operations, require sustained staff study and consultation with responsible officials. The president should be able to make the final big decisions on the basis of such advice and then to put his recommendations before Congress (I take it) *as a whole*. The formulation of presidential policy requires more discretion for the president—more "privacy and confidentiality in the preparation of staff papers. The President also needs considerable control of the legislative agenda in order to select the priorities and exercise timing."[13]

This scheme would enable Congress and the president "to give more weight to the ends of policy and the general values that determine them than to the technical means or to bureaucratic procedures." This "more democratic and responsible arrangement" will "focus the attention of the electorate and Congress as a whole on the main general issues, which they are interested in and competent to decide, rather than on technical or procedural details, which they are not." This trenchant analysis is reminiscent of the stress placed on the division of political labor by Ernest Barker and Joseph Schumpeter, two renowned commentators on political institutions who admired the parliamentary system.

Price acknowledges the difficulty of achieving this scheme because of the American distrust for political authority, combined with faith in science and the law. Such faith has bred a great reliance on scientific and legal standards to constrain political power. Nevertheless, Price finds some virtue in the distrust. He holds that "better policy choices may emerge from free-wheeling debate in an undisciplined legislature with free access to private scientific advice." This may be true even if it is "less tidy than the classic parliamentary system of responsible government."[14]

And yet the result may be to fragment policy and responsibility. Bits and pieces of policy are accountable to bits and pieces of the legislature and, in a sense, to bits and pieces of the electorate; "narrow and special interests" are encouraged to appeal to science or the law.[15] Perhaps the major influence toward this result are "the present procedures and institutions of the unwritten constitution"!

Changing the Unwritten Constitution: Accent Again on Accountability

These procedures and institutions, if changed "by general consent . . . to emphasize a higher degree of delegation and a higher concentration of interest on the major issues of policy [might enable] both science and the law [to] support a more balanced type of accountability.[16]

Price briefly discusses the necessity and insufficiency of both science and the law unless both are informed and guided by political institutions that "raise the level of public attention to the major issues and . . . political leaders see their obligations to society in broader terms than the interests of local constituents or the enforcement of rigid specific rules."[17]

Now Price comes to the nub of his argument. We have seen his rejection of both aggregate cost-benefit calculations and of the choice between the programs of two disciplined political parties as the essential means of resolving policy disputes; both may ignore the values of justice and freedom. He opts for general philosophical and legal principles to guide and inform the formation of policies that both the president and the Congress will leave to subordinates to spell out and implement, presumably with local differences worked out by compromises with affected interests. "Politics is the art of agreeing on values and purposes in situations that are not covered by established law and that are too complex to be subject to measurement by recognized disciplines."[18]

"Accountability," Price continues, "must be a political matter to be worked out within the context of our unwritten constitution." What this means is explained: Accountability "depends, not on precise Constitutional distinctions between the roles of the Congress and the President, but on political cooperation between them." (I cannot resist a snide reminder of Carl Friedrich's definition of cooperation: "I operate and you coo.") True, Price presents an alternative. Accountability may be achieved not only by cooperation between the two branches; it may also depend "on political controversy that illuminates broad issues and thus helps the voters make their fundamental decisions on election day as between competing candidates and parties."[19] I return to this later.

How is accountability to be measured? "Congress would need to provide for a far greater degree of party discipline." So Price, too, reaches for the same instrument as the advocates of parliamentary adaptation. Price says that party discipline could be sharply increased if the electorate would "delegate to the Congress a greater measure of responsibility." Another fascinating statement. For the present, please note that we are back again to the stress on *delegation*. Price contrasts the "reformist impulse" that "requires the instant reporting of every political negotiation and the independent voting of every member under the pressure of television commentators and special interest lobbies." The electorate says to Congress, in effect: "You govern, except . . ." "With such political discipline Congress could delegate generally to the President the authority necessary for administrative coordination and management but . . ." I will return to these two statements later.

Up to this point it appears to me that Price has tried to create substantially what is ideally achieved by the parliamentary system. The establishment would govern. It would presumably do so on the basis of a majority party so that we should have party government. Yet institutions would remain separate. Instead of being fused together by the vote of confidence and the power to dissolve, they would be joined by cooperation: each would look at the other and say, "For the good of the whole, we must agree."

Now for the *except* or the *but*. The Congress should still "reserve to itself the right to intervene on some measures that it may consider important, especially if they involve questions of fundamental rights, distributive justice (such as the competing interests of the several regions), and political freedom." Only the congressional committees (retained as a practical matter) could "intervene . . . with the right to challenge the leadership of the parties or the President."[20]

So Price wants some discipline and coherence but not too much. "If one were to insist on achieving the full extent of party discipline and coherence of policy of the classic parliamentary system, it would be necessary to abolish such a role of committees." Committee challenge would express a lack of confidence. But with the fixed and independent tenures of the president and members of Congress, "there is good reason to maintain the double channel of responsibility." The overlap can be constructive "provided that the committees are made more accountable to the Congress as a whole, and their policies are effectively subject to review and reversal by congressional leadership in negotiation with the President."

So the electorate says, "Both of you govern, and we expect you to work together." Price says that political authority should not be absolute but had better not be precisely defined by law. Let the Congress and the president negotiate about who shall do what and about what accountability means.

This system of continuous revision has its cost, says Price. Neither political nor civil servant may know where responsibility lies. By contrast, Price says, the British know precisely where responsibility lies, what accountability means, and who has the power—or they did know until the emergence of the Loyal Opposition "introduced uncertainties into the traditional ideas of obedience to royal authority."[21] I shall return to this in a later discussion of Price's views of the parliamentary system.

Price then says that if the Congress can achieve a more predictable and responsible system in its internal procedures—presumably organizing itself to act more continually and effectively *as a whole*—then the Congress may be able to establish a relationship with the president: and the United States "might attain a tolerable balance, for a federal system in a technological era, in its system of accountability."

Price concludes that the United States can work things out without constitutional amendments and, indeed, even with few statutory changes.[22]

This skeletonized sketch is no substitute for reading Price's rewarding argument; but it will enable readers to understand my perspective in order to evaluate my answer to him which begins with a discussion of the triangles of power that he repeatedly notices but does not, in my judgment, give sufficient weight.

Price and the "Triangles"

In his attack on the feasibility of adaptation of the main features of the parliamentary system, Price discerns a temptation to overstress the inherent conflict in the American system between the president and the Congress, which misleads many Americans to advocate parliamentarianism as a cure. But this celebrated presidential-congressional conflict is "not as difficult a problem as . . . the conflict between Congress and itself—between Congress as a whole and its own committees and staffs."[23]

Price complains that Congress prefers "as an organized and disciplined entity, not to exist. It rather prefers to leave its undisciplined parts in control of pieces of its business." He denies that this process is real delegation which would imply accountability, and says that there is no way to make the committees and staffs accountable "fully and publicly . . . to the whole Congress." Nor can Congress delegate "in the Constitutional way—to the President and the legally accountable heads of departments and agencies."[24]

There is, I think, a better way of analyzing the phenomenon that Price is attacking: Consider again the whirlpools of power, the bureaucracy, subgovernments, the iron triangles, or simply, triangles. The triangles are produced by strategically located legislators, bureaucrats, and interest groups who combine to form quasi-independent entities or organizations that run their own programs. This fragmenting tendency, originated perhaps in the rivers and harbors pork barrel, grew lustily in the New Deal, and really burgeoned in the 1940s.[25]

The triangles are not confined to the Congress. They extend their disruptive influence into the executive. Indeed, they undermine and fragment the entire government. In my understanding the triangles appear not because the Congress prefers to forego acting as a whole. Rather, they are the natural consequences of the separation of powers. Thus, Charles H. McIlwain concluded his *Constitutionalism: Ancient and Modern* with a slashing attack on the separation of powers, which he castigated as destructive of government (gubernaculum) itself.[26] "Among all the modern fallacies that have obscured the true teachings of history, few are worse than the extreme doctrine of the separation of powers and the indiscriminate use of 'checks and balances.' " Calling for "full political responsibility to the . . . whole people," McIlwain declared that power must be concentrated to be held accountable. With us, he wrote, the inability to fix responsibility has been the main stimulant of "pressure groups" and has "led to 'log-rolling' and every other form of crooked politics."[27]

Price maintains, nevertheless, that "this conflict between Congress and its own parts would make it futile, for the purposes of settling the problems between the Congress and the President, to . . . abolish the separation of powers."[28] By contrast, I think that the only way to control and neutralize the adverse effects of the triangles is to attack the separation of powers itself.

The comparison between Price and McIlwain is revealing. Both approach the awe-inspiring problems of free government from the vantage points of lifetimes of devoted study, mixed, on Price's side, with an unexcelled experience as a (sometimes participant) observer of the highest levels of American political-administrative life for nearly fifty years. Both profit from intensive scholarly acquaintance with British government. Their grasp is informed by their profound sense of the importance of beliefs (philosophical, ideological, and religious) on the human approach to the organization and control of power. Both seek to strengthen the ability of government to view, analyze, and act upon divisive issues from a comprehensive perspective. And yet McIlwain concluded that the separation of powers was a natural enemy of the strong gubernaculum that he thought such comprehension required while Price professes that the separation can be bridged by cooperation.

Experience warrants some pessimism about cooperation. The presidential side of the potential bargainers was strengthened greatly by the Executive Office of the President. In a seminal article in 1965 Richard E. Neustadt discerned the same problem that agitates Price.[29] He delineated the emergence of triangles as semi-independent, disruptive, and largely unaccountable entities (he called them bureaucracies, but he described them as triangles). Neustadt stressed the role of the presidency in trying to reassert coordination and direction over the triangles. The presidential response came through the Executive Office of the President (EOP) established in 1939 and legitimized "in the nick of time"; without it, the presidency "would by now have been a hollow shell." The EOP was the fruit of the Brownlow Commission, named after its chairman and Price's mentor, Louis Brownlow.

A significant part of the unwritten constitution, the EOP, although essential, was in Neustadt's view, still insufficient. "Politicians at the two ends of the Avenue unite! You have nothing to lose but your pieces of power—and even these may be slipping out of reach." His foreboding was confirmed eighteen years later by Price who found that the EOP had expanded beyond manageable limits, only to be matched and overmatched by the mushrooming of the congressional staff (perhaps exemplifying Daniel Patrick Moynihan's "iron law of emulation") first for committees, then for subcommittees, and finally for individual legislators. Price recommended shrinking the EOP but then acknowledged that it would be unable to cope with a congressional staff now ten times as large. "A very large proportion — my guess is three-quarters to nine-tenths — of the time of the Executive Office staff and of the congressional staff is spent in defensive maneuvers against each other, with no benefit either to the substance of policy or to accountability."[30]

As the impression of the intractability of the triangles seizes people some of them are likely to think of more drastic remedies. The one striking alternative that would abolish the separation of powers is the parliamentary system. This change, Price writes, would purport "to give the legislature and the executive mutual control over each other's tenure — as the executive may dissolve the legislature and as the legislature may vote no confidence in the executive, forcing him to resign . . . both sides of the struggle appeal to the voters for a final decision."[31] Very succinctly put. But this, Price says, fails to understand the essentials of the parliamentary system.

Price on the Parliamentary System

The American system may confuse accountability, says Price. Neither politicians nor civil service may know who is responsible — the president or some one in his entourage or his administration, or the Congress, or one of its committees (or, I should add, a quasi-independent triangle formed of an executive agency, one or a few powerful legislators, and an organized clientele or other directly concerned group that is nominally outside government). Price says that by contrast the British know precisely who is responsible, who has the power — until the emergence of the Loyal Opposition.[32] If I read him right, Price seems then to suggest a parallel between Britain and the United States. Just as the British have learned to live with the Opposition, so Congress and the president may learn to live with each other — if the Congress can achieve a more predictable and responsible system in its internal procedures (presumably organizing itself to act more continually and effectively *as a whole*), then this newborn Congress might be able to establish a relationship with the president: and the United States "might attain a tolerable balance, for a federal system in a technological era, in its system of accountability." Price concludes that this might be done without constitutional change, indeed, with few statutory changes: the changes would be in the unwritten constitution.

Price's conception of the British system dwells heavily on the monarchy and the establishment, which in the late–eighteenth century, was the Church of England.[33] Somehow this monarchical system has continued to invest late-twentieth-century British government with an inherited centralization: an enduring establishment. The trappings of monarchy survive. The Church of England establishment is reincarnated in Her Majesty's Civil Service And the ruling politicians, the "masters," all life-members of Privy Council, have learned "to respect the integrity and continuity of H. M. Civil Service, the administrative embodiment of the monarchy." This inbred, commonly accepted devotion infuses prime ministers, Cabinet members and backbenchers alike with the spirit of the unitary state; hence, the uncertainties introduced by the rise of the Loyal Opposition—uncertainties in the "traditional ideas of obedience to royal authority."[34]

But was it not the emergence of the opposition that gave modern parliamentary government its true character? Modern parliamentary government has developed the party discipline that facilitates the cohesive policies that Price wants the United States to achieve by cooperation between the president and the Congress—although he hastens to add: not too much. In England, party discipline developed rapidly in the nineteenth century, between 1860 and 1891 (following Allen Potter, drawing on A. Lawrence Lowell).

Whence came this party discipline? I refer to the internal arrangements that enjoin the membership, especially and specifically the party membership in the legislature, to concert policies and then to support their party's position thereon. This, it will be remembered, is the central Price assumption for his newborn legislature that will be able to achieve a proper cooperation with the president: discipline (but not too much).

In explaining party cohesion in Britain, Samuel H. Beer cites

Leon Epstein's conclusion that "members of a majority party share in the partisan desire to keep their leaders in office." They want "to keep their party in and the Opposition out." The argument in reverse motivates cohesion in the Opposition. In short, the chief motivation in each party is the fear of the opposing party. This is the culminating motive, as Beer points out, noting other motivations — "the threat of dissolution, the disciplinary power of the whips, the possibility of expulsion, the leadership's control over political advancement, pressure from constituency parties, and the like."[35] I should add: partisan control over nominations, over who shall run for office with the party label.

If members of Parliament are to rally to support the government (or the opposition, as the case may be), they must perceive the life of the government to be in danger. From what? An adverse vote of confidence "The incontestable and defining convention of the [parliamentary] system has been that the Government must have the confidence of the House."[36] Yet this convention became operative only about 1840 Afterwards, for a time, the House remained quite undisciplined.

What brought about the change? At the risk of *post hoc ergo propter hoc*: population rapidly increased (it tripled between 1831 and 1931). Parliament kept enlarging the electorate (5 percent of the population over twenty years of age in 1830; 7 percent after 1832; 16 percent after 1867; 28 percent after 1884 — and eventually 96.7 percent after 1928). Political parties set out to organize the expanded electorate. The workers begin to emerge into class consciousness (Hobsbawm) that prepared the ground for a transition from Tory-Whig (Church and chapel) political dichotomy to the Tory-Labour dichotomy in the twentieth century (Lipson). Party discipline suddenly crystallized in the House of Commons. As late as 1860, 90 percent of the Conservative M.P.'s voted together in only 31 percent of the votes, compared to 25 percent of the Whigs. By 1871 a sharp rise in discipline was evident and in 1894 90 percent of the Conservatives voted together on 91 percent of the votes; the comparable figures for Liberals and Irish Nationals was 81 percent. Party government shone clear and rapidly put an end to "the old Corruption."[37] H. M. Civil Service, freed from patronage, emerged to become the bulwark of the establishment that Price perceives.

In considering the significance of the British development for the United States, it might be noted that if Britain was uniquely hospitable to party government it was not apparent yet in 1860. It seems to have emerged as the consequence of several dynamic characteristics of the English socio-economic-political scene interacting together: the rapid rise in population, the extension of the suffrage, the galvanization of parties in order to organize the electorate and to maintain control of nominations, the emergent social dichotomy, the clarification and establishment of the principle of collegial responsibility—the convention that the government must have the confidence of the House—all these combined to facilitate and even perhaps to ensure party government.

Above all, party discipline and H. M. Civil Service emerged from the continuous conflict between Whig and Tory, between Gladstone and Disraeli. Opposition appears as essential to parliamentary government. Rather than causing uncertainties in accountability, it *defined* accountability: accountability of the government to the House and of both the government and the Opposition to the people. As W. Ivor Jennings wrote: "To find out whether a people is free it is necessary only to ask if there is an Opposition and, if there is, to ask where it is."[38]

The rapid evolution of the British unwritten constitution in the nineteenth century seems to suggest the following. First, it casts doubt on some interpretations that the Framers of the American constitution of 1787 had the model of the British centralized constitution "before their eyes"[39] and rejected it. There is a sense in which such statements are true, but they cannot be taken to mean that the Framers consciously considered and rejected parliamentary government as it is now looked upon as a model for adaptation That parliamentary government did not exist in 1787.

Second, the rapid evolution of the British parliamentary system in the nineteenth century casts some doubt on Price's warning that America's intransigence toward authority is so deeply embedded in a variety of dissenting religious beliefs that the American ethos cannot sustain the deference toward government that a centralized parliamentary system requires. In Britain all the elements seemed hospitable to emergent parliamentarism. But the influence of such specific conventions as the ability of the monarch to convene and dissolve parliaments that readily transferred to the government simply did not exist in the United States But was this because America's pluralis-

tic and antiauthoritarian religious beliefs made it impossible? I
doubt it. The rapid American evolution (much against the intention
of the Framers) of the virtually directly elected presidency could occur: despite the strength of "irresponsibility as an article of faith" it
virtually dictated a two-party system (such as it was and is) in
America. It is also quite capable of nourishing the possibly dangerous loyalty inherent in a plebiscitary presidency.

Third, the very malleability and virtuosity of the British unwritten constitution brings out even more starkly the rigidities of the
American Constitution of 1787. Take federalism. James Q. Wilson
wrote: "Suppose the Founders had adopted a centralized, parliamentary regime instead of a decentralized, congressional one." But
federalism was a given in the Constitution of 1787. Indeed, it had to
be invented and then it was frozen into the written document—
frozen so hard that the allotment of two senators to each state is not
amenable even to the formal amendment process. Also frozen are
the separation of powers and rigid calendar elections. Where the
British unwritten constitution could evolve the written American
constitution cannot.

Fourth, the radically different, modern parliamentary system
that evolved in England toward the end of the nineteenth century
was, like Minerva, born in full bloom. Institutionally tough, it
formed a structure and process that governed the behavior of participants—sometimes too strictly as in the excesses of party discipline.
But it produced a government with the coherence and cohesion that,
up to a point, Price aspires to for the United States. By contrast,
Price's formula for cooperation between the president and the Congress would, in a manner of speaking, require both sides to achieve
the miracle of the born-again Christian every day of their lives They
would have to act as though consanguine when their mode of existence puts them apart and infuses them with mutual suspicion.

Price Wants Greater Coherence, Except . . .

I have noted that Price wants greater coherence in government,
wants Congress to act as a whole much more than it does now, and
wants it to delegate consciously as a whole to the executive who will
then be able to develop a more comprehensive approach to policy-

making and to administration, both, in Price's view, clearly executive functions.

But Price warns that too much coherence and discipline may threaten two "crucial political values."[40] First is the value of justice with respect both to fundamental rights and to the distribution of benefits and costs among the various regions and groups. Second is freedom from arbitrary political power especially in a federal system with inbred distrust of centralization.

Price raised these questions in a Committee on the Constitutional System meeting, September 1984. In a letter to me of November 30, 1984, he restated them. He thought that the complex CCS agenda needed a unified approach to avoid inherent conflicts over inarticulated purposes.

"To avoid this, I suggested three questions that seemed to me crucial: (1) do we want our policy leadership to be more unified or less unified—in either case to what extent? (2) do we want that leadership to be from a chief executive chosen by popular election . . . or from the leadership of a legislative body (Congress, or some variations of parliamentary system)? (3) do we want full control of leadership in a national government, or control over it by the states?"

This was one of the more trenchant statements in the CCS debates. Price suggests his answers in *America's Unwritten Constitution*, calling for much more centralization within Congress and the executive, for much more comprehensive delegation to the executive, for a much firmer corps of permanent and generalist civil servants, and for much greater party discipline—all to create and support much more cohesion in government—but, again, not too much. And he wants to accomplish all this while retaining and observing the separation of powers.

Price may well be right that this is our only hope. If so, I think that it is a forlorn one. Supported by McIlwain, I think that the separation of powers is inherently destructive of that firm, resilient, and effective government (gubernaculum for McIlwain) that is essential for both the preserving of justice with respect to fundamental rights and to freedom from arbitrary political power: both these are substantially protected by the rule of law administered by an independent judiciary (jurisdictio for McIlwain).

Elsewhere I have asserted, with some supporting evidence, the destructiveness of the separation of powers on government itself, its inexorable fragmenting tendency. Its fruits are too often triangular—with hard edges that tend to stick in the throat and then rip the guts of the body politic. They are not aberrations but the natural products of the separation of powers.

As for the scrutiny of the distribution of benefits and costs among various sections and groups as well as in the arbitration of the claims of the states, I agree that federalism was in the beginning and remains today an abiding condition of the viability of the United States of America. Our system lavishes care on many interests ensconced in state politics. In doing so it benefits many regional interests. If it has hindered the rise of a centralizing elite comparable to H. M. Civil Service, it has proliferated numerous elites, many of them highly (although still separately) centralized. Agriculture is rife with examples as are related natural resource entities—water, forests, and public lands—not to mention the military, the army, the navy, the marines, the air force, and indeed, the special services!

But John Marshall's reference in *McCulloch v. Maryland* to "the exigencies of the nation" remains compelling. Ours is the first era in which each of two nations, the United States being one, appears to have the power to make the planet uninhabitable. The military budget, enormous, insatiable, and nearly ubiquitous in its manifestations, nourishes the "defense triangles" throughout the country, peaking on the Potomac. Our diplomatic weight is a factor in numerous countries around the globe.

These preeminent defense activities of the federal government are undeniably nationalizing. So are many aspects of economic policy. The Framers of the 1787 Constitution firmly vested fiscal and monetary control in the federal government. National fiscal and monetary policies have recently brought its dominance to fruition. The national debt itself, the value of the dollar internationally, international trade, international lending policy—all are irresistably centralizing. The entitlement programs have a nationalizing effect. Social Security and its retirement brethren show that this nation has revised and adopted Marx's golden rule to read: "From each according to his productivity; to each according to his longevity." The overriding policy on health care—how much, for whom, how it's provided, how it's distributed, how it's paid for—is inescapably national.

Moreover, the nationalizing force of economic policy has an

ominous geopolitical effect, according to Helmut Schmidt, *A Grand Strategy for the West*. I quote from David P. Calleo's review:

> The analysis is compelling. Profligate American fiscal policy, caused by inadequate taxes and a grossly inflated military budget, combines with a low savings rate to result in massive bargaining, much of which comes from the rest of the world's taking advantage of preposterously high American interest rates. These rates produce an overvalued dollar that feeds protectionism and crushes debtors in the third world and at home. Everywhere, the high dollar destabilizes financial institutions and discourages serious investment—the latter desperately needed in Europe to transform its old industrial base. The whole situation grows politically and economically intolerable. The world's richest country cannot go on sustaining its prosperity by borrowing from the rest of the world.[41]

Certainly decentralizing along federal lines is an indigenous principle of the United States system. As an early "farm hand" studying the Soil Conservation Service I never found a good answer to the question: Why should the federal government be running terrace lines? At the same time the exigencies of soil science seemed to demand first a national and then a global taxonomy. But these are technical matters. Many political issues can surely be resolved or compromised locally; many community objectives can be articulated locally. On the other hand, we might well remember that the unarticulated major premise of many early defenders of states rights was the preservation of white supremacy.

This leads me to question Price's placing fundamental rights and "the distribution of benefits and costs among various regions and groups" under the same rubric: justice, Price's first value.[42] Fundamental rights include assurance of a quick trial in open court, with proper restrictions upon seizure, arraignment, the right to council, the protection against imposed self-incrimination (confessions secured by torture), etc. This seems to be a different order of things from the scramble over the distribution of federal public works.

Similarly, his second "value of freedom from arbitrary political power" seems to me to hark back to his first: the protection of fundamental rights. But here he talks immediately about a large federal system that will engender claims from a diverse population, claims

that will be negotiated out through the familiar committee-domi-
nated legislative process in the Congress. To be sure, this process will
be reformed from within. But will Price's reforms take hold or will
plus ça change plus c'est la meme chose prevail? The natural tendency for the separation of powers to nourish disruptive triangles will
die hard. Can we really cure the fragmenting tendencies by a potion
of the hair of the dog that bit us?

To be sure, Price has some powerful arguments. Local control,
"home rule," is often appealing. Centralization is not necessarily
good. Party government may become too rigid.

Moreover, Price's institutions are vested by two centuries of history. And yet recent history may be misleading, especially American
history, because of the exceedingly favorable conditions unique to
the United States until the 1950s. I turn again to McIlwain for a
contrasting appeal to history against separation of powers.

McIlwain could find no good precedents in history for the separation of powers that he called "this dissipation of government"
which has "worked disaster ever since it was adopted." "Unlike the
legal limitations in our bill of rights, it is not the matured result of
centuries of trial and error." The separation of powers "is a figment of
the imagination of eighteenth century doctrinaires who found it in
our earlier history because they were ignorant of the true nature of
that history. These political balances were unknown before the eighteenth century, were almost untried before the nineteenth, and have
been disastrous wherever they have been tried since." McIlwain
feared that if the dissipation of government developed much further
it would precipitate a reaction that might sweep away "every protection of any sort, legal as well as political, to leave the individual
naked and unprotected against the ever-present danger of arbitrary
government."[43]

Both Price and McIlwain fear arbitrary political power. If their
perspectives on the origins of its threats and on the counter measures
against it appear to differ, both look to accountability to the people
as an important, indeed, a crucial part of a saving system. McIlwain
calls for "full political responsibility to the . . . *whole* people."[44]
Price wants America's unwritten constitution to be changed so that
Congress acts more as a whole and conceives itself as a whole which is
strong enough to delegate power to a strong executive that "needs to
be given a greater degree of freedom in the formulation of policy."
The president should be able to organize his office properly and to

formulate policy proposals to be presented to the Congress as a whole. The formulation of policy requires great discretion vested in the president—"more privacy and confidentiality in the preparation of staff papers. The President also needs considerable control of the legislative agenda in order to select the priorities and exercise timing."[45]

This scheme would enable the Congress and the president "to give more weight to the ends of policy and the general values that determine them than to the technical means or to bureaucratic procedures." This "more democratic and responsible arrangement" will "focus the attention of the electorate and Congress as a whole on the main general issues, which they are interested in and competent to decide, rather than on the technical and procedural details, which they are not."[46] And this brings us ultimately to the role of the people.

The Role of the Public

Price begins with the problem of the role of the people and repeatedly returns to it. He laments the "loss of any consensus—even within any one of the major contending intellectual or political factions—on how to approach the problems. We are confused on what government should do, how it should do it, and how we may hold it responsible for what it does."[47]

On the role of the public, Price also writes: "*A free citizenry can hold government responsible only if it can choose from time to time which elected offices should hold power and what the limits of that power should be. It can do so only if the contending political leaders, while disagreeing on policies, agree in large measure to maintain government as a going concern and to respect the legal processes by which they hold or give up their power.*"[48] (Italics added.)

And, somewhat later, while contrasting the British idea of sovereignty, first in the king by divine right, then in the crown as the instrument of a sovereign parliament, but always centered, exactly located, and authoritative, with American sovereignty dispersed among the people (but still, I take it, somehow real and collective), Price turned to an eminent member of the Constitutional founders of 1787, later a justice of the Supreme Court: James Wilson. Denying sovereignty in either a royal or an ecclesiastical center, Wilson "asserted that the 'sovereign power of the society rests in the citizens at large,' who should always be free to change that constitution whenever expedient. 'The dread and redoubtable sovereign, when traced on to his ultimate and legitimate source, has been found, as he ought to have been found, in the free and independent man.'"[49]

In the final chapter, Price writes: "After the divine right of kings lost out to the voice of the people as the ultimate basis of political power, it became necessary to work out some new way to translate that power into practice, with proper responsibility." But the vox populi might not be clear. Government had to "obey the democratic decisions of the electorate" by relying on experts to "translate them into action." Could this possibly serve the public interest? "Those who make an earnest effort to make the public interest a reality have to work out some notion of how the will of millions of voters, expressed through polls or elections, may exercise some coherent control over the diverse functions of government."[50]

These statements are helpful. My only reservation is regarding the "will of millions of voters, expressed through polls or elections," exercising "some coherent control over the diverse functions of government." This smacks of the general will and also suggests too much credence in the egregious pretensions of the pollsters.

One must tread carefully. There is no denying the potential of popular demands. In the nineteenth century the westward surge persistently overrode efforts to plan the development of the frontier. In the twentieth century Americans washed the prohibition amendment out of the constitution with rivers of rotgut whiskey. Gabriel Almond has alerted us to the changeability of public moods. But there is something vastly greater in the concept of the people, "the dread and redoubtable sovereign." We cannot now speak only of constitutional government. It must be *constitutional democracy* or *democratic constitutionalism*. Both words must be operative.

At just this point, however, the Framers of 1787 bequeathed us a problem not only in the separation of powers but also in the concept of the people and in the definition of the popular role and function in the government of the United States. True, the most important words of the constitution are arguably the first three, "We, the People. . . ." Introduced late in the day by the Committee on Style this language was adopted without debate in Philadelphia and with almost no debate in the state ratifying conventions. Perhaps the words were inspired by the common vision of the "dread and redoubtable sovereign." But the proximate motivation seems to have been to frustrate the anticipated efforts of what we would now call the "states righters"—those who would urge that the Constitution, having been created by the states, could be interpreted and changed by the states. But the actual role of the people was hedged about, filtered, and checked so that, reinforced by institutions that naturally emerged to implement the structure issued from Philadelphia, the voters' choices were fragmented and multiplied until their proper function, to create a government and an opposition, became obscured. Except that the voters came to choose the president who may become ascriptively the embodiment of the popular will, a situation fraught with danger.

Nevertheless, the arrangement and its rationale served in the 150 years of insulation that the United States enjoyed when we were "bounded on the north and south by weak neighbors and on the east and west by fish"—and had only the Indians and ourselves to fight. Our institutions survived the era of "vote yourself a farm," "deal me in," and "a little plum for everyone." Now that the world has become a dangerous stage on which we ineluctably hold the center, we need another set of institutions that will not only enable the people to elect a government *and* an opposition but will *charge them with doing so.*

The Meaning of Accountability

Constitutional, democratic government should be responsible to the people, and the people, in turn, should be responsible for maintaining, as Edmund Burke wrote, "the partnership not only between those who are living, but between those who are living and those who are dead, and those who are yet to be born." The preeminent function of the election must be to show that the constitution is alive and flourishing. Of course, people will vote their interests. There will be a "competitive struggle for the peoples' vote" between the political parties. But the overriding significance of the constitutional function of the electorate should be to ensure the vitality of the institutions.

To that end the written constitution needs changing. The indicated changes appear to be many and complex even though the result should be a simpler political process with accountability more clearly established all around. Elections should not recur too often but often enough to remind all parties, all governors, and all leaders of oppositions that their tenure is limited. Campaigns should be drastically shortened; it is monstrous to continue having interminable campaigns when the chosen governments dispose of apocalyptic military power (as well as enormous power to do economic good or ill). Governing should be the chief function of such a gubernaculum, not campaigning. Governments need majorities: the vote should clearly designate majority winners and minority opposition losers. In this way the fact and responsibility of creating the government and the opposition would be brought home to the people. Government and opposition would emerge from the election; they would not be created afterwards by political brokers building coalitions. T. V. Smith's *Legislative Way of Life* in which the voters kept their moral purity by shifting the burden of choice to the legislators would be drastically changed so that voters would share some sense of responsibility—as much, indeed, as they can share—for governance.

Elsewhere I have suggested a program of reform that might achieve these ends. Such massive changes can be brought about only after long debate They can be accomplished only by a number of changes in the written constitution. If such changes occur, "We the people" will have to take a much more decisive and magisterial part than our ancestors did in 1787. The only conceivable way that this can come about is through a long and vigorous educational program.

During that period of constitutional education there will be time to try Price's approach of working with the unwritten constitution. His consul is to "imitate the parliamentary system's essence," at least to the extent of recognizing the fundamental need for a division of political labor in which the voters delegate to government and, within government, the legislature organizes itself as a whole to delegate to the executive so that it can exercise its proper functions. This large part of his analysis, with its emphasis on the crucial relationship between delegation and accountability, on the need for party discipline and for a permanent civil service built around a corps of generalists will help to prepare the public understanding of the kind of changes called for.

But we will still need a prolonged and thorough examination of the shortcomings of our written constitution. We have to go right on talking about the separation of powers.

8

Constitutionality of
Gramm-Rudman-Hollings

ON February 7, 1986 a three-judge federal court struck down the "automatic deficit reduction process," a key part of the Gramm-Rudman-Hollings Act, because it violated the separation of powers. The decision has been appealed to the Supreme Court. This chapter will argue that the three-judge court oversimplifies the separation of powers, reduces its flexibility, and greatly increases its rigidity, thus worsening the institutional problems that now beset the Constitution of the United States.[1]

From Schechter to Synar

In 1935 the United States Supreme Court unanimously struck down the National Industrial Recovery Act of 1933 (NIRA). Chief Justice Hughes cited Article I, sections 1 and 8 of the Constitution and declared: "The Congress is not permitted to abdicate or to transfer to others the essential legislative functions with which it is vested." *Schechter Poultry Corporation v. The United States*, 295 U.S. 495. Concurring, Associate Justice Cardozo wrote: "anything that Congress may do within the limits of the Commerce Clause for the betterment of business may be done by the President upon the recommendation of a trade association by calling it a code. This is delegation running riot."

Since 1935 the Supreme Court has "consistently rejected delegation challenges." Then in 1985 the Congress passed and the president signed the Balanced Budget and Deficit Control Act, the Gramm-Rudman-Hollings Act. (Henceforth, G-R-H.) Both the NIRA and G-R-H were passed in times of severe, though strikingly different, economic crises. In 1933, the fourth year of a deep depression, 24.9 percent of the civilian labor force was unemployed. In 1985 the national debt approached two trillion dollars, having doubled since 1981; the United States was spending twenty-four dollars for each nineteen dollars it collected in taxes, and endless annual budget deficits of at least two hundred billion dollars were projected.

In 1986, by contrast with the famous Schechter decision, a three-judge federal court held that G-R-H is "remote from legislative abdication."[2] *Synar et al. v. United States* went on to find a key provision of G-R-H unconstitutional not because of an excess of delegation but because the Congress had failed to delegate enough! Or, perhaps, as the court would prefer to put it, because the Congress had presumed to appropriate a uniquely executive power and then to vest this purloined power in its own creature, the comptroller general.

The *Synar* decision held that "since the powers conferred on the comptroller general as part of the automatic deficit reduction process are executive powers, which cannot be constitutionally exercised by an officer removable by Congress, those powers cannot be exercised and therefore the automatic deficit reduction process to which they are central cannot be implemented." Lest the court be misunderstood, the decision went on to speak of "our invalidation of one small section of the Act."[3] If it was a small section, the automatic budget control was at or near the heart of the act.

The *Synar* decision seemed to imply that had the president been given the assignment rather than the comptroller general, that delegation would have been valid: "if the present statute had not inserted the Comptroller General between the president and the Directors of the CBO and the OMB, and if the determinations to be made under the Act by the Comptroller General had been assigned instead to the President himself."[4] Then, the court went on, the Congress, under the *Chadha* decision (*INS v. Chadha*, 462 U.S. 919, 1983), would have been unable to exercise a legislative veto over the president's action and the decision in *Synar v. United States* would presumably have vindicated G-R-H completely.

The *Synar* decision appears to have anticipated this conclusion and to have sought to refute it or, at least, to render it ambiguous. Earlier on, the court had asserted that the statutory grant of authority to the comptroller general was a "carefully considered protection against what the House (of Representatives) conceived to be the pro-executive bias of the OMB. It is doubtful that the automatic deficit reduction process would have passed without such protection, and doubtful that the protection would have been considered present if the Comptroller General were not removable by Congress itself—much less if he were removable (as validation of his functions under this legislation might constitutionally require, a point we do not reach) at the discretion of the President, like the Director of the OMB himself."[5]

In this convoluted judicial prose, the three-judge court seemed to say that if the comptroller general were removable by the president, the insertion of the comptroller general's function would have been constitutional—but then the judges deferentially retreated: "a point we do not reach." Perhaps, however, their vindication of such delegation would constitute an obiter dictum. The court had said that it would offer its views obiter dicta on the general question whether G-R-H violated the prohibition against delegating legislative powers; thus, fifteen pages of the mimeographed decision are included so that the Supreme Court, if it thought it necessary to consider the larger question, "would have the usual benefit of having a lower-court opinion."[6] Hence the implied cure for the diseased part of G-R-H might be designated as obiter almost dictum. To underline the point, as it were, the *Synar* decision genuflected to the president who had brought the participation of the comptroller general to the attention of Congress when he signed G-R-H into law, December 12, 1985: "[E]xecutive functions may only be performed by officers in the executive branch. The . . . Comptroller General [is an] agent of Congress, not [an] officer in the executive branch . . . My administration alerted Congress to this . . . problem throughout the legislative process in an effort to achieve a bill free of constitutionally suspect provisions . . . [W]e were unsuccessful in this goal."

On the face of it, then, the *Synar* decision seemed to fault G-R-H not because of a too fulsome delegation of legislative powers but because the delegation did not go far enough. But the three-judge court persisted in putting it differently, appealing to Montesquieu in finding that the Congress had wrongfully appropriated an intrinsically executive power.

Inviolable Executive Powers: Invoking Montesquieu

The *Synar* decision is at pains to identify normal executive decisions. These must be performed by the president or by someone he appoints (perhaps by and with the consent of the Senate, perhaps not) and whom he alone can remove. To do otherwise violates the separation of powers. "We are confident . . . that congressional removal power cannot be approved with regard to an officer who actually participates in the execution of the laws. Once an officer is appointed, it is only the authority that can remove him, and not the authority that appointed him, that he must fear and, in the performances of his functions, obey."[7]

To give such power over executive functions to Congress (the court argued) violates the fundamental principle expressed by Montesquieu upon which the separation of powers rests: "When the legislative and executive powers are united in the same person, or in the same body of magistrates, there can be no liberty." And the opinion also quotes *Federalist* No. 48 that no one of the three branches of government "ought to possess, directly or indirectly, an overruling influence over the others, in the administration of their respective powers."

But in *Federalist* No. 47, Madison put a very different interpretation on Montesquieu's famous dictum quoted above—"he did not mean that these departments ought to have no *partial agency* in, or no *control* over, the acts of the other. His meaning . . . can amount to no more than this, that where the *whole* power of one department is exercised by the same hands which possess the *whole* power of another department, the fundamental principles of a free constitution are subverted." This famous statement of Madison is the solid ground for Richard E. Neustadt's celebrated summarizing phrase: "separated institutions sharing powers."

G-R-H lays down a formula by which federal appropriations and spending are to be rigorously controlled over a five-year period. Recall the Constitution: "No Money shall be drawn from the Treasury, but in Consequence of Appropriations made by Law." G-R-H was a law, signed by the president who could have vetoed it. In the law Congress stipulated and the president agreed that spending for five years should be restricted by a formula that would rigidly control both the president and the Congress. It was an act of both the separated institutions sharing powers.

But let us look at the *Synar* decision in more detail.

Essential Executive Powers, Yes; Essential Legislative Powers, No

Specifically, what are the "executive powers" in question? "Under subsection 251(b)(1), the Comptroller General must specify levels of anticipated revenue and expenditure that determine the gross amount that must be sequestered; and he must specify which particular budget items are required to be reduced by the various provisions of the Act (which are not in all respects clear), and in what particular amounts."

Then the *Synar* opinion says: "The first of these specifications requires the exercise of substantial judgment concerning present and future facts that affect the application of the law—the sort of power normally conferred upon the executive officer charged with implementing a statute. The second specification requires an interpretation of the law enacted by Congress, similarly a power normally committed initially to the Executive under the Constitution's prescription that he 'take care that the Laws be faithfully executed' . . . And both of these specifications by the Comptroller General are, by the present law, made binding upon the President in the latter's application of the law . . . In our view, these cannot be regarded as anything but executive powers in the constitutional sense."[8]

The *Synar* decision's analysis of "executive powers in the constitutional sense" contrasts sharply with its analysis of "core [legislative] functions." Objecting to the allegation that G-R-H delegates core legislative functions to the executive, the *Synar* decision said that not only had the Supreme Court never held any legislative function, even that of appropriations to be nondelegable, but also that "judicial adoption of a 'core functions' analysis would be effectively standardless . . . No constitutional provision distinguishes between 'core' and 'non-core' legislative functions, so that the line would

necessarily . . . be drawn on the basis of the court's own perceptions
of the relative importance of various legislative functions."[9]

But the *Synar* decision did specify what constitute "executive
powers." Observe the determination of the amount of spending to be
sequestered — this determination "requires the exercise of substantial
judgment concerning present and future facts that affect the application of the law"; and the court held this to be "the sort of power
normally conferred upon the executive officer charged with implementing a statute." This specification is not stated in the constitution. Rather, it is said to be inferred from practice (normally conferred). Who normally confers it? The Congress. But in G-R-H the
Congress conferred it on the comptroller general. This was the legislature's own perception of how and by whom the delegated authority
should be exercised. It offended the three-judge court's own perception of how things should be done. But whose perceptions should
prevail?

The objection to the *Synar* decision's point is even more fundamental: on examination, the substantial judgment conferred on the
comptroller general by G-R-H proves to be infinitesimally small, as I
shall indicate later. If the hands are the hands of Esau, the voice is
certainly Jacob's.

Against the Grain of History?

Does the *Synar* decision move against the grain of history? I
draw upon Frederick C. Mosher: *The GAO: The Quest for Accountability in the American Government* on the constitutional question of
the independence of the GAO.[10] Noting that the separation of
powers "was never intended to be ironclad," Mosher found the
answer to the question of who should have financial control ambiguous. The first Congress opted for the executive when it established
the comptroller in the Department of the Treasury, appointed by the
president, with senatorial consent, and removable by the president.

But the Budget and Accounting Act of 1921 "substantially re-
versed the original position." The act created the General Accounting
Office, "independent of the executive departments," and vested the
control of finances in it. The GAO was headed by a comptroller

general, appointed by the president for a single fifteen-year term, by and with the advice and consent of the Senate.

Noting that a strict construction might declare either the Treasury Act of 1791 or the Budget and Accounting Act of 1921 (or, perhaps, parts of both of them) unconstitutional, Mosher thought that view would now be questioned. For nearly a century the Congress, sustained by the courts, had created independent bodies, especially the regulatory commissions, in which legislative, executive, and judicial functions are joined. Clearly the comptroller general should be independent of the executive in his fundamentally legislative functions. "Congress can . . . utilize its own agent to make sure its laws and appropriations have been carried out. . . . All . . . agree that in these matters the GAO is accountable to Congress—although the Comptroller General insists on his independence even from Congress in selecting the majority of his projects and in the objectivity of his investigations and of the recommendations that grow out of them."

A stickier question (says Mosher) arises on whether the comptroller general's decisions are binding on the executive branch. "The attorney general has repeatedly, although rather infrequently, contended that the decisions of the Comptroller General are only advisory on the executive branch." The argument is buttressed by appeals to the Constitution: "The executive Power shall be vested in a President" who shall "take care that the laws be faithfully executed." Much has been made of these points in the *Synar* decision and of the fact that the comptroller general, though appointed by the president, is not removable by the president. In another example, Attorney General John Mitchell implied in 1971 that the act of 1921 unconstitutionally vested the powers to settle and adjust accounts in the comptroller general.

Comptroller generals have replied that, while the GAO is indeed ultimately accountable to Congress, that body has deliberately delegated to him "a number of powers of nonlegislative character primarily to assist [the Congress] in assuring the financial accountability of the executive agencies. In respect to these actions, the Comptroller General is an independent officer of the United States, substantially independent of either branch."

GAO protagonists also cite the "necessary and proper" clause of the Constitution, indicating that the Framers "intended that Congress exercise the ultimate powers of the government," including both the executive and the legislative branches: "To make all Laws which shall be necessary and proper for carrying into Execution the foregoing Powers, and *all other Powers vested by this Constitution in the Government of the United States, or in any Department or Officer thereof.*" (Emphasis added.) Hence the Congress can set up agencies, vest them with powers, and attach conditions to their performance as it wishes.

Mosher cites a decision by Judge Alexander Holtzoff of the District Court of the District of Columbia that found the comptroller general, "the chief accounting officer of the Government," to have "an executive function" in the performance of which he "acts as a member of the Executive Branch." Moreover, "The dual status of the General Accounting Office is not anomalous, for many regulatory commissions fulfill in part a legislative function and in part carry out executive duties."[11]

Although the presidential appointment supported, somewhat, the comptroller general's claim to be able to perform nonlegislative functions, Mosher noted also that the absence of presidential removal power "is key to Attorney General Mitchell's argument that he is an officer only of the legislative branch." Hence, after fifty-seven years the legal status and powers of the comptroller general were still subject to some dispute. Nevertheless, the "ambiguity and the allowance for dynamics that it permits may be an asset for the responsiveness and accountability of American government."[12]

And Mosher stressed the unique independence and insularity of the comptroller general and the GAO. The GAO's organization would "appear to include stability, continuity, orderliness, self-containment, and self-governance . . . a sense of insularity."

"It is a servant of one of the most 'political' bodies in the world, the U.S. Congress. But . . . Congress obviously is not a 'body' in any strict sense. [Top GAO officials] must obviously be politically astute . . . Yet the organization itself is nonpolitical." It has its own internal politics. "But it is not the politics of parties or of interest groups or even of program, as it is in so many government agencies." Its career personnel system seems to be immune from political pressures in hiring, promoting, placing, and firing. While most of the comptrollers general have been of the same political party as the president who appointed them, none, except perhaps the first one, has been widely accused of partisanship in the performance of his duties. The present Comptroller General, who served as deputy director of the budget under four presidents . . . deals evenhandedly with executive and legislative leaders of both parties. . . . His own political affiliation, if it is known, seems quite irrelevant, as do those of the Deputy Comptroller General and his predecessors."[13]

"The Comptroller General is unique in the powers, prestige, and influence that he enjoys within the GAO organization." The strength of his position "probably derives in part from his extensive powers . . . to shape the GAO organization . . . But more important is the legal fact of the fifteen-year term that is virtually assured if the incumbent is able and willing to fill it out . . . No other federal official is legally assured such longevity in office."[14]

An Assault on Liberty?

The *Synar* decision has no tolerance for this alternative analysis. It relies on a rigid interpretation of the separation of powers. In doing so it rejects the "doctrine of unconstitutional delegation" in favor of "the more technical separation of powers requirements." This is derived from Montesquieu who advocated "limiting governmental power and then dividing the remaining power among autonomous governmental compartments."[15]

The president is charged, according to this interpretation, with seeing that the laws of the United States are executed. Either he must execute them himself or he must appoint other officers who do so (or who appoint subordinates who do so). In order to control the execution the president must be able not only to appoint but to remove subordinates. It follows that any officer, although appointed by the president, who is dismissible only by the Congress cannot be constitutionally charged with executing the law. Under this decision many of the actions taken by the GAO throughout its history appear to have been unconstitutional.

The *Synar* decision does note that it "may seem odd that curtailment of such an important and hard-fought legislative program [as G-R-H] should hinge on the relative technicality of authority over the Comptroller General's removal." "But 'the decision goes on' the balance of separated power by the Constitution consists precisely of a series of technical provisions that are more important to liberty than superficially appears, and whose observance cannot be approved or rejected by the courts as the times seem to require."

The *Synar* decision makes no attempt to show by evidence that the comptroller general and the GAO have ever been a threat to liberty. It is enough to discover a rigid principle in Montesquieu and to construe it as requiring the absolute vesting of removal power in the president. There is no point in examining the history to see how many comptrollers general have been removed by Congress or even seriously threatened with removal. Once the principle is discovered and announced ex cathedra it is unequivocally binding.

On a number of matters, however, the *Synar* decision did indulge in historical or political institutional interpretation in order to strengthen its argument. For example, in pointing up the threat to the integrity of the comptroller general caused by his fear of removal by the Congress, the decision declared that "insofar as effect on balance of power is concerned, congressional power to remove is much more potent [than would be the president's power to remove], since the Executive has no means of retaliation that may dissuade Congress from exercising it—other than leaving the office vacant, thereby impairing the Executive's own functions. Congress, on the other hand, has many ways to make the President think long and hard before he makes a 'for cause' removal that Congress disapproves, ranging from budget constriction to refusal to confirm a successor."

Not only does this interpretation ignore the specific history of the comptroller general's security, insularity, and independence in office. It also overlooks the powers that vest in an active, skillful, and lucky president who enhances his reputation in the Washington community and burnishes his image with the public. The statement fails to recognize how much and how often members of the legislature must rely on the president to get what they want, a place in the executive program, budget, and agenda for their projects, an executive order signed, an appointment made, political support, etc. The influence that the president may achieve as occupant of the "bully pulpit," as well as his formal powers as commander-in-chief, his possession of the veto, and his power of appointment—including the appointment of Supreme Court Justices—all these powers, it must be assumed, are frequently in the minds of members of the Washington community.

Another example occurred when the *Synar* decision departed from its effort to find exactly what Montesquieu meant and to trace his revelation through the subsequent decades of judicial discovery and reiteration. This departure concerned the conception of the "independent regularity agencies." The *Synar* court found that Justice Sutherland's decision in *Humphrey's Executor* (1935) "is stamped with some of the political science preconceptions characteristic of its era and not of the present day . . . It is not as obvious today as it seemed in the 1930s that there can be such things as genuinely 'independent' regulatory agencies, bodies of impartial experts whose independence of the President does not entail correspondingly greater dependence upon the committees of Congress to which they are then immediately accountable; or, indeed, that the decisions of such agencies so clearly involve scientific judgment rather than political choice that it is even theoretically desirable to insulate them from the democratic process."[16]

Overlooking the jejune conception of "political science preconceptions" of the 1930s, the learned judges seem to be extending judicial recognition to phenomena of government in the United States with which students of its politics have been increasingly concerned: the emergence of partly independent centers of power based on alliances of strategically located legislators, high-ranking administrative officers, and leaders of organized clientele groups.

This phenomenon is not, repeat, *not*, manifest in the GAO. Recall Mosher: "It is not the politics of parties or of interest groups." The *Synar* decision has nothing to say on this point. But the triangles mushroom in government — sometimes in the independent regulatory agencies but much more significantly in the military and civilian executive departments where they manifest the inherent disruptive tendency of a government under the strain of the separation of powers.

A Different View of the Separation of Powers

Recall that the *Synar* decision finds its lodestar in the separation of powers according to Montesquieu. The inference is that all officers charged with the execution of laws must not only be appointed by the president (or by his appointees) but also dismissible by the president. That this would effectively wipe out the Office of Comptroller General can neither be escaped nor helped.

Frederick C. Mosher has a different interpretation. The separation of powers in the national government, he wrote,

> remains alive, and, if not perfectly well, is at least not critically ill. Despite recent concerns about the 'imperial presidency,' the alleged aggrandizement by Congress of presidential powers, or about unholy alliances between pockets of Congress and pockets in the executive branch, there continues a general recognition that these two branches have somewhat different powers (though some are shared), different constituencies, and different responsibilities. Conflicts between the two are endemic, built into the Constitution and supported through the development of a loose, relatively undisciplined two-party system. The GAO could hardly operate as it does without the separation of powers. There are few if any other nations in the world . . . wherein an official agency would, as a matter of normal operating procedure, publish reports critical of the policies and programs of another official agency — even when the two agencies are ultimately responsible to branches controlled by the same political party. This is routine for the GAO, some of the other congressional support units, committees of the Congress, and sometimes the Congress as a whole.[17]

Note that Mosher strongly criticizes the "unholy alliances between pockets of Congress and pockets of the executive branch." This is the same problem that the *Synar* decision observed. Mosher elaborates:

> One of the pervasive problems of American national government is the fragmentation of programs, functions, appropriations, and organizations within relatively narrow compartments . . . Such fragmentation has long been the subject of complaint and of efforts to reform in the executive branch. In recent years, with the development of strong subcommittees, it has become a problem of roughly comparable magnitude in Congress.

Mosher then finds that the GAO "with its almost unlimited scope of jurisdiction, its resources scattered among the various headquarters offices in Washington and in the field, is uniquely positioned to attack problems that cross both organizational lines in the executive branch and committee lines in Congress." He finds that the GAO's recent reorganization on the basis of broad functional areas (community and economic development; energy and minerals division, human resources division, etc.) and the development of a program built around issue areas (law enforcement and crime prevention; implementation of military preparedness plans; international economic and military programs) has facilitated such an approach. "The potential of the GAO for a unifying, integrating, and coordinating contribution is great."[18]

Conclusion

Until 1921 the United States had done without an executive budget. Until 1974 it did without a centralized congressional budgetary process designed to parallel and coordinate with the executive. With the high inflation of the 1970s, the escalation of military outlays and of entitlement programs, federal deficits began to grow. After the Reagan tax cut in 1981, they surged. By early 1986 deficits were running at $200 million a year and the national debt had doubled—had grown as much in 5 years as in the previous 192. Congress passed the Gramm-Rudman-Hollings Act in desperation. Even Senator Rudman called it "a bad idea whose time has come." This was a radical effort to cut federal outlays by $36 billion annually until 1991, when the deficit was projected to be reduced to zero. Reductions were to be achieved by applying rigid formulae, so precise that they were labeled "automatic."

G-R-H instructed the Office of Management and Budget and the Congressional Budget Office (OMB and CBO) by January 10, 1986 (and by August 15 in after years) to make quarterly estimates of economic growth and of the deficit, to calculate whether spending under the budget would exceed specified limits in 1986 and, in future years, would exceed such limits by more than $10 billion, to calculate the budgetary cuts necessary to bring spending down to specified limits, and to produce a "base line" of automatic cuts that, with the exception of Social Security and certain other programs, would be apportioned half to the military and half to the civilian budget.

The base line must be reported to the comptroller general of the

GAO who has five days—*five days*, hardly enough time to check the OMB/CBO arithmetic—to prepare the "Sequester Order" to transmit to the president. How much discretion the GAO has is evident in the extremely brief time allotted to it and also in the congressional instructions that where the CBO and the OMB differ the GAO is to take the average! The comptroller general has perhaps enough discretion to decide whether to split an infinitive. He is more like a proofreader than a discretionary executive.

The *Synar* decision underscores the essence of what it finds repugnant to the Constitution in this sentence: "*And both of these specifications by the Comptroller General are, by the present law, made binding upon the President in the latter's application of the law.* Act 252(a)(3)."[19] Just so. But what G-R-H made binding on the president is the will of the Congress expressed in law. Congress has seen in the budget crisis an extremity that requires a coherent act of governance, binding in extraordinary fashion on itself and on the executive. The extent to which the Congress has bound itself is apparent in its stipulation that in floor debate any proposed increase in budgetary items over the specified limits would be subject to a point of order that could be overridden only by three-fifths of the representatives present in the House and three-fifths of the entire Senate.

Despite its numerous references to Supreme Court and other federal court cases, the *Synar* decision bases its appeal to the separation of powers on Montesquieu.[20] In that the enshrinement of Montesquieu is accomplished by quoting "a respected Scholar," Krattenmaker, it is fitting to reply by quoting the late Charles H. McIlwain, a towering figure in constitutional law and political theory. In *Constitutionalism: Ancient and Modern*, McIlwain wrote: "Among all the modern fallacies that have obscured the true teachings of constitutional history, few are worse than the extreme doctrine of the separation of powers and the indiscriminate use of the phrase 'checks and balances.' "[21]

So far as McIlwain could see there was little historical background for the theory of the separation of powers "except the fancies of eighteenth century doctrinaires and their followers. Political balances have no institutional background whatsoever except in the imagination of closet philosophers like Montesquieu."

Deriding "this dissipation of government" which has "worked disaster ever since it was adopted," McIlwain wrote: "Unlike the legal limitations in our Bill of Rights, it is not the matured result of centuries of trial and error." McIlwain feared that if the dissipation of government developed much further it would precipitate a reaction that might sweep away "every protection of any sort, legal as well as political, to leave the individual naked and unprotected against the ever-present danger of arbitrary government."[22]

What are the merits of Gramm-Rudman-Hollings? What of its wisdom? Its prudence? The *Synar* decision is innocent of any consideration of these questions. Perhaps it should be. But it seizes on a "relative technicality" to impose a rigid construction of Montesquieu's glittering generality. It does so in order to ensure liberty, although it made no effort to show even a superficial connection to liberty.

By contrast, G-R-H perceived the ballooning deficit, with its inherent threat of unleashing a devastating inflation, to be a clear and present danger to the polity. G-R-H sought to overcome that threat by heroic measures to control the dissipation of government that alarmed McIlwain by forging the entire government into one coherent force to attack it. The methods of G-R-H and the formulae it prescribes may be grossly mistaken. Senator Moynihan discerned in it a "suicide pact." Surely Gramm-Rudman-Hollings deserves the most thorough examination. The three-judge court's *Synar* decision is woefully inadequate.

9
Separation of Powers and Arms Control

THE American separation of powers between the president and the Congress tends to fracture or rupture the government of the United States. It does so by encouraging informal coalitions of strategically located legislators, ranking administrators, and leaders of relevant organized groups. These coalitions are the triangles that achieve significant degrees of control over parts of United States public policy over pieces of the United States government. The formation and operation of triangles has frequently been discerned in pork-barrel politics. Examples are building dams, improving harbors, locating defense plants, and maintaining costly subsidies long after their original rationale has eroded. This chapter argues that the natural formation of triangles helps explain the recent extended deadlock in arms control negotiation with the Soviet Union.

My focus will be on efforts to achieve an agreement on nuclear arms control between the United States and the USSR during 1981-83. The result has been termed by Strobe Talbott: "the most serious and protracted break-down to date" in such negotiations.[1] After the Russians withdrew from Geneva talks in December 1983, resumption was postponed fifteen months to March 1985. The first round ended in April, and both sides characterized it as fruitless.[2]

To repeat, the years 1981 through 1983 (and actually through mid-1985) were marked by a virtual cessation of meaningful negotiations between the United States and the USSR on nuclear arms control. In part, this was attributable to the United States stance on such negotiations. The United States may have simply been implementing a policy not to negotiate because the USSR was conceived to be so dishonest that any arms control agreement with it is worthless. Or a non-negotiations policy may have been masked by combining it with another policy of seeming to negotiate. Whenever the USSR walked out of negotiations, the United States could then say: "We have made every effort to negotiate in good faith; but the Russians, typically, have broken up the talks."

My interpretation begins with the argument that the stance of the United States was unclear because President Reagan himself was ambivalent. In the struggle for the soul of the president one side held that worthwhile arms control agreements can be negotiated with the Soviets and that it would be in the interests of the United States to do so. The other side held, in effect, that a policy of no-negotiations or, at least, of no serious negotiations (the United States making demands that the USSR would categorically refuse) was preferable.

No negotiation won out in 1981–83. The breakdown occurred. My interpretation is that the breakdown is significantly attributable to a rupture or a fracture or a division within the United States government; one severe enough virtually to ensure it. I say "virtually" because the president could have overridden the opposition and supported the protagonists of serious negotiations. To have done so he would have had to pay the costs. Part of the costs would appear to have been to confront and override his conservative supporters on what many of them deemed to be an extremely important issue. Part of the costs would have been personal; he would have had to pay close attention to the issues, to have studied them deeply, and to have achieved and maintained an understanding of them certainly beyond his wont and perhaps beyond his capabilities.[3]

The Constitution attempts to endow us with a strong executive but it lets us open not only to the inadequacies of individual presidents but also to the continuing propensity for government by presidential whim or impulse. The "struggle for the soul" of the president, an ancient ritual, requires courtiers to strive unremittingly to get and keep the president on their side. My assumption is that President Reagan, despite his jaundiced view of the USSR and his determination to "make the United States strong again" might still have opted for serious negotiations. His words and actions in 1984 and increasingly in 1985 seem to bear this out.[4] If so, the victorious protagonists of no-negotiations in 1981–83 were not merely the president's tools.

Nor were the victorious protagonists for no-negotiations simply more profound in their grasp of the issues and more persuasive in their arguments. (Although, as Talbott points out they had the advantage of being "naysayers"; it is usually easier to keep things from happening than it is to make them happen.)[5] Government-by-discussion assumes that after a reasonable time for debate a decision is reached in which either of the two final alternatives prevails. A rupture of government occurs if one side achieves an all-or-nothing position. This is what seems to have happened during 1981–85 in the development of American policy on negotiations with the USSR.

The debate on policy among the leaders did not take place in a situation that would be resolved by a conclusion that would commit the power base of the government. Here the power base itself was divided. A triangle of power, the Pentagon civilians, the conservative bloc in Congress, and presumably some important constituents of that bloc, all coalesced or appeared to have coalesced behind the no-negotiations position. They would win unless the president was willing to move against them in the spirit of "Damn the torpedoes; full speed ahead!" This triangle of power grew directly out of the separation of powers.

The Mischief Wrought by the Separation of Powers

My intention, to repeat, is to provide additional evidence of the destructive effect of the separation of powers between the legislative and the executive on organized government in the United States. As elsewhere, I draw on Charles H. McIlwain's discussion of constitutional government, which culminated in a sharp attack on the American separation of powers.[6] In this understanding constitutional government is limited government. It is limited by the institutionalization (an independent judiciary) of due process of law: McIlwain called this limit jurisdictio. For jurisdictio to exist a strong government is necessary; McIlwain called it gubernaculum because he found the roots of constitutional government in Ancient Rome. Hailing both jurisdictio and gubernaculum, McIlwain concluded that the reconciliation between the two "remains probably our most serious practical problem." He argued that both of them must be strengthened; and he wrote that among "all the modern fallacies that have obscured the true teaching of constitutional history, few are worse than the extreme doctrine of the separation of powers and the indiscriminate use of the phrase 'checks and balances.'"

How is government (gubernaculum) ruptured or fractured in consequence of the separation of powers? Richard E. Neustadt provided one theory. The 1940s saw "an extraordinary element added to the government of the United States: an executive establishment, a body of official which, for size, scale, and corporate survival was a new creation, unlike anything our governmental system knew before." In an effort to control the bureaucracy—that is, to control the government—the president acted according to his genius which was to manage things by coordinating, synthesizing, and integrating them. The creation of the Executive Office of the President established and legitimized the doctrine "in the nick of time"; without it the presidency "would by now [1965] have been a hollow shell."[7]

But under the separation of powers the Congress is authorized to organize the government. Congress had a different genius for managing things. Instead of coordinating and centralizing, it controls by dividing things up and parcelling them out, thus creating quasi-independent bureaucracies. "The gainers [Neustadt wrote], are of two sorts: on the one hand, effective agency careerists; on the other hand, well-placed committee members, especially seniority leaders (or their staff)." And later: "If clients and constituents are brought into the combine to the satisfaction of all sides, so much the better." Hence, the triangle.

McIlwain provided the magisterial criticism of the separation of powers as potentially destructive of gubernaculum. Neustadt advanced the theoretical explanation (the model) of one very important way that this destruction takes place. We hear much of the "fragmentation" of government. This is how it can and does happen. Neustadt's theory illuminated what I had observed in agricultural policy and administration: in the Soil Conservation Service, in the credit agencies (beginning with the old Farm Security Administration), in the Cooperative Federal-State Extension Service with its famous link between the county agents and the Farm Bureaus, in the tobacco, the dairy, the cotton, the sugar, and other commodity programs and, overarchingly, in the price-support, production control programs—the Agricultural Adjustment Administration and its successors. Some of these quasi-independent bureaucracies or triangles emerged well before the 1940s when Neustadt discerned the bureaucratic explosion. Even earlier predecessors appeared in rivers and harbors, the water policy agencies and programs, and in pork barrels generally.[8]

A Denial of Neustadt's Theory

Is there more irony than iron in the triangle? Arthur Maass, whose *Muddy Waters* is the prototype for the triangle theory, has declared, in *Congress and the Common Good*, that the triangles manifest "pathological forms of bureaucratic intercourse."[9] "Although whirlpools and iron triangles can be found at any time, they do not describe the normal pattern of American executive-legislations relations." His theory follows:

> For each substantive policy area—agriculture, civil rights, transportation—there is an independent and unique decision-making subsystem, consisting of an executive bureau, a congressional subcommittee, and the relevant pressure groups. The major objective of all participants . . . is to insure that the subsystem aggregates and retains the political power and influence necessary to make and control public policy in its area . . .
>
> This alternative method of studying committees . . . describes a great deal of routine governmental activity where the President and Congress as a whole have elected not to intervene, but can do so at any time they choose. Beyond this it describes what we have called the pathological form of bureaucratic intercourse. Indeed, it confuses the pathological and normal forms. Although whirlpools and iron triangles can be found at any time, they do not describe the normal pattern of American executive-legislative relations.[10]

Maass cites the problem for his model of executive-legislative relations that surfaces "when the relations between bureaus and the committee are so intimate and so ubiquitous that they preclude the President and the whole House from participating in the legislative and administrative process when they want to participate." This means that the "bureau-committee relations are so intimate as to challenge the President's control over bureaus and Congress's control over committees. This . . . can be called the pathological form of bureau-committee relations, in the sense that it is a deviation from the normal or typical form." He provides an example:

> Presidents Franklin D. Roosevelt and Harry S. Truman were frustrated in their efforts to adopt national policies for the development and use of water and land resources by the U.S. Army Corps of Engineers and the congressional committees that authorized the planning and construction of water-resources projects. The Corps considered themselves to be "engineering consultants to and contractors for the Congress of the United States," and as such they resisted and ignored directives from the Executive Office of the President and from the President himself. This pathological form of bureau-committee relations was terminated in the 1950s when the Corps and the committees changed their approaches to executive-legislative relations. The Corps began to clear its policies and projects with the President's office before sending them to Congress and to participate actively in interagency committees for the purpose of developing uniform policies for the executive branch. The congressional committees altered their conduct to accommodate the new form of executive-legislative communications.[11]

An Answer to Maass

First, the triangles seem to be very durable although they may have to change their organization and tactics. Early on the dairy interests were able to outlaw yellow colored margarine. ("God made butter yellow!") That tactic was overridden. So were the penalty taxes imposed on margarine. But arbitrarily high supports for dairy products and the swollen governmental stocks thereof remain. The Corps of Engineers may seem to have come or to have been brought into line. But familiar signs of the survival of triangles in water politics recur. The enormous Tennessee-Tom Bigbee Project was completed in all its expensive redundancy. And it is only one of many examples.[12]

Second, the efficacy of a triangle need not require that the president and the Congress as a whole be entirely frustrated in controlling it. There are degrees of intransigence that the triangles may exploit even when the president and the Congress both have theoretical powers of control over them. It is often difficult and costly to intervene. If a triangle can turn opposition into obstruction, it may cause delays in the developing of policy that may be damaging to the country's interests. The present chapter argues that the *delay* in serious negotiations on arms control may have been damaging in itself. It did not have to be permanent nor did it have to be unequivocal in the sense that it could not possibly have been overridden.

Third, and more fundamentally, Maass's finding that the triangles are pathological may be countered by showing (as much as these things can be shown) that the triangles emerge as logical consequences of the separation of powers. They are normal products of our received system of government.

What is normal for Maass? It is the "discussion model" (Chapter 1 of *Congress and the Common Good*). This model explains executive-congressional relations, relations between congressional committees and the whole house, voting in the Congress, the relations of the Congress to its constituencies, and the resolution of congressional concerns over narrow versus broader interests. All these are explained as controlled and propelled by public opinion expressed by citizens in their communities and then interpreted by the governmental process. "A constitutional democracy is based on the capacity of its citizens to debate and determine the standards by which they wish to live in the political community." A community is "basically one of voluntary association."[13] Its function "is to foster a process of discussion that results in an agreement on standards."

The citizens do not ask only what is good for them but also what is good for the community, both the local and the national community. But individual citizens cannot determine what would be good policy on complex issues. They can elect representatives, the president and the Congress, who can use special techniques to analyze more information than their constituents can. These representatives comprise the state. The state (McIlwain calls it Gubernaculum) takes note of the agreements that the communities have reached by discussion. Using more sophisticated techniques, the state translates them into law. As I understand him, Maass says or implies that in addition to the small communities there is a national community and that the standards arrived at in it must be superior. But the standards still come from the people. The president who alone is chosen by a national electorate is uniquely able to comprehend and interpret the national will. The president leads—but the Congress controls. For the Congress is also chosen by the people expressly to carry out collectively their separate visions of the public interest. "There is probably no better index of the degree to which the executive proposals are actively or passively acceptable to the community than the voice of the legislature."[14]

Professor Maass provides more than a counsel of perfection. He offers a model of which the natural outcome approaches perfection. In his theory the pristine will of the people is refined and interpreted faithfully and well. Excellent results are inevitable, or almost so. Maass stresses the orientation of the individual voter, not just toward maximizing his own narrow economic interest, but toward achieving the public interest, the nation's economic well-being, as he sees it. And the voters and others form into "issue networks," that, quoting Hugh Heclo: "involve self-conscious efforts to develop good public policy rather than simply adjustments of narrower interests."[15]

On the contrary, I think that the natural consequences of our political institutions is to emphasize elections as the voter's opportunity to look out for himself. The protracted campaigns, the multiplication of elections, the separation of elections for executives from those for legislators at all levels, the spread of primaries with the assumption that the voters choose not only who shall win and hold office but who shall run for office—all these prompt the candidates to appeal to the voter's self interest. Moreover, the voter's vision of the public good is readily seen through the prism of his own interest. Narcissism acquires an altruistic aura. What's good for General Motors is good for the country. Agricultural fundamentalism assures the farmers that their prosperity is essential to society's well-being. Meanwhile, legislators "take care of the home folks first." When government rapidly expands, laws multiply, and agencies proliferate, the services to interest flourish. Agencies seek to consolidate their legislative bases. Affected interests are encouraged to organize. Triangles emerge naturally; they thrive in quasi-independence.

Maass writes:

> The unique contribution of the popularly elected legislature—institutionalization of the lay mind, and of the open mind, and representation of a different constituency than the

President's—all apply to the Congress as a whole, not necessarily to specialized and sometimes unrepresentative committees of Congress.[16]

Example.   In 1968 President Lyndon B. Johnson proposed the development of an antiballistic missile (ABM) system which both houses of Congress then approved by large majorities, although a number of members were strongly opposed. The next year President Richard M. Nixon proposed further development and deployment of the ABM, and this time opponents used the institutions and procedures of Congress to focus national attention on the issue. As a result, the pros and cons of the ABM became a great national debate, and two close roll-call votes in which the Senate opponents were defeated (52–49 and 50–50) assumed the character of an exciting national drama.

On February 4, 1969, a bipartisan group of senators, including Mike Mansfield (D. MT and majority leader), J. William Fulbright (D. AR and chairman of the Foreign Relations Committee), John Sherman Cooper (R. KY), Edward M. Kennedy (D. MA), Jacob K. Javits (R. NY), Edward W. Brooke (R. MA), and George S. McGovern (D. SD) made concerted speeches on the floor opposing the ABM, which attracted great attention in the mass media. These opponents then helped to organize an impressive group of anti-ABM scientists whose testimony before the Foreign Relations and Armed Services Committees was widely reported and used for additional floor speeches. Finally, they debated the issue on the floor for approximately one month before the hairbreadth votes of August 8. The congressional opponents were unable to convince a majority of their colleagues, but they were able to use Congress's means for controlling the legislative process to elevate a fairly technical question to an issue of broad national concern. Subsequently the ABM was scaled down, in part due to the thorough debate on the subject in 1969.

The ABM debate is an impressive example of what the American governmental process can produce as was the debate on the Civil Rights Act of 1964. Unfortunately, so was the act of 1924 halting Japanese immigration to the United States that E. S. Corwin called a "particularly wild romp of the Congressional bull in the diplomatic porcelain shop," and so was the notorious Smoot-Hawley Tariff of 1930. On the Executive side so were the unprecedented overcommitments of the United States in the 1950s when John Foster Dulles

went "around the world promising every nation that would accept
. . . an American military guarantee . . ." as well as the legacy of a
succession of presidents plunging America into the Vietnam
quagmire. We have also witnessed the dangerous ballooning of the
entitlement programs, the combination of an excessive tax cut in
1981 with soaring defense expenditures, and the exploding deficit.
In one glittering example of presidential whim, Ronald Reagan, in
his rousing ride from one electoral landslide to another, proposed the
SDI — and threatened single-handedly to dash the memory of the
ABM debate. And all these, too, are typical of what the American
system regularly produces. Both kinds of outcomes are "normal."

Walter Dean Burnham proffered an alternative theory to that
advanced by Maass. Noting the differing relationships of president
and Congress to their constituencies, Burnham finds the congressional elections particularly "in this era of permanent campaigns"
exhibiting the candidates' "doing everything they can to develop
broad-based but completely localistic appeals." Voters agree with
criticisms of big government except those chunks of it that benefit
them — they are "ideologically conservative" but "operationally liberal." (This is akin to what Hugh Heclo calls the "compensatory
mentality.")

Burnham suggests that voters tend to choose the more conservative presidential candidates and the more liberal congressional aspirants who specialize in appealing to their particular constituents
and, in doing so, who sharpen the interests of their constituents. "In
terms of government, what this means — as it has always meant in
parallel cases in United States history — is that the separation of
powers laid down in the Constitution receives a huge reinforcement
by behavior at the polls."[17] But which comes first, the chicken or the
egg? Burnham could also say that this behavior at the polls is rooted
in the separation of powers.

The Pervasive Influence of the Triangle

The triangle. The iron triangle. Drop the "iron," a bit of facile
alliteration that conveys too much brittleness and rigidity. The real
triangles are often flexible and protean as well as ubiquitous. Nor are
they so unfailingly obvious as iron implies. But they are there. "As in

geometry and engineering, so in politics the triangle seems to be the most stable type of structure," Theodore Lowi wrote in 1969. Stable? Durable and inevitable would be more descriptive. In 1978 Hugh Heclo noted the received opinion on how political administration works in Washington: "Control is said to be vested in informal but enduring series of 'iron triangles' linking executive bureaus, congressional committees, and interest group clienteles with a stake in particular programs." And then: the "iron triangle concept is not so much wrong as it is disastrously incomplete."[18]

Granted, the triangle does not account for everything. For example, Congress has declared war five times, although it debated the merits of doing so only once, in 1812.[19] But it is beside the point to say that the triangle is "disastrously incomplete," because it does not account for everything or even almost everything. If it illuminates some important policy situations, such as the persistence of high price supports in agricultural policy, the triangle is a factor to be reckoned with. If the triangle helps to explain the grievous expansion of the arms race in the 1960s it is as absurd to label it disastrously incomplete as it is to argue that it is pathological.

It is tempting to go farther. The triangle is the manifest destroyer of gubernaculum that worried McIlwain. The rupture of congressional government (and executive government, too) exhibited in the triangles nourishes the dangerous creed of plebiscitary democracy. Despairing of the Congress we are repeatedly drawn to the president as a savior. He becomes the providential magic helper. And, on the other side of the coin is the reification of public opinion—the unremitting effort to invoke the public, the people, as the arbiter of all grave political questions. Both of the unfortunate tendencies, the extravagant elevation of the savior president and the desperate appeal to the public—what Walter Lippmann called the "phantom public"—both are efforts, sometimes frantic ones, to reconstitute gubernaculum, to create a government that can govern.

The roots of the problem go deeper than the triangles. The separation of powers imbedded in our constitutional structure inexorably brings the triangles into being. The obvious agents to govern the triangles and bring them in to line are the political parties: a governing party representing the ruling majority. Equally vital if the government is to be both democratic and constitutional, a strong, organized opposition party is needed. Strong parties would profoundly change the situation in which debate takes place. The protagonists would no longer have the independence created by the triangles. They would have their power bases but these would be integral parts of the governing party or of the opposition. If protagonists chose to be intransigent they would risk splitting their party. Except in exceedingly rare circumstances they would debate and win or, on losing, they would more or less gracefully concede. Under the separation of powers, by contrast, the triangles it nourishes have often been intransigent, leading to the fragmentation of government or to stalemate.

The American separation of powers works against the development of strong political parties and the party government they would provide. The famous separation requires fixed calendar elections which engender interminable campaigns that, among numerous other ill-effects, eventually deny the parties the control over their own nominations, control that is necessary to party discipline and to party government.

I do not want to gloss over this point. The issues raised by the triangles should add to the accumulation of evidence that will at last bring us to a searching examination of our constitutional system.

The Triangle in Arms Control

The triangle that I discern in Talbott's *Deadly Gambits* has some peculiarities. Here Hugh Heclo's analysis is helpful. After lamenting the incompleteness of the iron triangles, Heclo suggests a supplementary concept, the "issue network."[20] Although I shall retain the term "triangle," Heclo's concept usefully suggests expansibility and contractability. He lays stress not on "the technocrats or people in the white coats" but on those who "care deeply about a set of issues." These are the policy activists who are more likely to expropriate the policy process. This applies to what I shall set forth. So does a degree of uncertainty about the players and their organizations: "it is almost impossible to tell where a network leaves off and its environment begins." But in my paper there is no question that Richard Perle is usually in charge, a contrast to Heclo: "no one, as far as one can tell is in control of the policies and issues."

In my account the argument will often be by inference and

interpretation. For example, there is nothing here about the third leg
of the triangle, the constituencies of supporting groups. No one is as
obliging as President Edward A. O'Neal of the American Farm Bureau Federation who shortly after Pearl Harbor loudly told an acquaintance in a crowded Washington Hotel lobby: "We've got the
Secretary of Agriculture by the short hairs of his chest, and we can
move him this way or we can move him that way!"

How does one know that the third leg of the triangle, the constituency component, is present? One infers it. If legislators appear
to be teamed up with administrators, one may assume that constituency support is present. Members of Congress live with uncertainty.
"Of all the many sources of uncertainty, the most constant—and
usually the greatest—involves the challenger." Members of Congress
assiduously nurse their districts. To do so is an essential part of being
a "representative." They do so to the extent of running and hiding
"when a defense of Congress is called for . . . members of Congress
run *for* Congress by running *against* Congress." They are so successful
that 90 percent of those who seek reelection win. Richard Fenno's in-
depth study of the "Home style" of members of Congress obviates
the necessity of showing the third leg of the triangle: if it is not
there, congressional support will not be, either.[21]

Reasons for congressional support of the "no-negotiations position" are apparent in the political economics of being hard-nosed as
well as in the kudos to be reaped by macho appeals. In 1985 what
major upthrust the monthly leading economic indicator index
showed was repeatedly due to increased factory orders, most of which
were from defense industries. A hard line toward Russia resonated
well among a member's supporters in these industries. Recall that
Richard Perle ascended into power with the benediction of Henry
Jackson, D. Washington, also known as "the Senator from Boeing."
Jackson's constituency became Perle's constituency, and so did those
of other like-minded legislatures. When Perle became assistant secretary of defense, his legislative constituency remained intact.

The argument of this paper is then that the triangles, nourished
by the separation of powers, tend to rupture the government (the
state, the gubernaculum). The leader or leaders in the given triangle
openly or tacitly assume that their piece of the action is the government. *L'etat c'est moi*! That is the motto: whether it be for tobacco,
or sugar, or diary products—or whether it be for nuclear armaments

(the size and character and deployment of our nuclear weaponry and the deals we make thereon with allies or potential enemies: these are the true and proper bailiwick of the triangles). Trespassers, beware!

If this is true, the story of nuclear arms control policy in the first Reagan Administration is much more than a struggle between Perle and Burt, as Talbott suggests.[22] Just as issues of foreign policy may involve much more than feuds between Secretaries Schulz and Weinberger as Philip Taubman implies.[23] Important as the personal clashes are, they take place within the controlling framework of the structural problem that I have called the triangle.

Talbott revealed the phenomenon when he discussed Fred Iklé, under-secretary of defense and John Lehman, secretary of the navy in the Reagan Administration. "Iklé and Lehman were members of what was sometimes called 'the Perle mafia,' the wide circle of Perle's former associates, proteges, and mentors scattered throughout the new Administration and, of course, still in place on Capitol Hill."[24] This is a clear acknowledgment of two legs of the triangle. Unfortunately, the term "mafia," is misleading. There is nothing sinister nor even underhanded about it. This is simply the way our system works. It is sanctioned and even celebrated as a manifestation of pluralism.

At this point I wish to emphasize two things that strongly suggest the presence of an arms control triangle. One of these is the extraordinary leverage that is repeatedly and successfully exercised; the other is the continuity of the triangle from 1972 through 1983 (and, apparently, to 1985).

A striking example of the influence of the triangle occurred in 1972 when Fred Iklé was brought into the Nixon Administration. In 1972 Senator Jackson had demanded that President Nixon purge the SALT delegation (United States participants in the Strategic Arms Limitation Talks) and the Arms Control and Disarmament Agency. "Perle played an important part in picking Iklé, then at the Rand Corporation, as the new director of the ACDA."[25] When a twenty-seven-year-old member of the staff of an opposition senator has a decisive voice in selecting a key executive branch administrator, something more than personal influence must be at work.

Again in 1972 Senator Jackson drafted an amendment to the SALT 1 Interim Agreement that was designed to make the reduction of Russian throw weight the chief target of United States negotiators. The amendment was "largely drafted by Perle himself." In the 1980s

Perle frequently carried a draft of the amendment, together with excerpts from the floor debate; it became known as "Perle's bible."[26]

Continuity was maintained when Perle became a "*bête noire* of Henry Kissinger's" in 1974. In 1976, Perle prevented Kissinger "from tying up the loose ends of SALT and getting an agreement." On that occasion Perle had an assist from Ronald Reagan, then bidding for the Republican presidential nomination, as well as from Fred Iklé and John Lehman, then in the Arms Control and Disarmament Agency. Again, in March of 1977 Senator Jackson and Richard Perle were the effective advisers who shaped Carter's Comprehensive Proposal that anticipated the Reagan zero option and that was "rudely and categorically rejected by the Soviets."[27]

Signs of the triangle also appear in Perle's repeated successes in gaining privileged access and in his apparent extraordinary leverage. A prime example occurred in 1982 in the heated internal debate over chief negotiator Paul Nitze's initiative in the "walk in the woods," designed to facilitate a resolution of the impasse in the INF talks with the USSR. Assistant Secretary Perle was promptly and covertly brought into the arcanum even though he was at a conference in Aspen, Colorado. Secrecy was so tight that the highest ranking participants (Cabinet Secretaries) were supposed to have only one aide apiece. Perle, in effect, had two. Back in Washington, working with Secretary Weinberger, Perle was able first to divert and then actually to replace the memorandum on the subject prepared by the Joint Chiefs of Staff at the request of the president. Perle moved into the penultimate counsels, shoving his nominal superior, undersecretary Iklé, aside. He dealt curtly with Paul Nitze; and his abrasiveness with the Joint Chiefs apparently contributed to their reticence when the president was present—using Perle's brief, Weinberger dominated the final session and secured the president's favorable decision. (Let me anticipate a riposte that Perle was merely Weinberger's subordinate and spokesman. Often he must have been exactly that. But if the triangle was in fact there it would be equally true that at critical times Weinberger becomes Perle's spokesman. Charles G. Dawes' celebrated remark is in point; "The members of the Cabinet are the President's natural enemies.")[28]

Then, too, there is the arrogance. Not that the characteristic is rare among governmental officials as Mark Twain noted, but Perle's is world-class. An example was his contemptuous dismissal of the venerable Paul Nitze. "Nitze doesn't deserve a damn thing." Repeatedly he has been publicly abrasive toward senior military officers, including members of the Joint Chiefs. In February 1985, British Foreign Secretary Sir Geoffrey Howe publicly criticized the SDI and even implied that it might be compared to the Maginot Line. Richard Perle, who happened to be in London, vehemently answered him; "it may have been the first time that a sub-Cabinet-level official of one government attacked a minister of another, and on the minister's turf."[29]

There is much more, including an effort at a direct use of power to intimidate. Undersecretary Lawrence Eagleburger headed a European mission in March 1981, to clarify the new administration's posture to its allies. His intention was to indicate that the arms control process would continue. But Eagleburger found that Perle's representatives were ubiquitous. He was accompanied to Brussels by one of them, Michael Pilsbury, who fought against language in the communique, indicating that on arms control, efforts would continue. Indeed, Pilsbury threatened that senatorial confirmation of Eagleburger's undersecretarial post would be denied him! (If Eagleburger did not delete the paragraph, Pilsbury said, "Your ass is grass.") Eagleburger persisted. Pilsbury was replaced. But Pilsbury joined the staff of the Steering Committee, a collection of right-wing senators.[30] The triangle provided him with a "safety net."

Conclusion

As late as July 1985, arms control talks with the Soviet Union continued what Talbott called "the most serious and protracted break-down to date." In so far as the United States was responsible for the break-down, part of the cause may be in the peculiarities of the president himself. In discussing American preparations for the INF and the START negotiations, Talbott wrote:

> In both dramas, the president would step to center stage to deliver his lines in set speeches. But behind the scenes, where decisions were made and policy was set, he was to remain a detached, sometimes befuddled character. Even though he chaired sixteen National Security Council-level meetings on START, there was ample evidence, during those meetings and

on other occasions as well, that he frequently did not understand basic aspects of the nuclear weapons issue and of policies
being promulgated in his name.[31]

Of Henry Kissinger's experience in consulting with President
Reagan, Talbott wrote:

> And yet, on a number of these occasions, Kissinger notices
> something unsettling about the President: Reagan seemed
> strangely uninterested in international relations as such. He dis-
> played little knowledge or even curiosity about the interaction
> of states and forces in the world arena. Even more disturbing, he
> seemed remarkably *blasé* about U.S. foreign policy. It was as
> though long-term strategy was something other people were
> paid to worry about. Kissinger found that, when he advised
> Reagan on what the government ought to be doing, the goals it
> should set and the methods it should employ, Reagan seemed to
> tune out. The best way to get Reagan's attention was to suggest
> to him what he personally should say publicly about a foreign
> problem or a policy. Then the President would sit up, and his
> eyes would come back into focus. What he cared about was
> speeches — particularly his own speeches. He knew that his
> smooth delivery and easygoing, winning manner were huge as-
> sets. He would work at fine-tuning a speech with an enthusiasm
> that he rarely devoted to other duties.
>
> It was this aspect of Reagan's approach to the presidency
> that led him to see the announcement of the proposal as an end
> in itself. If the speech worked as a speech, then the policy must
> be a good one. If the speech came off, the policy could be
> sustained.[32]

Presidential idiosyncrasy as an explanation of the American contribution to the breakdown is supplemented by the intransigence of
the triangle led by Richard Perle. To reiterate, it is most important to
recognize that much more than interpersonal clashes, specifically,
Perle versus Burt, is involved. It is not just Perle himself nor his
official position as assistant secretary of defense that gives him power.
It is his leadership of the triangle. In a manner of speaking, the
triangle is his oyster. In the conception of the members involved, the
triangle is the government. *L'etat c'est moi.* This is a telling example
of the fragmentation of gubernaculum that McIlwain warned about.
The separation of powers may, indeed, contain the seeds of destruction of that constitution it is supposed to ensure.

10
Separation of Powers
as Destructive of Government

PROFESSOR James Q. Wilson in "Does the Separation of Powers Still Work?" ignores the argument that the separation of powers is destructive of government itself.[1] Rather, he denies the claim that our constitution too often produces deadlock and stalemate. This is a very important issue. Those who raise it propose steps to reduce the recurrence of deadlock-generating split governments by increasing the likelihood that the same political party will control both the presidency and Congress. Wilson's bristling counterattack is formidable but not invulnerable. I shall let others answer his strictures against the stalemate argument in order to address an even graver issue, the undermining of constitutional government itself.

Asserting that the critics provide little analysis of the case for constitutional reform, Wilson writes that Lloyd N. Cutler's essay, "To Form a Government," "is almost the only systematic effort to explain why we need to modify the separation of powers."[2]

On the contrary, the late Charles H. McIlwain attacked the separation of powers in his Pulitzer Prize book, *The American Revolution* (1923); and he maintained, elaborated, and strengthened his argument in *Constitutionalism: Ancient and Modern.* The works of a number of other writers also contradict Wilson's statement, but McIlwain is authoritative, succinct, and explicit.[3]

The Destruction of Government

The separation of powers fragments government. Leaders of the fragments continually try to take over a piece of the government, each proclaiming *L'état c'est moi*. Now the imminent danger is that one of the fragments, the military—at once the largest and most menacing—will succeed and because of its nature will take over the whole government. Elsewhere I have pointed to the destruction of government by the separation of powers: the inflation of the executive, the denigration of the Congress, the reification of public opinion, the nourishment of an unhealthy resonance between the president and the public (the plebiscitary presidency), and the fragmentation of government.[4] All of these are involved in what follows, especially the inflation of the executive, the denigration of Congress, and the fragmentation of governments.

In his polemic James Q. Wilson reduced the critics of the separation of power to the ultimate solipsism: "Separation of powers are a fine idea, it would seem, except when they prevent me from having my way." But is not this the genius of the separation of powers: to declare an open season on government for groups to pursue their own ends?

So say a number of leading political scientists. Every interest has its group, every group its interest. Numerous factions seek and get their own laws, their own programs, their own agencies. Standards become more and more malleable until they disappear altogether, according to Theodore Lowi. In the evolution of "interest group liberalism, the requirement of standards is replaced by the requirement of participation" and "the requirement of law . . . by the requirement of contingency." The Constitution itself disintegrates. "What's a Constitution among friends?"[5] In a similar and reinforcing interpretation, Grant McConnell discerned the dissolution of government into private power. As government dissolves, formality is lost and, with it, the means of setting limits on private action, of distinguishing between what is public and what is private. Formality is "close to the heart of constitutionalism." Government is the means of limiting conflicts between and among interest groups. "To give this service, however, government must be formal and distinct. It can not be either if it is broken into units corresponding to the units which have developed power."[6]

In an interpretation quite harmonious with these views, Richard E. Neustadt cited the problem inherent in the explosion of bureaucracy: in the 1940s "an extraordinary element was added to the government of the United States, an executive establishment . . . unlike anything our government had known before . . . [F]or a quarter of a century our system has been struggling to assimilate it."[7]

In Neustadt's interpretation the Constitution institutionalizes a ceaseless struggle for power between the president and Congress. The president's genius is to control by centralizing, coordinating, synthesizing, integrating; by contrast Congress controls by dividing and distributing to committees and subcommittees. In the struggle, the bureaucracy often escapes control by either entity and emerges in power clusters or whirlpools or sub-governments or iron triangles of quasi-independence. Examples multiply; but, again, the looming threat is that of the military.

The military was a prime concern of James Madison.

James Madison's Forebodings Are Suddenly Relevant

No one was more dismayed about the danger of the military than James Madison, the fourth president of the United States, and perhaps the first among equals of the Framers of our Constitution. On June 29, 1787, in the Philadelphia convention Madison dwelt on the threats to individual states if they failed to unite in a strong union, threats that would grow out of the armed forces both of neighboring states (that sometimes would have larger populations and more resources) and also in their own states, created for their self-defense.

> In time of actual war, great discretionary powers are constantly given to the Executive Magistrate. Constant apprehension of War, has the same tendency to render the head too large for the body. A standing military force, with an overgrown Executive will not long be safe companions to liberty. The means of defense agst. foreign danger have been always the instruments of tyranny at home. Among the Romans it was a standing maxim to incite a war, whenever a revolt was apprehended. Throughout all Europe, the armies kept up under the pretext of defending, have enslaved the people.[8]

Again, on August 23, 1787, in a discussion of the proposed constitutional language concerning the militia, Madison declared: "As the greatest danger is that of the disunion of the States, it is necessary to guard against it by sufficient powers to the Common Government. And as the great danger to liberty is from large standing armies, it is best to prevent them by an effectual provision for a good militia."[9] Madison had also urged providing in the Constitution for the proper training of the militia; left to themselves, the states would ignore this as they had ignored the confederation's requests for money.

And on Friday, September 14, 1787 (nearing the end of the convention), Colonel George Mason, noting that he was sensible that an absolute prohibition of standing armies in time of peace might be unsafe, wished at the same time to provide language that would point out and guard against their danger. He proposed that Article 1, Section 8, "To provide for organizing, arming, and disciplining the militia, etc." be prefaced by the words: "And that the liberties of the people be better secured against standing armies in time of peace . . ." Governor Randolph seconded Mason's motion, James Madison supported it, declaring that it "did not restrain Congress from establishing military force if . . . necessary, and as armies in time of peace are allowed on all hands to be an evil, it is well to discountenance them by the Constitution, as far as will consist with the essential power of the Government on that head."[10]

Emergence of the "Military-Industrial Complex"

My argument is that the separation of powers leads to fragmentation; and one of the fragments now threatens to recreate the whole in a martial image. To stress the contrast with James Q. Wilson's interpretation, his only comment on the role of the military in *The Public Interest* article is to urge Congress to relax its supervision of the CIA and to eliminate the legislative veto on arms sales. Few question that a large military establishment is necessary in the contemporary world. But what we have is a huge military, enormously extended to undertake the reckless global commitments that recent presidents have made. It is ironical that our latest great military figure to become president (and all the more so because his own secretary of state was the proximate author of much of the worldwide commitment debauch) laid out the problem in 1961 in his Farewell Address:

"Until the latest of our world conflicts," Dwight D. Eisenhower declared, "the United States had no armaments industry. [But now] "we have been compelled to create a permanent armaments industry of vast proportions. Added to this 3.5 million men and women are directly engaged in the defense establishment.

"In the councils of government we must guard against the acquisition of unwarranted influence, whether sought or unsought, by the military-industrial complex. The potential for the disastrous rise of misplaced power exists and will persist."

To be sure, the United States had hitherto enjoyed a seemingly providential exemption from overweening military influence, let alone the serious threat of a military dictatorship. The nation had a number of presidents with distinguished military careers, beginning with George Washington, himself, and including Andrew Jackson, William Henry Harrison, Zachary Taylor, Ulysses S. Grant, Theodore Roosevelt, and Dwight D. Eisenhower. In addition, military officers were often unsuccessful candidates, John C. Fremont and George B. McClellan, as well as strong aspirants who failed to secure nominations, Winfield Scott, Leonard Wood, Douglas MacArthur, and (probably) Alexander Haig. But, however often the electorate seemed enamored of military heroes, Alfred Vagts, found the United States blessed with a military staunchly devoted to serving as the instrument of the civilian government.[11] Even so, in the country's greatest military convulsion, the Civil War, both General McClellan and General Joe Hooker showed some susceptibility to the temptation to usurp the Union government (for the good of the country, of course). But they did not attempt it.[12] And our historical tendency after wars have ended has been to demobilize and disarm as rapidly as possible—until 1945.

In recent years, as President Eisenhower noted, the military has loomed large in the economy. In late 1986 it accounted for 10 percent of the nation's employment and 30 percent of the nation's budget.[13] The share to the military of federal funds for research has increased from 50 percent in 1977 to 70 percent in 1988 (proposed).[14] In some areas, like United States shipbuilding, the military demand approached monopolization of the industry; commercial

ships of one thousand tons or larger under construction in United
States private shipyards numbered seventy-five in 1979 but dwindled
steadily to less than five in 1987; whereas naval vessels, seventy-five
in 1979, expanding to over one hundred in the Reagan buildup, and
were still seventy-five in 1987.[15] In appraising the health of the
economy, analysts frequently stress military's demands. As one of
many examples, new factory orders in April 1987 were reported by
the United States Department of Commerce to increase by 0.2 percent. "The small rise . . . reflected a sharp 8.1 percent gain in defense orders."[16]

As Anthony Lewis pointed out in November 1985, the lure of
Pentagon spending, especially in the unfolding promise of Strategic
Defense Initiative (SDI) procurement, was enormously attractive to
industry. The *Washington Post*, writing about the upcoming Geneva
Summit, found arms contractors worried lest arms-control cost them
lucrative contracts. The *New York Times* identified SDI contracts
awarded to TRW, $424 million, to Boeing, $217 million, to Lock-
heed, $192 million, etc. The *Times* went on: "The most lucrative
. . . contracts have gone to many of the same companies . . . that
also build Minuteman missiles, the MX missile and military satel-
lites." Lewis also quoted a Boston defense analyst to the effect that
aerospace companies had to look to Star Wars because the traditional
defense budget was not going to grow much—"if they want to be a
long time player, they can't let SDI get away."[17]

So the armament industry has become a huge, dynamic, evolv-
ing, changing economic interest that, like all such, requires unremitting, flexible, and imaginative support from those involved (the
companies, the unions, and the defense communities) in order to
maintain and increase the flow of political funds. The military-industrial complex emerges as an exceedingly powerful player in the interest group jungle that Lowi, McConnell, and Neustadt have pic-
tured, pursuing the familiar tactics of creating quasi-independent
triangles of power, but on a grander scale.

The momentum and growth of military expansion is influenced
by other developments. First of these is the conception that the
ultimate enemy not only of the United States but of constitutional
democracy itself (or, more grandly, the "free world," an undis-
criminating collectivity) is totalitarian communism. As the conception sharpened, the wonted demobilization ended after World War

II. President Truman laid down his doctrine, initially to protect Greece and Turkey from the communist threat, and later extended it to Europe. The doctrine was reaffirmed and extended by succeeding presidents to include virtually the entire noncommunist world. It was also made clear that the guarantee was not only against foreign threats but also against internal communist subversion. The doctrine not only required the development of formidable American military capacity but the export of military missions to those nations, old and emergent, that would ask for or, at least, accept them.[18]

To show the extent of American military overseas commitments in terms of bases: in 1973 there were 323 sizable installations outside continental United States. In 1983 there were 359, "not including foreign military bases to which American forces have access but not control." Although informed persons differed on the total cost of keeping troops, ships, and planes abroad, there was general agreement that "forward deployment is the single largest cost in the military budget." One estimate was that the United States commitment in Europe, Asia, and the Persian Gulf region would cost $212 billion in fiscal year 1984.[19]

Second, the projection of American military might overseas meant the association of our military representatives with those of host countries wherein the conception of the role of the military has often been very different from ours. Consider Central America where American military assistance to its allies or clients increased from $14.2 million in 1981 to $212 million in 1986. In the countries concerned, especially El Salvador, Guatemala, Honduras, and Panama, civilian government leaders were "concerned about prospects for weak governments that must deal with [their] vastly strengthened armies." These worries, the leaders said, were "justified . . . in a region where the army has often left the barracks to occupy the presidential palace and where army officers are essentially a separate elite, better organized and more unified than most civilian administrations."[20]

American military personnel are extensively and intensively exposed to situations wherein their military counterparts in host countries are not only the makers and unmakers of governments but also the champions of those forces opposed to the designated enemy, communism. The concept of a "higher law" may begin to crystalize, and it may encourage a shift in the traditional American concepts of the proper role of the military vis-à-vis the state.

Third is the development and rapid expansion of covert action. This has meant the installation as a central part of our government of an agency devoted to the subversion of government by any means, always, of course, in the service of the higher good by working against the consummate communist evil (as identified in secret, naturally, by the subverting agency itself). In World War II the Office of Strategic Services was created not only to gather intelligence but to deploy armed forces behind the enemy lines. After the war the Central Intelligence Agency (CIA) was soon created (1947); and in 1951 the CIA was formally authorized and given the resources not only to gather intelligence but also to engage in covert action.[21]

The combination of espionage activities and covert military actions was consummated during the presidency of Harry S. Truman, who later regretted the act and called for its reversal. "I never thought . . . when I set up the CIA that it would be injected into peacetime cloak-and-dagger operations." The CIA should be "restored to its original assignment as the intelligence arm of the President."[22]

The threat to democratic constitutionalism embodied in this combination is formidable. Spying is an ancient calling. Its professionalism, however necessary for reasons of state, calls for the indoctrination of its participants with the peculiar mores of such work: lying, cheating, dissembling, stealing, entrapping, betraying; all these plus the use of ruthless violence that are normally proscribed are taught and learned as the proper virtues of the spy. Learned so well that when the spy comes in from the cold, he will normally bring his perverted code with him. This situation creates problems for constitutional government as illustrated by Peter Wright's allegations of a British secret service plot in 1974–76 to undermine Prime Minister Harold Wilson. Of this, more later. Here, my concern is to point up the increased danger if the hazards of the spy's code are multiplied by the association with an agency prepared, equipped, and authorized to subvert other governments by covert action. The danger lies in the galvanizing, purpose-instilling ideas of a paramilitary organization institutionalized at the vital center of one's own government. Will not the skills of subversion be hypothetically, at least, applied at home? Note that this is not a conspiracy theory;

what would ordinarily be conspiracy has become, in effect, normal operating procedure.

But the web was even more entangled. To focus on the CIA may be too narrow. Indeed, the role of the executive, the president, must be considered. When in the mid-1970s Congress sought to subject the CIA to more control, part of its intention may have been to remove the cover of "deniability" from the president for any covert actions that might fail or prove embarrassing. Nevertheless, the CIA's role may have become stereotyped as overly independent. Richard Helms, a former CIA Director, remarked: "Perhaps the most unfortunate phrase [to come] from the Church Committee was 'rogue elephant.' If you look back at . . . all the charges and wrongdoings, with only a few exceptions, they were ordered by the political level of the U.S. Government, and the CIA was carrying out instructions."[23]

Fourth is the privatization of covert action. After Congress applied vigorous controls and reporting requirements on the CIA in the 1970s, the Iranian arms sales–Contra aid development in the mid-1980s shifted the base of covert action to the National Security Council staff (NSC). Also dating from the Truman years, the NSC, a presidential agency, was free from congressional oversight. But it was handicapped by its small size, 186 staff members, including 59 professionals (twice as many of whom were, under President Reagan, military officers), compared to the thousands of employees of the CIA. Nothing daunted, the NSC developed its operative muscle in paramilitary organizations led by retired Major General (and formerly Deputy Assistant Secretary of Defense) Richard Secord. Authority was shifted from the CIA to the NSC and thence to General Secord. The CIA became a "banking and shipping agent." (Reportedly, the CIA had over one thousand bank accounts in Switzerland.) If the CIA could not be the overt covert action agency, the transfer of arms to Iran required CIA participation as well as the Department of Defense. But the president could make all these things possible through the leadership ensconced in the NSC staff. (The late director of the CIA claimed that the NSC "was operating this thing.")[24]

Before this thought propels the analysis into the aggrandizement of the presidency, one should emphasize that the "privatization of covert action" adds another and very disturbing dimension to the evolution of the military: the country has counted on the formal creeds of the armed services, nourished by the military academies, to implant the traditional conceptions of a military as a servant of the civilian state. With the privatization of covert action, this inculcation may be seriously diminished.

The Aggrandizement of the Presidency

This shift to the NSC brought forth an argument that the president has, under the Constitution, a carte blanche in foreign policy. If this is staggering, we might recall a propensity in wartime to inflate executive powers. The Reconstruction Finance Corporation (RFC), established under Herbert Hoover, retained and greatly enlarged under FDR and vastly expanded in World War II, furnishes an example. After the war, the doughty Jesse Jones, who, among other exalted positions, became president of the RFC (then authorized to lend up to $30 billion, double the then current federal budget) was anxious to kill off the agency. The RFC, Jones testified before Congress, could lend any amount of money, to any borrower, for any purpose, at any rate of interest, with or without collateral, for any length of time. Congress was flabbergasted. The only explanation that legislators could offer was that Congress liked and trusted Jesse Jones.

But the current White House claim that the president is endowed with supreme powers in foreign affairs is not based on anything so ephemeral as an act of Congress; it claims to rest on the Constitution, itself. And the power is not delegated to an agency that can be easily abolished. Rather, it inheres in and greatly enhances the majestic presidential office.

In 1987 the White House made the ultimate assertion about the power of the president when Chief of Staff Howard Baker opined: "There is a strong argument" that Congress cannot "limit the president's authority under the Constitution to administer the foreign policy of this country." By "administer" Baker apparently meant not only to conduct foreign policy but also to formulate it. This appears to be the interpretation of L. Gordon Crovitz, a *Wall Street Journal* editor, who concluded that if any crimes had been committed in the Iran-Contra affair, Congress has been the guilty party. "The better view is that any likely 'crimes' are *unconstitutional* laws passed by

Congress." Thus in 1983, during the debate on funding for the Contras in the Defense Appropriations and Intelligence Authorization Acts, Representative Tom Harkin (D., Iowa) "proposed a bar on anyone 'carrying out military activities in or against Nicaragua.' " The White House sent word "it would veto any such broad bill as an *unconstitutional usurpation of executive authority*." (Italics added.) Mr. Crovitz applauded the White House position, only regretting the "greatest failure of President Reagan in the Iran-Contra affair," namely, "ducking his duty to himself and future presidents to fight back when Congress first began usurping executive authority."[25]

In support of the claim to unlimited power for the president in foreign affairs, Chief of Staff (and former Senator) Howard Baker cited Justice Sutherland in *United States v. Curtiss Wright Export Corporation*.[26] "A political society cannot endure without a supreme will somewhere." In external, as compared to internal, affairs, "participation in the exercise of . . . power is significantly limited. In this vast external realm, with its important, complicated, delicate, and manifold problems, the President alone has the power to speak or listen as a representative of the nation." Sutherland then cited John Marshall (later, our most famous Chief Justice) in the House of Representatives in 1800: "The President is the sole organ of the nation in its external relations."

The issue in that case, however, was whether Congress could delegate the implementation of its foreign policy to the president. Congress had laid down the policy: to prohibit the sale of arms or the munitions of war to those countries (Bolivia and Paraguay) engaged in war over the possession of the Chaco, if such prohibition were based on a presidential finding (after presidential consultation with such governments as he deemed necessary). Congress also laid down penalties, fines and/or jail, for violators of any such prohibition.

In short, Congress was making foreign policy and delegating a crucial part of its implementation to the president. The Sutherland decision did not find Congress to be presumptuous. It did not explicitly say that the president could spell out any foreign policy he chose and implement it in any way he wished, and that Congress was barred from interfering with his decisions and actions. Even Sutherland's extravagant dicta did not go that far. Indeed, E. S. Corwin found the practical conclusion of Justice Sutherland to be that "the constitutional objection to the delegation of legislative power does not apply to a delegation by Congress to the President of its 'cognate' powers in the field, that, in short, the merged powers of the two departments may be put at the President's disposal whenever Congress so desires."[27]

Threats to Constitutional Government

The separation of powers threatens constitutional government. Such government has been the result of slow, sporadic, risk-filled growth. The concepts of limited government began to be enunciated by judicial officers. The concepts of representative government began to distill out of the corporate sense achieved by members of the various estates summoned to early meetings to hear the demands of monarchs for increased grants of money. If the judges have led in defining the rights that have become the essential constitutional limits on government, the meetings that became parliaments or legislatures eventually provided first the beachheads and later the forums and platforms for the consolidation of popular forces able to challenge and eventually to prevail in the power struggle with the monarchs—and so create constitutional governments.

In dividing the executive from the legislature, our Constitution inexorably pits the president against Congress in a way that has been characteristically accompanied by the denigration of the latter. That scorn and derision has been tempered by one of the hoariest bits of political science's lore: "The people may despise Congress, but they love their own Congressmen!" (In 1986, over 98 percent of incumbent Congressional candidates were reelected.) But the old adage, once humorously benign, may now conceal an ominous development. Earlier, liberals often disparaged Congress for obstructing the ameliorative programs of the equalizing state. Recently, conservatives have heaped contempt on Congress for dragging its feet against the worldwide crusade against communism.

This onslaught is accompanied by a conservative (but not only a conservative) claim for virtual presidential sovereignty in foreign affairs. Meanwhile, foreign affairs tends to envelop politics. (Who was it said "All politics is local"?) The economy, financial institutions and their operations, and, to a considerable extent, the movement of population become internationalized — along with the vast extension of military commitments already mentioned. What emerges is a President, smartly saluting as commander in chief, leading enormous and greatly extended military forces, supported by a mighty military-industrial complex — and opposed to and by what is caricatured as an inept, bumbling, confused Congress. In this light, the rising problems of the military-industrial complex become even more threatening.

Back to the Military

In a 1976 discussion of the CIA, Garry Wills touched on the military, rejecting the fear of some liberals that the military would someday "supply us with a dictator." "Our military is not aristocratic in tradition. The inability of the services to maintain even the minimal professional exclusiveness is witnessed by the fact that the academies have had to accept women." The fault of our military (he went on) "is not autocratic haughtiness but timorous evasion . . . This means, fortunately, that the military cannot defy Congress or the public the way the CIA does."[28]

But in 1987 Garry Wills discerned "The Military Coup in the White House." He thought now that certain military officers had engaged in a coup. Not an "overt junta's coup [in which] military forces take the government away from effete civilian authorities (what Patrick Buchanan likes to call 'the pygmies on the hill')" but a "silent coup — one that did not overthrow the government, but sealed off most of it from the 'real' action, sealed off not only Congress but whole parts of the executive branch, including the Secretary of State."

What prompted the action of these military officers, Wills suggests, may have been their shared patriotic humiliation and revulsion at having been "stabbed in the back" by a "contemptible government" that had refused to win in Vietnam and had finally withdrawn in defeat. "The Contra story (Wills concludes) is not one of yesterday's communism. It is part of an older story of empire (we ruled Nicaragua, directly or through surrogates for three decades of this century) — and the military coup quietly effected in the White House has many imperial forebears. The 'stab in the back' justifies any actions outside the law to punish the contemptible government that delivered it."[29]

Elizabeth Drew deplored the government-within-a-government that carried out the Iran arms sales/Contra support deal, but asserted that we do not have a coup mentality in the United States; that is, "a proclivity for deciding that established civilian authorities can't get things done and having coups d'etat that put the government in the hands of a group, usually the military, to cut through the tedious legitimate methods of governing."[30]

However, John Walcott and David Rogers of the *Wall Street Journal* gravely warned of the danger.[31] Lt. Colonel Oliver North, from the vantage point in the NSC, had developed the network of ships, planes, and operatives that he called "Democracy, Inc." to arm the Contras, in spite of the apparent will of Congress to the contrary. Now he wanted to use the same organization to support rebel leader Jonas Savimbi in Angola. Speaking of North's network, Senator Paul Sarbanes (D., Md.) said, "It was sort of a junta within the executive branch . . . It had this quasi private-public character which really allowed it to maximize its advantages . . . All of this was unaccountable. Secord denied he was trying to run a private CIA but that is in effect what they were doing." To quote further from Walcott and Rogers: "Testimony last week revealed that in a last effort to keep alive an opening to Iran, Col. North's associates said the U.S. would help to oust Iraqi President Sadam Hussein and go to war with the Soviet Union if it invaded Iran.

' "I thought it was appalling,' said Michael Armacost, undersecretary of state for political affairs. 'I thought that I had heard everything, . . . but it keeps getting worse. The idea that you could negotiate with another country through CIA annuitants, a retired general, and an Iranian businessman only a recently naturalized citizen is shocking.'

"The network's organizers respond that they could act more quickly and creatively than the CIA or the Pentagon. 'The system has to be unlocked, and I'm not holding my breath until we get a president who is strong enough to do that,' says General Secord.

"The memory of Vietnam, where virtually all the military officers in the network served, plays a part in shaping this outlook. The war was a bitter lesson in the strength of modern Soviet-backed forces, and it left those officers with an attitude of disdain for Congress and the press. Five years later, the disastrous attempt to rescue American hostages in Iran helped convince . . . Secord and . . . North that the Pentagon wasn't serious about unconventional operations.

" 'It was very easy for these people to talk themselves into the position where whatever they did was justified,' says one senior House Democrat.

"In separate conversations, a senior intelligence officer and a top congressional investigator each compared Col. North and his colleagues to 'the Algerian colonels,' the group of French military officers who in 1958 tried to overthrow the French government . . . 'These people were dangerous,' says the intelligence officer."

Conclusion

No doubt exists that the separation of powers still works: it works to demolish constitutional government. It wrenches the executive and the legislature apart and exalts the executive (Madison's "overgrown Executive") in proportion as foreign and military affairs expand to preempt much public concern; and it undermines the legislature by isolating it, insulating it, and heaping contempt upon it. It nourishes the growth of a gargantuan military-industrial complex, not least by endowing successive presidents with delusions of their grandeur as commanders in chief of the forces of the free world, each of whom seems to want to outdo his predecessor in enlarging America's overseas commitments and in showing "resolve" to fulfill them. In spite of this vast expansion by presidents of both parties, the conservatives, when not engaged merely in liberal bashing, have cried, "they lost China!" and "they surrendered in Vietnam!" And now, unless the United States makes good its domination of the Persian Gulf, they are preparing to cry, "they lost the Middle East!"[32]

Meanwhile, the separation of powers has recently proved hospitable to the emergence of juntas, militarily based, but sufficiently privatized (ah, the magic of the market!) to escape accountability, yet remaining "national" enough to inspire patriotism as the instrument of righteousness against the communists — and to vindicate the appeal to the country against those who "sold it out" in Vietnam.

Constitutional democracy in this country is gravely endangered. It has been shaken by one crisis after another. Douglas MacArthur, Joseph McCarthy, Vietnam, Watergate, Iran, and the Iran-Contra imbroglio. We hang on the edge of future crises, such as a repetition of the oil shocks of the 1970s or any one of several other imaginable economic catastrophes. We do so with an enormously inflated presidency (in terms of asserted power) and a Congress increasingly ineffectual, and (so far as its detractors can achieve), widely discredited. On the ineffectuality of Congress, consider the War Powers Act of 1973 in light of the subsequent war-making proclivities of successive presidents; consider the Chadha decision of 1983 that cut down the legislative veto that had been employed for nearly fifty years by Congress to attempt to counterbalance and restrain the modern presidency; consider the self-denying effort of the Gramm-Rudman-Hollings effort to achieve budgetary control with what Senator Moynihan called a "suicide pact"; and consider the growing pressure on the legislator's time by the demands of his office and the escalating (and quite possibly corrupting) need for campaign funds.

This is where the separation of powers has brought us. Would a fusion of powers between the executive and the legislature, plus a division of powers between government and opposition, restore a government, a gubernaculum, that would have a better chance of sustaining constitutionalism in these parlous times? Difficult as it is to conceive what an alternative would be like and then to make the transition to it, there are strong arguments for shifting our full intellectual powers to face the question.

At this point, opponents will say, "Ah! You are talking about a parliamentary alternative, and the British prototype has recently proved itself worse!" They refer to the allegations by Peter Wright, formerly a member of MI5, the British counterintelligence agency, that an MI5 group conspired to "undermine and overthrow the elected [Labour] government headed by Harold Wilson" in 1974–76. "This would seem an even worse scandal than ours since, if it took place, it involved an attack not just on the laws but on democracy itself." Contrasting the plethora of American inquiries into the Iran-Contra affair with the British determination to sweep Wright's allegations under the rug, Arthur Schlesinger, Jr., concluded that the separation of powers is vastly superior. "Through a written constitution, a bill of rights and the separation of powers accountability is built into our system as it is not built into the British system."[33]

But Professor Schlesinger (like James Q. Wilson) does not come to grips with McIlwain's argument against the separation of powers. Elsewhere I have analyzed the role of British parliamentary government in coping with that country's recent and contemporary problems, concluding that some elements of parliamentarism remain attractive for consideration in the United States. Respecting the Wright allegations, Harold Wilson survived whatever plot there was in 1974–76, to be succeeded by another Labour prime minister, Sir James Callaghan, whose regime lasted until 1979. In 1977 Sir James ordered a probe of the alleged MI5 effort to undermine Wilson who had been elevated to the peerage. In 1987, the issue having surfaced again, Sir Antony Duff, MI5's current director-general, "completed an exhaustive internal inquiry," concluding "that there is no truth in [Peter Wright's] allegations." Sir James Callaghan and others have recently called for a more independent and far-reaching inquiry.[34] As to the British proclivity to suppress books, papers, and stories on such matters, it would seem that a revival of the Duke of Wellington's policy is called for: "Publish and be damned!"

The Wright allegations, however, allege a behavior in MI5 that illustrates the proclivity of spies to practice their art on their own government. The same proclivity is rife in the United States, and we even build monuments for sufficiently successful practitioners like J. Edgar Hoover. Indeed, an American CIA agent, James Angleton, is said to have stimulated the MI5's attempt to discredit Prime Minister Harold Wilson, by proving that he was a Russian Communist mole!

Heinous as it was (if true) the MI5 attack on Wilson was ad hominem. It was not aimed at government, at gubernaculum, itself. But the destruction of government, of gubernaculum, is what the separation of powers gives us, not in any underhanded way, but forthrightly. What we are seeing is an incremental process (but with larger and larger leaps) of separating the executive from the legislature, of expanding and canonizing the former, and of pulverizing and denigrating the latter. This at a time when the military-industrial-scientific-populist-patriotic complex waxes in strength, with shadowy reinforcement from paramilitary organizations, and with an invidious credo combining the chorus that "we are the only true anti-Communists" with a counterpoint refrain: "the liberals have stabbed us in the back in China, in Vietnam, and their dagger is poised again in the Persian Gulf." This is the present dimension of the military threat that James Madison foresaw, without quite realizing that the separation of powers would eventually aggravate it so grievously. I repeat the theme of this paper: To survive this threat we need a government in which the executive and legislature are fused. This does not mean scrapping the separation of powers: it means changing it—powers would then be separated between the government and the opposition.

James Q. Wilson closed one of his essays celebrating the success of the separation of powers: "To learn from experience about constitutional 'reform,' we will have to take a precipitous leap into the dark." He is right about the leap; but we are already in the dark from the leap into the separation of powers taken in 1787—and it is getting murkier and murkier.

11
Constitutional Reform
The Role of Education

I N 1986 I was asked by the *American Political Science Review* to review James L. Sundquist, *Constitution Reform and Effective Government* (Brookings, 1985).* I did so:

In December, 1979, C. Douglas Dillon, former Secretary of the Treasury, Under Secretary of State, and ambassador to France, declared, "I very much doubt that . . . we can long . . . afford . . . the division of power and responsibility between our Executive and Legislative branches of government . . . I have no pat answers. But I do know that until we are prepared to examine the basic structure of our federal system . . . rather than indulging in continuous . . . recriminations, our problems will remain . . . and, in all probability, increase in severity."

This speech led to the organization of the Committee on the Constitutional System (CCS) in 1981 and to its incorporation in 1983, co-chaired by Mr. Dillon, Lloyd N. Cutler, formerly counsel to President Carter, and Senator Nancy Landon Kassenbaum (Suite 410, 1755 Massachusetts Ave., NW, Washington, D.C., 20036). The CCS workbook, edited by Donald L. Robinson, is *Reforming American Government* (Boulder: Westview, 1985). The CCS includes present and former Senators and Representatives, Cabinet members, presidential advisers, state governors, ranking members of major party organizations, business and labor leaders, journalists, and academicians. Members

---

This review, first published in the *American Political Science Review* for December 1986, is reprinted by permission.

combine reverence for the constitutional ideal with a conviction
that the uniquely favorable circumstances of its provenance and
the evolution of our Constitution's particular structures have
virtually disappeared.

Now CCS charter member James L. Sundquist publishes a
magisterial account of the constitutional origins, the history of
suggested reforms, and an intensive and detailed analysis of
contemporary proposals.

In the latter he deals with forestalling divided government
(the team ticket that mandates straight-ticket voting for President and Congress, bonus Congressional seats to insure the winning President a majority, etc.); with lengthening the terms of
office (especially the 4-8-4: electing the President, the House,
and half the Senate—given 8-year terms—every 4 years); and
with replacing failed governments. He then discusses lesser proposals for fostering inter-branch collaboration and altering the
checks and balances (including incisive critiques of the presidential item veto and of the possible rehabilitation of the Congressional veto devastated by the *Chadha* decision).

In the bicentennial, this book, together with Robinson's,
should inform the celebration of the Constitution by insisting
on a thorough re-examination of its present adequacy. I dissent,
however, from Sundquist's espousal of incrementalism — "the
parliamentary system represents only a source of ideas for incremental steps that might bring more unity to the American government, each such step to be considered on its own merits in
terms of its adaptability to American traditions and institutions."

Normally incrementalism is the proper approach to change.
But in 1787 the farmers radically departed from incrementalism, thereby creating a system which, if it is to be fundamentally changed has to be approached as comprehensively as the
framers did. Charles H. McIlwain capped his illustrious career
with *Constitutionalism: Ancient and Modern* (Cornell, 1940,
1958). "Among all the modern fallacies that have obscured the
true teachings of constitutional history, few are worse than the
extreme doctrine of the separation of powers." He could find
little historical background for the theory "except the fancies of
eighteenth-century doctrinaires." Excoriating the separation of
powers for dissipating government, McIlwain stressed its departure from incrementalism: "Unlike the legal limitations in our
bill of rights, it is not the matured result of centuries of trial and
error."

Suppose the CCS fixed on the 4-8-4 as an incremental step. This might (a) consolidate elections so that voters could learn-by-doing that they are creating a government and an opposition and (b) give the government enough time to develop and apply its program. But it would not cope with failed Presidents for which a vote of "no confidence" is the obvious solution. Yet if we favor keeping a popularly-elected President to help insure a unified executive and a governing majority, can the "people's choice" be voted down by legislators chosen in single-member districts? Can this dilemma be resolved by educating voters to perceive the President as a leader of a governing majority rather than as the embodiment of the sovereign people? Another problem: both history and logic tell us that only one house of the legislature can properly be vested with the vote of confidence. What to do about the Senate? Meanwhile, the vote of confidence alone would unbalance the constitution unless paralleled by vesting the power to dissolve the government in the executive. Careful readers will note that this is *not* a plea for simple adoption of a parliamentary system but rather an argument that constitutional reform is ineluctably complex. It cannot be properly approached piecemeal.

History shows the actual drafting of viable constitutions to be the work of relatively few people. Our vigorous democracy would stipulate that this small group be surrounded, informed, and interpreted by Carl Friedrich's "constituent group." Political science can lead in the fearful task of forming the constituent group by focusing intensive study and debate on the Constitution. But can we sustain such prolonged national questioning without undermining that reverence necessary to the maintenance of any regime? Plato's nocturnal council (*Laws*, Book 10) haunts us. Yet we may be able to have our inquiry and still hold fast to our devotion by distinguishing the essence of constitutionalism from the particular structures devised to implement it. Again, McIlwain is a good place to start.

Before publication I sent a short paper based on my review to a number of political scientists (and a few others) with the following cover letter.

"Enclosed is a paper based on my forthcoming review of Jim Sundquist's new book . . . I should be interested in your reaction to the argument over an incremental vs. a comprehensive approach . . . Beyond this, I should like to know what you think of the wisdom and timeliness of incorporating a serious discussion of constitutional alternatives in the political science curriculum. Should this be attempted? If so, 'should it be done primarily in advanced political science courses or can it also be made a part of the introductory course in American government?

"Realizing that the "desperate brevity" of my review of Sundquist omits many aspects of the argument over constitutional reform, I first tried to expand this letter to include them. But the list got out of hand; and since my main purpose is to elicit your comments, let me simply ask you to suggest one or two (or more) aspects of the subject that ought to be included in the teaching program. I know, of course, that a lot of highly relevant teaching is already taking place. In response to earlier, more tentative inquiries, Professor William P. Kreml of the University of South Carolina wrote that he discussed the issue in the introductory political science class as well as in other classes, such as Constitutional Law, where appropriate. Professor Edward A. Kolodkjiez, the University of Illinois, Urbana, sent his impressive syllabus for P.S. 450A, "Evaluating the Practice and Performance of the American Political Process." And Ross B. Talbot, Iowa State University reported a lively and critical discussion of an earlier CCS tentative agenda, but wrote that there might be a willingness to devote P.S. 215, the basic national government course, to the subject.

"I can report that in the winter quarter, 1986, at Davis, Professor Larry Berman focused P.S. 105, Contemporary Problems of the American Political System, on a critical examination of the overall framework of government devised in Philadelphia in 1787. His reading list featured Robinson . . . Except for strengthening political parties, most of the 150 students rejected proposals for fundamental constitutional change; but the vast majority thought that the issue of reform should be taken seriously, and were enthusiastic about the course."

Twenty-five persons answered, between June 1986 and May 1987. All favored the inclusion of this controversial subject in teaching programs in political science. Some would begin such teaching in introductory classes. Most thought that it should be postponed until students "are already familiar with the political grammar and where their input would be potentially enlightening," as one put it. But let them speak for themselves. Austin Ranney wrote:

> "In response to the questions you raised in your letter of June 9, I have no doubt that a critical evaluation of the performance of the Constitution in the 1980s and of the various proposals for reform, ranging from the balanced-budget and school-prayer amendments to the kinds of proposals discussed in Robinson's *Reforming American Government*, should play a major role in Political Science curricula, should have been doing so all along and should continue to do so long after the special occasion of the 1987 bicentennial has passed. The curricular question, of course, concerns the point at which such studies and discussions should take place. We are all tempted, I think, to give them a major role in the big freshman-sophomore introductory course so as to be sure to catch the maximum number of students. My experience, however, has inclined me to believe that we should wait until students have had at least one introductory course or have otherwise demonstrated some understanding in how the constitutional system works now. I have found that a surprisingly (and disappointingly) large proportion of the freshmen and sophomores I have encountered at Illinois, Wisconsin, and Georgetown are really quite ignorant about the fundamental operating principles of the present system—especially such matters as the relative power of the president and Congress, the role of the courts, the place and role of the bureaucracy, the principle of limited government and its application in the bill of rights, the guarantees to persons accused of crime, and so on (I realize that Davis freshmen and sophomores may be much more sophisticated in this regard). So I have concluded, perhaps wrongly, that we must first do our best to make sure that they know and understand how things are before we can engage them in serious discussions about how things ought to be changed.
>
> "Accordingly, it seems to me what Larry Berman did with P.S. 105 in the last winter quarter is the way to go. In short:

make sure that you get students who know at least the fundamentals of the present system, and then allow them—no, provoke them—to consider how it should be changed.

I don't know if this makes sense to you, but that is how it
seems to me. Perhaps we can do something along those lines in
the winter and spring quarters of 1987."

After leaving the AEI to join the Berkeley faculty, Austin Ranney was a visiting professor at Davis for the winter and spring quarters of 1987 when, at his suggestion, he and I led an informal and
irregular not-for-credit seminar on whether fundamental constitutional reform is advisable, feasible, and practical in the United
States. The consensus was that the seminar augured well for a teaching program on the subject.

From Harvard Richard E. Neustadt wrote:

"For what it is worth I do think the issues of constitutional
alternatives should be broached in political science courses—
wherever applicable, introductory and advanced—although the
best way to do it may be by means of comparison to, say, British
and French constitutions, just to show that 'our way's' not the
only one! In my upper-college course on the Presidency, I do
that for a couple of lectures and then go on to a day on current
issues of US reform, followed by a section-discussion of the
subject.

"But I fear I *don't* agree that the 1787 constitution-makers
broke from 'incrementalism.' On the contrary, I see them as
Englishmen intent on 'restoring' (and of course adapting) an
improved, perfected version of the English Constitution under
William and Mary! They didn't *talk* that way, but it is what they
did."

Neustadt may be right about what the Framers thought they
did. But the magnitude of the change they wrought on British institutions by introducing the formal separation of powers may constrain
us to undertake an heroic approach. And Neustadt's comment gives
one pause. If it is true that drafters of a reformed American constitution would need to be *consciously* more innovative than even the

Framers of 1787, the task is awesome, indeed.

An extraordinarily experienced visiting professor (who has legislative service, has been a diplomat—ambassadorial rank—and a leading corporate executive—communications—and whom I shall keep anonymous) wrote:

"A comment from a non-resident alien on your letter of June 9 . . . is probably unwanted and almost certainly an impertinence. But for what little it's worth here goes.

"1. *Is the serious study of constitutional alternatives wise and timely?* Yes. If the criticisms of the constitution as is are to be taken seriously, the study of the alternative exemplars is essential. And where will this be done seriously if not in a university and probably in the Pol. Sci. Department? There are as many objections to the alternatives of which I am aware as to the existing constitution, and the finding of viable alternatives which will be satisfactory in the long-term requires deep and complex consideration.

"From my very limited experience of UCD undergraduates I should be reluctant to see this undertaken in an introductory course on American government. To do this would, I fear, lead to misunderstanding and a proliferation of half-baked ideas—to confusion, in other words, rather than clarity. It seems to me to be well suited to an advanced, or preferably graduate, course where the students are already familiar with the political grammar and where their input would be potentially enlightening.

"2. *Incremental vs. Comprehensive.* I put this question second because I don't think it should be answered a priori. It is not until there are manifest signs of a degree of academic consensus about what, if anything, *ought* to be done that the dimension of the resulting political problem can be perceived with any certainty. And it is only at that stage that confident judgments can be made about how the process can be set in hand with any possibility of success. I would venture the guess that in any event constitutional reform would come about incrementally—if only for practical reasons: a Congress which traditionally can't even pass a coherent Budget—an annual, well-established, necessary operation—will surely find it very difficult to enact comprehensive constitutional reform. If you are right in believing that this is what is required, then its best (perhaps only) chance would be after the establishment of a massive consensus on what needs to be done. That, I imagine, would require a decade of study, disputation and propaganda, which would have to go far wider than the boundaries of Academia, but would have to be grounded in the universities."

"Does that make sense, I wonder."

Aaron Wildavsky, the University of California, Berkeley, wrote:

"I am not longer certain that our politics can be described as incremental or that I know which way they are tending. Gramm-Rudman and tax reform, for instance, are the most radical changes in spending and taxing in any country of the Western world I know about in the last century. These are not incremental changes. Nor can I imagine any Western democracy seeking to balance its budgets in so short a time or to cut tax rates so drastically at one time. Moreover, these measures are almost entirely generated by legislative elites with little or no input or interest by the general public. On the one hand, these measures lend support to those who say that incremental change may be infeasible, whereas radical change may become feasible. After all, tax reform went from being utopian to unstoppable in about three months or three days. On the other hand, those disturbed by these measures may just tell you that that's what you get when you depart from time-honored methods.

"I know what you mean by reverence. I can recall seeing pictures of American flags being burned but never of the Constitution suffering that fate. I would be careful. But I am open to the argument that only substantial change would make a substantial difference. In any event, as I work my way through a volume on the great battles of the budget, a volume that is essentially concerned with the capacity to govern, I shall give this matter more thought."

Arend Lijphart, University of California, San Diego, wrote:

"I support your argument that a comprehensive approach to reform is preferable to incrementalism. Basically I believe that there is no good intermediate system between presidentialism and parliamentarism such as the 4-8-4 plan or French-style strong presidentialism combined with a parliamentary system. As far as the latter is concerned, it is interesting to note that Greece and Portugal, which originally flirted with the French model, have now both abandoned it.

"I also support the idea of introducing this kind of fundamental debate in the curriculum wherever it is appropriate. I do not teach American politics, but it seems to me that there are all kinds of good opportunities to deal with these issues in courses on the U.S. Constitution, the presidency, etc. It also seems to me completely appropriate to have one or more special courses devoted to the debate. In my comparative politics courses, I always try to make students think of alternatives to established American patterns, such as parliamentarism, proportional representation, and so on.

"What worries me most about presidentialism is actually not so much the American case—in my opinion, the U.S. system does not operate all that badly, although there is clearly room for improvement—but how presidentialism works, or fails to work well, in other countries, especially in Latin America. There seems to be a strong tendency for presidentialism to lead to autocracy. I wish that I could make this clear to the current constitution-writers in the Philippines. I fear that they will draft another presidential constitution, and I am convinced that this is not optimal for them."

These remarks on presidentialism are arresting. I have maintained that we should attempt to formulate a system that would combine parliamentary features with a directly elected president, but Lijphart's letter adds to my uneasiness on this point. Nevertheless, faut de mieux. . . .

Philippa Strum, Brooklyn College of the City University of New York wrote:

"Obviously, I agree with you in the incremental vs. comprehensive debate. Discussions of specific institutions, without reference to the larger context, are likely to be mired in arguments about details, and sight will be lost of the larger goals (as well as of the larger questions). There's also the problem of how something put together in bits and pieces is ultimately going to hold together.

"The question of the appropriate courses in which to raise the subject is, I think, unanswerable, because it depends upon the nature of the student body in each institution. Students at Brooklyn have virtually no knowledge of the American system, and by the time they get enough sense of it to explore possible alternatives the course will be over. The students I've taught at New York University, however, walked in fairly well-educated about their political system, and would no doubt be stimulated by an approach that raised serious questions about it. Whatever the level of the course, however, I can't see any way of eliciting real thinking about the system without making the major question that of the entire system (something along the lines of 'Should the current system be replaced by parliamentary government?') Of course specific institutions would be examined as the debate went on, but again—the picture makes little sense if it's confined only to certain parts.

"My only discomfort with the comprehensive approach stems from my total belief in the necessity of safeguards for civil liberties and my skepticism about the majority of the citizenry (or members of a constitutional convention) doing that which is necessary to provide them. *Maybe* this problem could be solved by the 'educating' done by political scientists, but I'm neither convinced that they'll inevitably do a good enough job nor that they themselves, taken in their totality, are fully cognizant of the need. You scarcely need to be reminded of the periodic studies done by Americans' attitudes toward civil liberties (the most recent comprehensive one having been done by McCloskey and Brill) or of the way political scientists act within their own professional organization.

"This discomfort preceded my studies in Israel but has been emphasized by them. There I found a supposedly Westernized society in which *the* definition of democracy is majority rule—with absolutely no reference to the rights of individuals or minorities. This is scarcely the place (the book I hope to write this year is) to explore the historical reasons for this phenomenon. Perhaps it will suffice here to say that the state was founded by articulate, politically aware and involved people, who held passionate debates about the nature of the proposed state and who had been socialized to take freedom of speech and association and a dynamic press for granted, and who nonetheless simply ignored civil liberties in their emphasis on institutions and processes. We're not Israelis and we do have an intelligentsia at least a segment of which does understand the need for protection of rights and liberties, but the current climate of intolerance for unpopular ideas, the emergence of a yearning for a simplistic yesteryear that never existed, the popular support for capital punishment, the Roman Catholic Church's delegitimizing of meaningful debate (and I should imagine that the fundamentalist churches that account for over a quarter of the population are no different)—all leave me with a queasy feeling that the comprehensive approach might result in establishment of a government able to function with great effectiveness and impervious to the claims of civil liberties."

Professor Strum's concern for the preservation of the bill of rights and all that it implies in *any* season of constitutional reform expresses a frequent worry of political scientists (and some others, including Justice Stanley Mosk of the California State Supreme Court and Clark Kerr, former president of The University of California) with whom I have corresponded in the last seven years.

Frederick C. Mosher, Professor Emeritus, The University of Virginia, wrote:

"I think it would be a very good idea to include constitutional change in one or more political science courses and even courses, graduate and undergraduate, directed to it. My reasons are somewhat different from yours. It would, I think, be a wonderful way to teach and to learn how the government works under the constitution, its beauties and its warts; what the 'essence' of the constitution really is; how and in what ways it has obstructed progress and democracy; how we have lessened the impact of some of its rigidities. On the last point, the separation of powers is probably the key issue. The separation was softened somewhat in the constitution itself, and over the two centuries a number of other devices have been invented to relieve it — regulatory commissions, the budget, impoundments, legislative vetoes, GAO, etc. But recently, the Supreme Court seems to be widening it into a chasm.

"However, I am pessimistic that there will be a major change in the constitutional structure of our government short of a sweeping catastrophe. And I doubt that teaching college students will affect the probabilities significantly. I think that you are right on the desirability of comprehensiveness, and Jim Sundquist on the greater likelihood of something happening with an incremental approach. In the current political climate, I would be scared to death of a national convention. I am afraid it would produce a bunch of junk on abortion, school prayer, AIDS, creationism, budget balance, secrecy, states' rights, — and even a more rigid separation of powers in favor of the president."

Dwight Waldo, Professor Emeritus, the Maxwell School, Syracuse University, wrote:

"On logical grounds — if that's the way to put it — I agree with your 'It cannot be approached piecemeal.' But I rate the chances of any overall review and substantial change in any "forseeable" future as near zero. Indeed, the effect of the Bicentennial is likely to increase the reverence for THE CONSTITUTION that makes any examination of it in the light of 200 years of history a possible enterprise. Change the Const." — 'Forbid it Almighty God.' If this can be the response of a political scientist — you once so quoted one of your correspondents, what can you expect from others?

"It would be 'nice' if the political science fraternity were to make the adequacy/appropriateness of the Const. a focus for its study and discussion at this bicentennial period. But this would be quite out of character. Only, it's hard to find its 'character' nowadays. Query: if political science did not exist, would it now be created? For what purposes? In its present spirit(s) and configuration?

"The cynicism of old age, I guess. But I am up on the idea of giving the subject of constitutional problems, alternatives, etc., attention in pol. sci. curricula. It is exciting. Maybe a generation of this, plus crises, could make change a real option. (Is that another lapse into cynicism? — I didn't mean it that way.)

"Personally, I'd start with the definitional problem (descriptive, positivist, behavioral definitions v. normative) and proceed to a respectable historical-theoretical treatment — McIlwain plus. And on from there. I'd put it both at the undergraduate and graduate levels. A *piece* of it in Pol. Sci. 1."

Quentin Quade, Executive Vice President of Marquette University, wrote to express his preference for "the fusion of powers system" over the separation of powers. It has "a greater probability of producing effective *and* responsible action of promoting a rational and active political dialogue . . . because it has the greater possibility of producing disciplined, majority-oriented political parties, providing the electoral system itself encourages such parties."

After noting the reluctance of political scientists and practitioners, intensely aware of the heavy involvement of the present system with special interests, to consider fundamental constitutional changes, Quade continued: "By contrast, young college-age people, not so wedded to the *status quo* and usually ignorant of the vested interest problem, were always open to and ready to deal with systemic evaluation and the possibility of basic change, in the years that I taught."

"I think this leads to a brief response to your second topic: incorporation of root system evaluation in political science course work. It was always my judgment that one cannot effectively study institutional policies *except* comparatively. To study American government without reference to a) other democratic methods and b) the norms against which to measure such methods is not to study at all in a fully human way, for it does not approach the basic political questions as they truly exist; always normatively, always choosing and discriminating, always, in short, exercising human judgment. To study American politics without integral reference to alternatives and norms is, in my view, to proceed in a circular and finally inauthentic mode.

"Now back to the beginning: even if one is not able to provoke or produce basic reform, one must develop the models with which to guide even incremental change. And those models are not found in the system one is going to change but in the comparative and normative models one should bring even to one-system study.

"What this brief letter does, Chuck, is provide in too brief and too hurried a fashion a synopsis of the method used by Tom Bennett and me in *American Politics: Effective and Responsible?*"

Thomas J. Bennett, Director, Research Services, Loyola University of Chicago, wrote:

"The American political science discipline is about the last place on earth that I would look for the kind of sustained effort in which you are interested. Even now, twenty years after the peak of the behavioral orthodoxy, a very large percent of our fellow political scientists are not only themselves un-interested in such work, but define it as pretty much a waste of time. And the notion of a discipline-wide dedication to ANY theme will strike our colleagues not only as a violation of their academic freedom, but as a request to improperly lead students down the garden path. On the other hand, when such analysis is incorporated into courses, it goes down pretty well.

"I incorporate a substantial section on institutional analysis into the Introduction to Politics course, using comparisons of three models of democratic governments. Students are quite willing to think first of the criteria to be used in asking if governments perform well, and then to apply them. There is no doubt that love of the familiar and patriotism get in the way, but one learns over the years how to cope. Anyone who has been living in Chicago, for example, during the past few years in which the Mayor and the City Council have been dancing their minuet, should have no trouble identifying the problems of separation.

"I also teach the undergraduate course in American Political Thought, and, as you know, a lot of the semi-philosophic speculation that makes up the body of such thought was expressed, from the days of Winthrop, in institutional terms. I find it useful to take a week out of the curriculum, at about the fourth or fifth week of the thirteenth week session, to do a review of comparative structures. Discussions later on of interest group liberalism, and the like, seem to be more easily grasped when there is some 'concrete' reference."

Thomas Payne, professor emeritus, University of Montana, after an examination of an incremental vs. a comprehensive approach to reform (siding with McIlwain) and a discussion centering on the separation of powers, noting the "defensive advantage" that David Truman has argued it provides, again suggested comparative governmental studies, particularly on the handling of the budget, between the United States and parliamentary systems.

All this led him to favor inclusion of the question of reform in the political science curriculum, in which he encountered "the same kind of opposition to constitutional change that Larry Berman found."

"Over the last ten years I have found it useful in introductory courses especially our P.S. 200 (American Public Policy) to spend some time in pointing out how the fragmentation characteristic of our system leads unavoidably to the system's slowness to respond to the widely felt needs of Americans, and how the response in policy making invariably is incremental in character. In two of the upper division courses which I have taught for years, P.S. 341 (Political Parties) and P.S. 342 (Political Interest Groups) I manage to get much more detailed and specific in the consequences for American politics of this fragmentation, explaining why American parties lack discipline and responsibility, and are unable to aggregate interests, and how interest groups have evolved specific tactics to gain access in coping with fragmentation. I retired in June of 1985 from full-time faculty status, but have a post-retirement arrangement that permits me to teach during Spring Quarter. Here one of my responsibilities is the graduate seminar for MPA students in the Budgetary Process. I devote a good amount of time in the seminar to showing how fragmentation leads to incrementalism in budgeting, as propounded by Lindblom and later Wildavsky, and thus to the disjointed nature of the process.

"Based on my experience, I am convinced that the issues of constitutional reform can be incorporated into the existing curriculum in political science, where such issues are relevant and implicit, and can be addressed at all levels from the introductory course to graduate seminars. I also believe there is much room for innovative experimentation with new courses, and that grants from foundations might be a means of stimulating such experimentation. For openers, I think that a course with several texts such as Sundquist, Burn's *The Power to Lead*, and some of Thurow's recent books (e.g., *The Zero-Sum Society*) could provide some of the corpus of materials for an exciting and useful course in contemporary American political issues."

Kenneth DeBow, California State University, Sacramento, wrote:

"I think that the topic of broad-gauged constitutional revision needs to be addressed in separate upper-division courses rather than woven into introductory level classes. For California State University campuses, the state education code mandates the general subject matter that must be incorporated in Government 1, and my perception is that this is the case for many state universities. (For instance, we are mandated to teach not only American Government, but State Government as well—all in one fifteen week course!)

"Special Problems courses, such as UCD's Political Science 5, can be an ideal forum, and in the hands of a sympathetic, knowledgeable professor such as Larry Berman, doubtless are. But these courses tend to be passed around the faculty, and would only periodically and sporadically be taught by professors with a concern for constitutional reform.

"Similarly, Constitutional Law classes, seemingly a natural home for discussion of basic constitutional aspects, tend in most cases to be taught along law school lines, emphasizing case briefs, court procedures, etc. In fact, there is a tendency in these classes to treat the Constitution as holy writ—just the wrong kind of atmosphere for the kind of analysis we need.

"A regular upper-division, catalogue entry course on reforms seems the best way to deal with these problems. Most
Political Science faculties, I assume, contain at least one or two
members who would relish the chance to teach such a class. In
most cases the course would be an elective rather than a requirement, and this would reduce the audience. On the other hand,
those who did enroll would start with at least some curiosity
about the subject and some inclination to take the endeavor
seriously. My experience is that the clientele for general education requirement courses is too diverse and, lamentably, often
too apathetic, to make such classes workable arenas for the discussion.

"Finally, I would urge that constitutional reform be incorporated into the graduate curriculum of doctorate granting
schools. Universities such as UCD prepare those who end up as
faculty at places like CSUS. Younger faculty, for whom Schattschneider, Burns and the 1950 APSA colloquium are dim his-
toric memory, need to be reinvigorated with a sense of urgency
about the workability of a two-hundred-year-old document's
prescriptions for political organization into the twenty-first century."

Some briefer comments follow. Robert A. Dahl, Yale, wrote:

"I like the idea of discussing constitutional reform in introductory political science courses. I'm dismayed by the difficulty
of getting our colleagues to take it seriously at all. In general, I'd
like to see American government courses taught with a more
comparative background so that students could gain a better
idea of the alternative constitutional and political processes of
other democratic countries. Too many of them tend to equate
'democracy' with 'American government.' "

Fred Greenstein, Princeton:

"If I were teaching introductory American politics, I would
be very much interested in including constitutional reform —
centrally. Indeed, I view this as a topic which might be discussed

at any level of the curriculum. Further, rather than taking a position on instrumental vs. comprehensive change, I can conceive that the student would be creatively engaged if he or she were encouraged to reason and muster evidence on this very great question."

Alexander Heard, Chancellor Emeritus, Vanderbilt:

"I would hope that all courses in American government would embrace discussion of alternative procedures, structures, and policies. I would think a serious discussion of constitutional alternatives would be an excellent instructional device for illuminating the weaknesses and strengths of the present condition, and the opportunities and obstacles to change."

Dorothy B. James, Dean, School of Government and Public Administration, The American University, Washington, D.C.:

"Certainly, facing the Constitution's bicentennial we should challenge students at all levels to clarify their basic assumptions and those of the framers. While courses in political thought have declined as a percentage of political science curricula around the country, these issues could be part of general introductory courses as well as constitutional law sections, and courses on the three institutions."

Christopher K. Leman, Graduate School of Public Affairs, the University of Washington, Seattle:

"The idea of addressing reform in introductory courses is a good one, and I especially like the idea of devoting an entire course to the subject. Edward Banfield used to teach a course on reform, although generally his viewpoint was critical that reforms have the impact expected. One addition I would make to your suggestions is the need for comparative study of other political systems. Such comparisons are often the most useful source of reform ideas, as well as providing a means to evaluate such ideas."

Nancy Altman Lupu, Harvard:

"I have begun to think about how to incorporate into the Kennedy School teaching some of the issues raised by the Committee on the Constitutional System. Most of the courses taught at the Kennedy School are directed towards public managers and seek to explore practical questions and problems of effective management. Nevertheless, I think a general discussion of the basic structure of our government and possible alternatives to it could be a useful backdrop.

"This spring I will be teaching a course entitled 'Political Management and Institutional Leadership.' I plan to revise it. As I do so, I plan to think through whether and how to include the issues of constitutional reform."

Richard Pious, Barnard College, Columbia University:

"Thank you so much for sending me a copy of your paper based on a review of Sundquist's new work. I used the paper as the basis for a discussion in my graduate summer school course on presidential-congressional relations and the prospects for reform, and it was most useful.

"You may be interested to know that next spring I'll be teaching a course to the public, sponsored by the 92nd Street Y in Manhattan, involving issues of fundamental constitutional reform. I expect to use both Robinson and Sundquist."

Ross Talbot, Iowa State University:

"Even so, I think it is a matter of such momentous importance that political scientists should make a concerted endeavor to see that the subject is discussed in our basic American Government courses, and in upper division and graduate courses, too, where the subject would be relevant to the content of the course. If there is one thing that I've learned over the years (along with, hopefully, a few others!) it is that what is of little interest today may be a burning issue tomorrow, and vice versa."

F. A. Hermens, whose classical analysis at the unfortunate consequences of proportional representation has illuminated that question
for generations of political scientists, wrote what I consider to be a
subtle criticism of an incremental approach.

"Incremental reforms do make sense as long as they promise to lead the way from the dynamics of the old and to fit in
with the dynamics which they create. There is, of course, no lack
of warning examples. The Brownlow report led to the creation
and eventual explosion of a White House staff which does more
to complicate our system than to make it work. W. Y. Elliott
warned, but hardly anyone is aware of that. Similarly, when
George Galloway (with whom I discussed the matter at that
time), advocated more Congressional staff, the result did not
make our system work better."

There were a number of brief but encouraging replies. Sheilah
Mann, Director, Project 87, wrote, "I appreciate receiving your review of Jim Sundquist's [book] along with your description of how
some political science faculty are introducing students to these issues." From the University of Virginia, Henry J. Abraham: "I have no
real suggestions and will simply commend you on your analysis."
Richard Fenno, University of Rochester: "I'm not sure I have much to
say on the matter other than that I think you do us all a service by
staying with this important question." A Visiting Scholar in Political
Science at Stanford, Virginia Schuck: "Thank you for your . . . new
proposal for a new major, emphasis in teaching political science. I
was delighted to learn the information you have and the reference to
Robinson's workbook." After commending an emphasis on the subject in the political science curriculum, Winston M. Fisk, Claremont-
McKenna, wrote: "I am convinced that such considerations . . .
should be as early and as penetrating as possible. Students tend to
rise to this challenge and to welcome this chance to use the analytical
tools of our subject."

Among other-than-political scientists C. Douglas Dillon wrote:

"Thank you for your letter of June 9th which has just
reached me. My reaction to your memo is mixed since I feel that
the only practical road to progress is via the incremental road

favored by Sundquist. At the same time I have considerable doubt that it will rectify all the problems. However, in the absence of a major crisis of the type none of us would like to see, the only possible way to move ahead is through incremental change.

"I am very much in favor of anything that will incorporate serious discussion of political reform in university curriculums. That indeed, is my first and immediate objective. Only through such discussions can we advance to agreement on actual changes. I would think that it is more practical to have these discussions start in the more advanced political science courses with the idea that it would then spread to undergraduates and even into introductory courses in the field of government.

"Based on the most recent discussions of our group, it seems to me that the one change of significance that has a real chance is the change in the terms of elected officials to the 4-8-4 system. I would hope that this will be discussed and studied as much as possible."

Finally, an eminent historian, John C. Greene, the University of Connecticut, wrote:

"You flatter me greatly in asking for my opinions about constitutional reform, a subject to which I have devoted no attention. Our present system has obvious defects, but I shudder to think what might happen at a constitutional convention dominated by single interest groups and penny-pinchers. The idea of including the question of constitutional reform in graduate and undergraduate courses is excellent, however."

At Harvard in 1938–39, John Greene and I took McIlwain's English Constitutional History together and audited his History of Political Thought. We have kept in close touch. He joined the Committee on the Constitutional System early. And yet, with his full agenda, the question of the constitution and of constitutional reform is rather peripheral in his thoughts. I suspect that this is true of historians generally, such eminent exceptions as James MacGregor Burns (also a leading political scientist), Barbara Tuchman, and Richard Wade notwithstanding. Davis has a very strong history department; but, other than James Shideler (with whom I have shared an interest in agriculture), my overtures have been unanswered. In the breadth, depth, and scope of the historian's world, the problems of government structures and processes rarely maintain that dominant position that the contemporary situation (I should say, "crisis") calls for.

Lawyers, again with notable exceptions like J. William Fulbright, Henry S. Reuss, and Lloyd N. Cutler (whose perspectives seem heavily shaped by their profound political experience), seem essentially concerned with the refinement of concepts as well as sharpening and distinguishing precedents. On the other hand, I found considerable interest among agricultural economists, like the late John D. Black, T. W. Schultz, James Bonnen, Jean Bowman Andersen, Marion Clawson, Willard Cochrane, Harold Halcrow, Chester O. McCorkle, Vernon Ruttan, and George Schuh. I think that this is perhaps because their analyses have necessarily and unremittingly involved the role of government.

But it is especially political scientists who cannot escape a feeling of responsibility. Political institutions and procedures, the formation of constitutions, the operations of government — these are their natural habitat. Since 1980 I have written to scores of political scientists, asking whether they believed that the problems of our constitution were serious enough to warrant intensive study undertaken with the intent to search for major reforms that they would seriously consider supporting. Responses were often filled with misgivings, skepticism, fears, and doubts, but — still — they were mainly affirmative. Paul Y. Hammond wrote from the University of Pittsburgh:

> "I have carried your letter of . . . around until it looks tattered and worn. I have been inclined to write you a negative response, but did not want to.
>
> "I am concerned that a constitutional convention would become a football for the extremes in American politics. Now, upon reflection, it seems to me that I am underestimating the capacity of competent people to manage the processes they undertake. In fact, I now have an opposite view in place of my original fear. Properly managed, a constitutional reform process could very well reinforce the centralist tendencies in American politics while it opened up issues that I would want to see

opened. But you already know this (although you would not know what issues in particular would interest me personally).

"Please include me in your plans, and forgive my tardy response."

Nevertheless, in addition to those already mentioned (and to my colleagues at Davis who, whatever their differences with me, have been very supportive), I can list nearly thirty political scientists, many of considerable eminence, who were willing to join in the search. Against these, I had only a handful of explicit rejections. I conclude that there is a widespread, if latent, willingness in the profession to share in a serious educational and research effort along the lines suggested, or some adaptation thereof, in this book.

12
A Grand Strategy
of Constitutional Reform

WE, the people of the United States, in order to form a more perfect union, should now give serious thought to the need for basic constitutional reform. The central structural principle of the 1787 Constitution, the separation of powers between the president and the Congress, has recently been criticized. Lloyd N. Cutler, former counsel to the president, wrote: "The separation of powers between the executive and the legislative branches, whatever its merits in 1793, has become a structure that almost guarantees stalemate today." C. Douglas Dillon, former secretary of the Treasury and undersecretary of state, questioned "whether we can continue to afford the luxury of the separation of powers . . . between the executive and the legislative branches." J. William Fulbright, former chairman of the Senate Foreign Relations Committee, urged "serious consideration to a merger of power between the executive and the legislature . . . under what we normally call a parliamentary system."

Congressman Henry S. Reuss, chairman, Joint Economic Committee, said that the advocacy of a parliamentary system for the United States is unrealistic but recommended examination of changes "of a milder nature," such as enabling Congress to remove the president by a vote of no confidence and, in the event of a "serious policy deadlock," enabling the president to dissolve the Congress and call for new elections in which the presidency would also be at risk.[1] He would thus incorporate two vital elements of the parliamentary system—and put an end to the separation of powers as we know it.

Inquiry into the need for constitutional reform with emphasis on the separation of powers has been undertaken by the Committee on the Constitutional System (CCS). Out of biennial CCS meetings a workbook entitled *Reforming American Government*; a history and analysis of suggested reforms by James L. Sundquist—*Constitutional Reform and Effective Government*; and *A Bicentennial Analysis of the American Political Structure: Report and Recommendations of the Committee on the Constitutional System* have emerged.[2]

The CCS *Report and Recommendations* dwells on measures to strengthen the organization and coherence of political parties, to enhance the role of congressional members and candidates in presidential nominating conventions, to permit meaningful regulation of campaign expenditures, and to relax the two-thirds rule for treaty ratification. But it properly goes much farther to propose that serious consideration be given to modifying the separation of powers by (1) adopting the 4-8-4 proposal (elect the president, the House of Representatives, and half the Senate every four years); (2) incorporating the power of dissolution to break (or avoid) deadlocks: enabling both president and Congress to seek a new popular mandate; and (3) permitting the president to appoint members of the Congress to serve in his cabinet without losing their legislative seats.

Toward a New Separation: Between the Government and the Opposition

With respect, the CCS Report does not go far enough. The United States has grown and thrived under uniquely favorable circumstances. With enormously rich resources and geographical insulation from other powerful countries, we have come this far despite a grievous constitutional flaw. To rectify our structure of government will require a more radical change than the CCS suggests, namely, *the replacement of the separation of powers between the executive and the legislature by a separation between the government and the opposition.* This would be the grand strategy of constitutional reform.

We see at once that we must think about this with the marked change in ambience in mind. Of about 3 million citizens in 1787, perhaps 500 thousand adult males could vote. Some 160 thousand voted on the adoption of the new Constitution, about 100 thousand of them favoring it. Today, such fundamental reform must seek acceptance in a mass democracy with a potential electorate of some 125 million. In devising their complex structure the 1787 Framers met from mid-May to mid-September virtually insulated from the public. Today's reformers would also need considerable privacy. Not every word and gesture would need to be televised. But frequent and extensive public debate would be not only inescapable but proper and necessary. For in a constitutional democracy characterized by a separation between the government and the opposition the explicit, practical, conscious role of the people on both sides of the separation is vital.

For political scientists devoted to the study of the organization and control of political power, the obligation is clear: to examine all sides of this issue of constitutional reform thoroughly and formally in order to ensure that the debate is as informed as they can make it. This view assumes the existence of Carl J. Friedrich's "constituent group."[3] Without implying their commitment to the specifics of my argument, I can say that the teaching obligation is strongly supported by an impressive list of the nation's political scientists.[4]

What may such teaching involve? One effort to define the problem ensues.

Constitutionalism

What does it mean? Here, it refers not merely to a description of how the government is organized but rather to a certain kind of government, one that is supposed to (and virtually always does) operate within limits designed to give meaning to "due process of law" and spelled out for us in the Bill of Rights. Much of our constitutional debate is over the precise meaning of phraseology in the Bill of Rights. But this assumes that there is a government that can act. Recall Madison's first requirement for framing a government of men over men: "to enable the government to control the governed." Only then could he state his second requirement "to oblige it to control itself."[5] Both requirements address political structure. Neither dwells on the refinement of the Bill of Rights.

Unfortunately, the Framers relied chiefly on the separation of powers to oblige the government to control itself. They appealed to

Montesquieu, "There can be no liberty where the legislative and executive powers are united in the same person, or body of magistrates." But, reading the British constitution over Montesquieu's shoulder, Madison immediately qualified the statement. "His meaning . . . can amount to no more than this: that where the *whole* power of one department is exercised by the same hands that possess the *whole* power of another department, the fundamental principles of a free constitution are subverted."[6] This interpretation informed Richard Neustadt's well-known description, "separated institutions sharing powers." It anticipated Paul Appleby's desideratum: "making a mesh of things." It opened the way, as Frederick C. Mosher put it, to "soften somewhat the separation of powers in the constitution itself, and over the two centuries a number of other devices have been invented to relieve it—regulatory commissions, the budget, impoundments, legislative vetoes, GAO, etc."[7]

This interpretation emphasizes the inherent flexibility in the American Constitution, notable in the first sentence of Article II on the executive, in the commerce clause, and in John Marshall's enunciation of the principle of "implied powers" in *McCulloch v. Maryland*. In this view, the constitution becomes almost infinitely adaptable. Fred W. Friendly and Martha J. H. Elliott declare: "The Constitution has been described as magnificently ambiguous."[8] Similarly, Don K. Price holds that "we can not deal with such fundamental problems by legalistic changes in the formal constitution but only by a political consensus to amend our unwritten constitution."[9]

But the written constitution is rigid and unambiguous on one crucial point that sharply constrains how the unwritten constitution may evolve. The constitution stipulates separate elections for the president and the Congress as well as separate elections for the Senate and the House of Representatives. The separation precipitates a continuing power struggle.

The Trouble with the Separation of Powers

Much emphasis is appropriately placed by the CCS on the contribution of the separation of powers, especially when it is exacerbated by divided government, to the production of deadlock or gridlock or stalemate. Divided government occurs when the president is confronted by a Senate or a House of Representatives, or both, controlled by the opposing political party. Except for 1874–1896 when it seemed endemic, divided government was rare in our history; but since 1954, it has been the rule whenever the Republicans have held the Presidency, 1955–1960, 1969–1976, and since 1981. Accompanied by a weakening of political parties, divided government is associated with repeated deadlocks in the most crucial question of foreign policy, the efforts to contain and limit the arms race, and, in domestic policy, the inability to control the budget.

There is, however, something other than deadlock or stalemate—indeed, its opposite. The United States government often produces explosive policy surges. If the 1920s brought a classic example of deadlock, the failure to approve the Versailles Treaty, it also witnessed the Immigration Act of 1924. There was also the protectionism of the Smoot-Hawley Act of 1930 that appears to have broadened, deepened, and lengthened the world-wide Depression.

The post–World War II period brought successive examples of policy surges. The United States repeatedly plunged into seemingly open-ended international commitments to defend the "free world." These included most poignantly the "presidents' war" (plural because a succession of them promoted it) in Vietnam, but it also included intervention and military investment in Iran that eventually contributed to a debacle that is still unfolding. These are not examples of deadlock but of imprudent governmental activities and programs.

In 1958 the United States provided military aid (ranging from very modest through substantial to the provision of nearly all training, weapons, and materiel) to forty-one nations. In these unprecedented global commitments we were, some thought, scandalously overextended. Walter Lippmann: "Dulles has gone around the world promising every nation that would accept . . . an American military guarantee. In this, Dulles has shown himself to be not a prudent and calculating diplomat but a gambler who is more lavish than any other secretary of state has ever dreamed of being with the promissory notes engaging the blood, the treasure, and the honor of this country."[10]

For John Foster Dulles, read President Dwight D. Eisenhower, operating under what was then thought to be virtual presidential carte blanche in foreign affairs, and gaining the strength to act from the resonance with the people that displayed itself in patriotic acclaim whenever the country flexed its military muscles — "the rally around the flag." Paradoxically, these executive upticks may be nourished by stalemate. If the latter occurs in domestic politics, "action-forcing" events may be devised to stir the lust for blood. The more the country seems deadlocked, the more inviting foreign adventurism appears. This may be both the seed and the fruit of the plebiscitary presidency which, in turn, is the legacy of the separation of powers.

Triangular Powers

Another perspective on the havoc wrought by the separation of powers is provided by the emergence of the iron triangles. Richard E. Neustadt provided a classic analysis of the development of the often durable alliances formed by combining strategically located members of Congress with leading bureaucrats and the heads of clientele groups. Calling it "bureaucracy," he found that it stemmed from the enormous expansion of government associated with World War II. His analysis illuminated the situation in agricultural politics in which the bureaucracy had mushroomed earlier: the personnel of the United States Department of Agriculture had expanded from thirty thousand to ninety thousand in the 1930s, not counting another one hundred thousand in the farmer-committee system in the production control-price support programs. Recognizing the phenomenon, Theodore Lowi wrote: "As in geometry and engineering, so in politics the triangle seems the most stable type of structure." Grant McConnell made telling use of a similar analysis.[11]

Interpretations of the triangles differ, however. Michael Barone and Grant Ujifusa refer to "the kind of 'iron triangles' which are so much a part of life in Washington — executive branch and congressional alliances in support of spending programs."[12] Here, the triangles are merely manifest in the pork barrel. Joseph S. Nye, Jr., views them rather benevolently: "the iron triangles of bureaucrats, Congressional staff and lobbyists [that] are part of the price Americans pay for the benefits of a pluralistic political system."[13] Most ironically, Arthur Maass, whose classic expose of the machinations of the Corps of Engineers in *Muddy Waters* was a central exhibit in any disquisition on the "iron triangles," has recently called them the "pathological form of bureau-committee relations, in the sense that it is a deviation from the normal or typical form."[14]

By contrast, it is argued here that the triangles emerge as logical consequences of the separation of powers. But they cannot always be dismissed as banal but affordable nuisances ("counting our money and throwing it away," Sandburg; "a little plum for everyone," Herbert Agar; "Deal me in!" David Potter). In addition to divided government (already noticed) the triangles help to precipitate stalemate. Cumulatively, they significantly contribute (along with prodigious defense spending and greatly reduced income taxes) to the zooming national deficit and the exploding national debt. And they breed some results that go far beyond the affordable pork barrel indulgences of our cherished pluralism. Triangular forces were instrumental in keeping agricultural price supports at their swollen World War II levels for a full decade after 1945, significantly contributing to the protracted boom in farm land values for which many farmers and much of the country is now paying dearly—and contributing, too, to wholesale dumping of American surpluses abroad in ways that significantly interfered with the nation's economic and political foreign policies.[15] Triangular forces also fueled the arms race in the early 1960s when the victorious Kennedy luminaries found that their touted missile gap was a hoax.[16]

The Results of Fragmentation

The separation of powers fragments government. It may encourage divided government. It has come to nourish the triangles. Despite Madison's sovereign appeal in *Federalist* No. 10 to "enlarge the sphere" as a means of diluting factions, it nourishes factions. Indeed, in campaign and election time, it forces an overweening localism on legislators. Budgets and nuclear warfare capabilities out of control? These be damned. "All politics is local."

In consequence of splintered government, of the disposition on the one hand, to blunder into disastrous courses of action, in Korea, in Vietnam, or in Iran, or in consequence of the failure to come to grips with looming domestic problems that seem to call for concerted national action, there are two resources, one real, the other mythical, but both seemingly connected, melded out of necessity into one—

the president and the people. The president is there, and often he can act. But he can act much more effectively if he somehow embodies the people—who are imagined as a collective entity inspired at once with universal vision, a complete grasp of events, an understanding of the alternatives of action, and the will to decide and proceed. The president articulates the people's will. But the popular will *must* be there. It must be discernible. On every question of public policy it knows the proper answer, if it can only be made or teased to divulge it.

We now confront the most grievous flaws in our system: the first is constant evocation of the people, the unremitting reification of the people—the "fallacy of misplaced concreteness"—the assumption of a popular will where one does not and cannot exist; with respect to specific and necessarily complicated solutions for particular problems.[17]

Parallel to, and resonant with, the reification of the people is the apotheosis of the president. He becomes the personification of the reified people. A hunger for leadership lurks in the nature of man, a restless search for Karen Horney's "magic helper," an inexhaustible source of human desire from which springs the divinity that doth hedge a king. The crescendoes of popular praise for presidents follow paradoxically on the heels of climactic moments or periods of widely perceived and felt national tragedy or danger that are blamed on the hapless incumbents. The greatest source of adulation for beloved Presidents may have been that they were *not* their unfortunate predecessors. FDR was not Hoover; Eisenhower was not Truman; Nixon was not LBJ; Reagan is not Carter. Out of this ill-starred mix of reified public and deified leader emerges the plebiscitary presidency. The ego cannot resist the worshipful tides. It swells. The king can do no wrong. FDR set out to "pack" the Supreme Court. ("Roosevelt's eyes got glassy whenever anyone disagreed with him.") Intoxicated by a belief in omnipotence, LBJ plunged deeper into Vietnam. Bemused by a messianic vision Reagan unreservedly commits himself and the nation to the SDI. After Reykjavik he boasted of his refusal to compromise on the SDI. Pollsters in Missouri found the quick popular response six-or seven-to-one in the president's favor, despite the repeated repudiation of the SDI by impressive numbers of persons most qualified to evaluate it.[18]

We may be living in a Greek tragedy. But as long as there is a straw to grasp at, we cannot simply resign ourselves. A straw may be bobbing in the process by which democratic governments are created, as Joseph Schumpeter put it, "by means of a competitive struggle for the people's vote."[19]

The Electoral System: The Fulcrum of Constitutional Democracy

I hope to have made a prima facie case that the separation of powers leads to a dangerous disruption and fragmentation of government. If the legislative-executive separation is to be replaced by a separation between government and opposition, the electoral system must be changed.

We now have elections riveted to the calendar. The alternative is to require elections at least every five years but to let their timing to the government-of-the-day. (They would typically be held about every four years.)

The only known method of providing elections on discretion is to invest the government with the power of dissolution. This is an executive function. It would be unthinkable without vesting a reciprocal power, the vote of confidence, in the legislature to force the hand of the executive by requiring him or her either to resign or to dissolve the government.

Sinnzusammenhang. The interrelatedness of meanings. Pull any thread in the constitutional system and learn how many others are attached to it. Once again, the intricate subject calls for intensive, thorough, long-range teaching and research programs if a significant number of the constituent group are to be educated sufficiently to act as bona fide opinion leaders in a period of reform.

Consider the substitution for calendar elections of elections on discretion. To list only the probable benevolent effects: the move should (1) restore to government a proper function of timing elections; (2) shorten campaigns, preferably down to three or four weeks, thus eliminating primaries and greatly strengthening political parties by restoring to them their essential control of nominations; (3) radically reduce the horrendous costs of campaigns, enabling simple campaign cost control laws to work; (4) virtually ensure that presidential nominees will emerge in the legislature, winning their nominations by their proven ability among their peers—and, overnight, eliminate the universal frustration of legislators who know that under the separation of powers excellence in their legislative work has almost no bearing on their eligibility for the presidential nomination; (5) end the opportunities that fixed elections now give to both foreign powers and to domestic mischief-makers to harass this country or to involve it in ill-considered policies during the electoral hiatus; and (6) by virtue of election of everyone at once, executive and legislature alike, and by strengthening party control and cohesion in the process, to enabling the people to perceive and knowingly perform their great function: choosing a government and an opposition.[20]

The Vote of Confidence and Dissolution

These two powers would mark the end of the separation between executive and legislature, substituting fusion between them. One would anticipate that dissolution would soon become *the* manner of fixing election dates. Its superiorities are overwhelming. On the other hand, the vote of confidence, while certainly occurring from time to time, would rarely topple a government. "A British Government whose party was elected with a majority of seats in the House of Commons has not been defeated in a vote of confidence since . . . 1886."[21] The same tendency would obtain in the United States if, as suggested later, steps were taken to ensure a government with a legislative majority.

The value and efficacy of the vote of confidence by no means depends on the frequency of governments' being overthrown by it. Rather, its function is to demonstrate the viability of the new division of powers between the government and the opposition in debates led by the president and by the leader of the opposition. The latter would be the defeated major party's presidential candidate who would win a seat (and the appropriate perquisites) in the dominant House of Representatives. Such candidates would be no stranger there, having emerged as their party's choice by dint of their legislative skill, acumen, and effectiveness as recognized by their peers. The repeated presentation by the two leaders of their countervailing positions should restructure the public's thinking about politics and its own role therein. Not one but *two* rallying leaders would be provided so that the separation of powers would not be confined to the formal institutions of government but would extend into the body politic—the populace—the electorate, itself.

Caveats are in order. First, the model suggested here of an emergent, superior, popularly elected body recognizes that the indispensable reciprocality of government and opposition, of executive and legislature, can take place only in one legislative chamber. The executive cannot be held to account in two legislative bodies. This fact has been repeatedly demonstrated in countries that have adopted the parliamentary system. There would be a continuing, honorable, and significant role for the Senate; but it would be a different role. The House of Representatives would perforce become the main political theatre.

Second, what is projected here would be a major departure from the parliamentary system in one crucial respect. If the direct election of the president is continued, the question immediately arises: How can a president elected by the people be voted out of office by a legislative assembly elected in single-member districts? Let me attempt an answer to this sticky question.

Direct Election of the President: The Keystone of Majority Rule

Whatever their intentions were the Framers of 1787 did not opt for a directly elected president, but that is what came about. It may contain a grave danger. The fragmenting effects of the separation of powers have prompted a search, greatly accelerated since World War II, for an authoritative sovereign power. The danger rises in a plebiscitary presidency perceived as the embodiment of a reified public whose omniscience and prescience is by definition instant and unfailing. "I want—the American people want!"

Despite the danger, a compelling argument favors retaining the direct election of the president. It is what we have (excluding as trivial in this regard the accumulation of the president's national majority by state majorities and the pro forma role of the electoral college). It continues to find eloquent justification in Hamilton's *Federalist* No. 70: "That unity is conducive to energy will not be disputed. Decision, activity, secrecy(!), and despatch will generally characterize the proceedings of one man." And finally it provides the capstone of constitutional democracy.

It is the instrument of majority rule. The single presidency is the primary reason for the two-party system in the United States. A faithful copy of the United Kingdom's parliamentary system in this country would assuredly produce a multiparty system: regional, religious, racial, occupational, and ideological parties—all would be stimulated to form. After elections the formation of the government would inevitably fall to brokers among the leaders of the five to seven larger parties. The direct sense of participation in creating a government or an opposition (which also needs concentration, a degree of solidarity, and group integrity) would be denied to the voters or, at least, would be greatly diminished.

By contrast, the suggested new dispensation would produce both a president and a leader of the opposition. It would explode the myth of consensus and give birth to a new overarching conception: a separation of powers between the government and the opposition. It would give fresh meaning to McIlwain's ideal of "responsibility to the whole people"—yes, to the whole people but the people divided into the supporters of the government and of the opposition, in signal verification of W. Ivor Jennings' criteria of constitutional government: "To find out whether a people is free it is necessary only to ask if there is an opposition and, if there is, to ask where it is."[22]

The Meaning of Majority Rule, of the Mandate, and of Accountability

In this system, majority rule would obtain, but it would acquire a different meaning. Majority rule would rest on the virtue of necessity: it would be the means of settling disputes.[23] It would not necessarily be right, as an opposition representing nearly half the country would constantly remind us. Central to our constitution, of course, would remain the "legal limitations of our Bill of Rights" which, as McIlwain said, were "the matured results of centuries of trial and error." Even in this sacred realm trial and error proceeds. A *fortiori*, in the general area of economic and social policies, whether promotional, regulatory, operational, redistributive, socialistic, or efforts to develop a mixed economy; or whether in the area of collective bargaining, in the stimulation of the development of countervailing power, or in the encouragement of cooperatives; or whether dealing with education, health, retirement, the environment, or immigration—in all these approaches and areas, policy; however vested it becomes, should be regarded as *provisional*.

Answers must be found to problems. Government must go on. But the answers will often be experimental—sometimes stabs in the dark. Under the regime of government and opposition, the myth of consensus would be dissolved. The chief executive would be challenged by the leader of the opposition who also ventures to speak for a large body of the public. This countervailing situation should strengthen partisanship and party coherence. It would provide an institutional reason that compels a Congressman to have a national point of view.[24]

As with the idea of majority rule, so with the mandate. Rapidly it would come to be perceived as a mandate to govern. As the myth of consensus is abandoned, so also should be the fiction that winning politicians are morally pledged to keep their specific campaign promises. To recall Pendleton Herring's witticism (that unfortunately loses something in the translation from the era of Pullman cars) "A platform is to get in on, not to stand on." Analysis unfailingly confirms what intuition tells us: people, including us, ourselves, are ill-informed on most policy issues to say nothing of their interrelationship with other issues and their evaluation in terms of their expense when (as they should be) opportunity costs are considered.

This is not to deny accountability but to cleanse the concept of its myriad of irrelevancies so that it stands inexorably stark. What the aspirants to public office are obligated to affirm is the continuing viability of the basic compact of constitutional democracy: the continuation of effective government *and* of due process of law that incorporates the Bill of Rights, along with the intention to confront and try to cope with the host of problems that the onrush of history compels modern governments to face.

The obligations of the citizen should be no less apparent. Adapting Burke, democratic constitutional government "becomes a partnership not only between those who are living, but between those who are living, those who are dead, and those who are yet to be born." In addition to giving the government a nudge in the direction preferred by his interests, the voting citizen discharges his fundamental responsibility to create a government or an opposition, in short, to preserve, protect, and defend the Constitution of the United States.

One More Hurdle: The Assurance of a Majority Government

One problem remains: to ensure that a winning presidential candidate shall have a House of Representatives controlled by his own party. For Democratic presidents this seems to happen regularly. For Republicans since 1956 it has proved unattainable. In part this has been because of the Democratic South. Even in 1952 when the Eisenhower victory brought in a Republican-controlled House, the GOP won only 6 House members in the eleven confederacy states. By 1984 the 6 had become 44; but still, and despite President Reagan's 1984 landslide, the Democrats emerged with 253 House members to 182 for the Republicans.

Part of the Southern disparity remains. In 1980 the Republicans scored 37,228,051 votes nationwide for House candidates; the Democrats, 39,166,261 — a difference of 1,938,210 votes. But in the confederacy states, 10,682,750 votes were cast for Democratic House candidates against 8,283,986 for Republicans — a difference of 2,388,764. Outside the South the Republican House candidates scored nearly half a million more votes than the Democrats.[25]

One way out would be to stipulate that the object of the election is to create a government that can govern and that, therefore, the party of the winning presidential candidate would if necessary be allotted a bonus of House seats sufficient to provide a majority of (say) ten. This could be viewed as a means of correcting the vagaries of the electoral system. It would also appear to be congenial to the desires of the electorate as far as these can be ascertained.[26]

A Short Digression into Voting Behavior

Under the separation of powers regime as we know it historically, party identification has recently declined, and people who describe themselves as independent have risen in numbers. Much is made of the preference of voters for the "best candidate" rather than for "party loyalty." A study of the 1980 electorate showed that only 9 percent of the panel disagreed with the statement: "The best rule in voting is to pick a candidate regardless of party label." Forty-one percent agreed, and other responses showed that the "agreed" end of the seven-point scale received 71 percent of the votes.[27]

But suppose that the question had been: "To preserve constitutional democracy, not only a strong government but a strong opposition is necessary; both must be organized by political parties. Hence, there is much to be said for voting for the same party's candidate both for president and for member of Congress, even though this conflicts with the adage, 'You should vote for the man and not for the party.' "

What the reasoned preference would be on this question is not known and probably unknowable. But if it is in line with voting behavior, even under the present dispensation, it can be argued that the voters would say "agree" quite overwhelmingly. Thus Milton C. Cummings, after a lengthy analysis of the rise of split-ticket voting, wrote "That it is only a minority who fail to heed the pleas for party loyalty, even in elections when ticket-splitting is widespread, should be emphasized. Even in the extraordinary election of 1956, only about 21 percent of the voters failed to mark a straight ticket at the national level."[28]

This figure of 21 percent may be questioned. A cruder but less challengeable figure is the percentage of Congressional districts that returned a majority for one party's presidential candidate while they elected the House candidate of the opposing party. Districts with such split results have, since 1948, fluctuated between 19.3 percent and 33.3 percent, except for 1972 when the score was 44.1 percent.[29] It is true that since 1948 there has been a considerable decline in the number of voters who identify themselves as either Republican or Democrats and a proportionate rise in the number of self-acknowledged independents. But most independents lean toward one or the other of the major parties and vote the way they lean. At the same time, it is worth noting that very few voters consciously vote for the presidential candidate of one party and the congressional candidate of the other in order to create a balance of partisan/opposition in government. Alan Baron wrote of the 1984 election: "Instinctively, ticket-splitters wanted to keep New Deal Democrats from running the country . . . and New Right Republicans, from running wild."[30]

Maybe so. Instincts are hard to prove or disprove. But "only 15 percent of those interviewed after the 1980 election could correctly identify which party had won the most seats in the House of Representatives."[31] If people had a burning desire for divided government, one would expect them to know when they had achieved it.

Despite the decline in partisanship, the political behavior of the American electorate as observed in the way they have voted and are voting in recent presidential and coinciding congressional elections shows that very substantial majorities typically vote for the same party's candidate for president and for member of the Congress. The conclusion is that if institutions can be designed to produce majority governments (president and a congressional majority of the same party) that will be balanced by, and from time to time, confronted by, an organized opposition that can be perceived as an alternative government, the demonstrated proclivities of American voting behavior will make them work as planned.

Conclusion

Impressive numbers of persons deeply experienced in politics now believe that the major political institutions of the United States need fundamental reform. The Committee on the Constitutional System has extensively examined the problems and is formulating a series of far-reaching recommendations to place before the Congress. Leading members of the CCS recognize that the problem seems to root in the separation of powers between the president and the Congress. But neither their analysis nor their recommendations quite come to grips with the problem.

The problem was analyzed by Charles H. McIlwain as a flaw in the separation of powers so fundamental that it fragmented government itself. This means that the very framework of the state is so undermined that the principle of constitutionalism incorporated into it by the institutionalization of due process of law is itself jeopardized.

The cure seems to lie in rooting out the separation of powers and replacing it with another structural principle, herein suggested to be the separation between government and opposition. This should create a structure that produces a popular and effective government but also incorporates with it a popular and vocal opposition. It would not only instill in government both the need and capacity to govern along with the necessity of control by the consistent presentation of a viable alternative: it would implicate the people themselves in both sides of this saving dichotomy.

But to bring all this about seems to require a comprehensive grasp that will permit a number of interlocking changes to take place nearly at once, including especially a thorough recasting of the electoral system to introduce elections at the government's discretion instead of by the calendar and the provision for the defeated major party's presidential candidate to be the leader of the opposition.

This might just come about if a constituent group came into being educated in the problem. Political scientists, God help us all, should hold themselves primarily accountable for providing this education.

Notes

Preface

1. Charles M. Hardin, *Presidential Power and Accountability: Toward a New Constitution* (Chicago: Univ. of Chicago Press, 1974).
2. From the preliminary statement of Donald L. Robinson, ed., *Reforming American Government: The Bicentennial Papers of the Committee on the Constitutional System* (Boulder, Colo.: Westview, 1985).
3. 97th Cong., 2d sess., vol. Nov.-Dec. 1982, 195–214.
4. Robert A. Goldwin and Art Kaufman, *Separation of Powers—Does It Still Work?* (Washington, D.C.: American Enterprise Institute, 1986).
5. Charles H. McIlwain, *Constitutionalism: Ancient and Modern* (1940; reprint, Ithaca, N.Y.: Cornell Univ. Press, 1958).

Chapter 1

1. Quoted in James Reston, "Where Are We Going?" *New York Times*, 23 Dec. 1979 (emphasis added).
2. Leon D. Epstein, "What Happened to the British Party?" *American Political Science Review* vol. 74, no. 1 (1980): 20.
3. Louis Fisher, *Congress and President* (New York: Free Press, 1972), 4.
4. Epstein, *British Party Model*, 18–19.
5. Ibid., 18.
6. Ibid., 18–19.
7. Ibid., 20.
8. Philip Rezvin, *Wall Street Journal*, 2 May 1980.
9. Winston Churchill, *The Second World War*, vol. 2, *Their Finest Hour* (Boston: Houghton-Mifflin, 1949), 15.
10. Quoted in R. T. McKenzie, *British Political Parties* (New York: St. Martin's Press, 1955), 47.
11. W. Ivor Jennings, *The British Constitution* (Cambridge, England: Cambridge Univ. Press, 1942), 192.
12. George E. Reedy, *The Twilight of the Presidency* (New York: World, 1970), Chapter 1.
13. Charles M. Hardin, *Presidential Power and Accountability: Toward a New Constitution* (Chicago: Univ. of Chicago Press, 1974), Chapter 3.
14. Charles M. Hardin, "The President and Constitutional Reform," in Thomas

E. Cronin and Rexford G. Tugwell, eds., *The Presidency Reappraised*, 2nd ed. (New York: Praeger, 1977), 286.

15. James David Barber, "Analyzing Presidents . . . " *Washington Monthly* (November 1969); cf. *The Presidential Character* (Englewood Cliffs, N. J.: Prentice-Hall, 1972).

16. Reedy, *Twilight of the Presidency*, Chapters 1 and 2.

17. Samuel H. Beer, "The British Political System," in Samuel H. Beer and Adam B. Ulam, eds., *Patterns of Government* (New York: Random House, 1973), 211.

18. Jennings, *British Constitution*, 78.

19. E. S. Corwin, *The President: Office and Powers*, 4th ed. (New York: New York Univ. Press, 1957), 30.

20. Richard Neustadt, *Presidential Power* (New York: Wiley, 1959), Chapter 5.

21. Walter Dean Burnham, *New Republic*, 24 March 1980.

22. Stanley Hoffmann reported that Europeans (not only Russians) had "been watching the American political scene with increasing bewilderment. The cascade of interrupted or failed presidencies, the rivalries within the foreign policy making process in the executive branch, the revolt and frequently destructive interventions of Congress, the dismal spectacle of the presidential campaigns, the apparent mediocrity of presidential personnel, the broad swings of public opinion, have been deplored, but neither perceptively analyzed nor understood." "The Crisis in the West," *New York Review of Books*, 17 July 1980, 41.

23. How bad is the need was recently suggested by Robert E. Osgood who, after listing "notable Western weaknesses," concluded: "and, most markedly in the United States, the fragmentation of political power and the policymaking process as the cold war consensus ceases to provide the integrating framework of a coherent foreign policy under presidential authority." *Limited War Revisited* (Boulder, Colo.: Westview, 1979), 95–96.

24. The "Special Interest State" was borrowed from Elizabeth Drew, "A Reporter at Large: Phase: Engagement with the Special Interest State," *New Yorker*, 27 Feb. 1978.

25. Theodore Lowi, *The End of Liberalism* (New York: Norton, 1969, 1979).

26. A. F. Bentley, *The Process of Government* (Chicago: Univ. of Chicago Press, 1908), 211 (passim).

27. Hardin, *Toward a New Constitution*, Chapters 4–6.

28. Don K. Price, "Irresponsibility as an Article of Faith," in Harlan Cleveland and Harold D. Lasswell, eds., *Ethics and Bigness* (New York: Harper and Brothers, 1962).

29. Lester C. Thurow, *The Zero-Sum Society: Distribution and the Possibilities for Economic Change* (New York: Basic Books, 1980).

Chapter 2

1. Robert D. Hershey, "Britain Being Prodded to Waken From a Long Economic Slumber," *New York Times*, 8 June 1980.

2. Samuel H. Beer, "The British Political System," in Samuel H. Beer and Adam B. Ulam, eds., *Patterns of Government*, 3d ed. (New York: Random House, 1973), 123. (Hereafter the 1962 and 1973 editions are Beer, *Patterns*.)

3. Ibid., 123.

4. Hugh Heclo and Aaron Wildavsky, *The Private Government of Public Money* (Berkeley: Univ. of California Press, 1974), 30.

5. Ibid.

6. Samuel E. Finer, *The Changing British Party System, 1945-1979* (Washington, D.C.: AEI, 1980), 18-19.

7. Beer, *Patterns* (1973), 233. TUC means Trade Union Conference.

8. Finer, *British Party System*, 143. During these same years unionization in the United States declined from 25 to 20 percent of the work force. A. H. Raskin, *New Yorker*, 25 August 1980, 37.

9. Finer, *British Party System*, 146.

10. "Labour's Dilemma," *Center Magazine*, Nov./Dec. 1975.

11. Finer, *British Party System*, 146.

12. Beer, *Patterns* (1973), 283.

13. Ibid., Chapter 2.

14. Beer, *Patterns* (1962), 208.

15. Ibid., 208, 213, passim.

16. Finer, *British Party System*, n. 5, 190-191.

17. Ibid., 192-93.

18. Ibid., 122-27.

19. Ibid., 134-35.

20. Ibid., 18-19.

21. Ibid., 124.

22. Ibid., 70.

23. Ibid., 225-26.

24. Ibid., 226.

25. Ibid., 230-31.

26. Lindsay Rogers, *The Pollsters* (New York: Knopf, 1949), Chapter 18; William D. Leuchtenberg, *Franklin D. Roosevelt and the New Deal* (New York: Harper and Row, 1963), 220-30; Alexander De Conde, *A History of American Foreign Policy* (New York: Scribners, 1963), 572.

27. Sir Kenneth Clark, *The Other Half* (New York: Harper and Row, 1977), 19, 31, 36.

28. Finer, *British Party System*, 27.

29. David S. Broder, "Dull Presidential Campaign Overshadows Spirited Contests," *Sacramento Bee*, 13 Oct. 1980.

30. Finer, *British Party System*, 210-11.

31. W. Ivor Jennings, *The British Constitution* (Cambridge, England: Univ. Press, 1942), 213.

32. Ibid., 63. For a discussion of the degree to which group politics and the exigencies of presidential electoral campaigns have disintegrated the one office that Hamilton thought in *Federalist* No. 70 would provide the needed "unity" in the system, see Elizabeth Drew, *New Yorker*, 20 Oct. 1980.

33. Jennings, *British Constitution*, 63.

34. Finer, *British Party System*, 230.

35. Jennings, *British Constitution*, 214.

36. Ibid., 78.

37. Finer, *British Party System*, 229.

38. Jennings, *British Constitution*, 19, 28-29, 60, 63, 78, and Chapter 9.

39. Charles M. Hardin, *Presidential Power and Accountability* (Chicago: Univ. of Chicago Press, 1974), 166-69. See also Beer, *Patterns* (1973), 301-2. Finer held

that the view that the winning party has a right to carry out its manifesto because the voters have mandated it is "entirely fallacious," *British Party System*, 125.

40. Finer, *British Party System*, 203–4.

41. Ibid., 190.

42. Austin Ranney, "Toward a More Responsible Two-Party System," *APSR*, June 1951.

43. Beer, *Patterns* (1962), 210. A different view of this complex problem is in John Logue, "The Welfare State," *Daedalus* (Fall 1979).

44. Except in Scandinavia. Logue, "Welfare State," n. 42.

45. Jennings, *British Constitution*, 35, 43, 47–50.

46. Beer, *Patterns* (1973), 280.

47. Ibid., 167, 192, 219ff.

48. Leonard Silk, *New York Times*, 11 Nov. 1977; Richard F. Janssen, *Wall Street Journal*, 10 Nov. 1977.

49. Allan L. Otten, *Wall Street Journal*, 1 Oct. 1980.

50. Finer, *British Party System*, 51.

51. Beer, *Patterns* (1973), 186–87, citing Lloyd Ullman and Richard Caves.

52. Dahrendorf, *Wall Street Journal*, 18 Aug. 1977.

53. Connor Cruise O'Brien, review of *The End of Ideology Debate*, by Chaim I. Waxman, *New York Times Book Review*, 16 Feb. 1969.

54. Edward C. Banfield, *Political Influence* (New York: Macmillan, Free Press, 1961), 331–35.

55. R. G. Collingwood, *The New Leviathan* (Oxford, England: Oxford Univ. Press, 1942), 95.

56. Cf. for example, T. W. Schultz, ed., *Distortions of Agricultural Incentives* (Bloomington: Univ. of Indiana Press, 1978).

Chapter 3

1. C. Douglas Dillon, "Remarks by Douglas Dillon" (The Fletcher School of Law and Diplomacy, Tufts University, 30 May 1982).

2. Lloyd N. Cutler, "To Form a Government," *Foreign Affairs* (Fall 1980).

3. Samuel H. Beer, *Britain Against Itself: The Political Contradictions of Collectivism* (New York: Norton, 1982).

4. Samuel H. Beer and Adam B. Ulam, eds., *Patterns of Government*, 3d ed. (New York: Random House, 1973), Chapter 3.

5. Samuel H. Beer, *British Politics in the Collectivist Age*, Vantage Random House edition (New York: Knopf, 1969), 80.

6. W. Ivor Jennings, *The British Constitution* (Cambridge, England: Cambridge Univ. Press, 1942), 35.

7. Beer, *British Politics*, 92.

8. Beer, *Britain Against Itself*, 210.

9. Ibid., Chapters 1, 2, 3.

10. Ibid., 180–84.

11. Ibid., 192–94.

12. Ibid., Part 3. Beer describes and analyzes the new populism in this part.

13. Ibid., 160.

14. Review of *Battle for the Labour Party*, by Kogan and Kogan, *Economist*, 6 March 1982.

15. Beer, *Britain Against Itself*, 5.
16. Beer, *Patterns*, 2d ed. (1962), 208.
17. Beer, *Britain Against Itself*, 37–40.
18. Ibid., 40.
19. Ibid., 45.
20. Ibid.
21. Ibid., 41–42.
22. Ibid., 55, 56–57, 84–90, 93–94.
23. Ibid., 228.
24. Allen Potter, "Great Britain: Opposition with a Capital 'O,' " in Robert Dahl, ed., *Political Opposition in Western Democracies* (New Haven: Yale Univ. Press, 1966), 13.
25. Jennings, *British Constitution*, 215.
26. Beer quoting from the *Economist*, 21 March 1981.
27. Beer, *Britain Against Itself*, 214–18. Beer also cites the unprecedented (and "un-British") riots that burst out in 1981, partly protesting unemployment, partly perhaps arising out of racial tensions, but most ominously appearing to manifest a revolt against the police, and, indeed, against ordered society.
28. Ibid., 210–20.
29. Ibid., 108–9, 212–13.
30. Ibid., 213.
31. Ibid., 213–20.
32. Ibid., 209.
33. "The Idea of the Nation," *New Republic*, 19/26 July 1982.
34. Benjamin R. Barber, "The World We Have Lost," review of *After Virtue: A Study in Moral Theory*, by Alastair MacIntyre, *New Republic*, 13 Sept. 1982, 29.
35. Jennings, *British Constitution*, 78.
36. Jack N. Rakove, "The Moral Militia," review of *The Glorious Cause: The American Revolution, 1763–1789*, by Robert Middlekauf, *New Republic*, 25 Oct. 1982, 39.

Chapter 4

1. "The Workbook for Constitutional System Review," Donald Robinson, prep. and ed. (Committee on the Constitutional System [CCS], Suite 410, Massachusetts Ave., N.W., Washington, D.C. 20036, Feb. 1984) [references in this chapter are to this unpublished manuscript]. See also Donald L. Robinson, ed., *Reforming American Government: The Bicentennial Papers of the Committee on the Constitutional System* (Boulder, Colo.: Westview Press, 1985).
2. Charles H. McIlwain, *Constitutionalism: Ancient and Modern* (1940; reprint, Ithaca, N.Y.: Cornell Univ. Press, 1958).
3. Ibid., 139.
4. Ibid.
5. Ibid., 141–42.
6. 97th Cong., 2d sess., two parts, 1982.
7. *New Republic*, 18 June 1984.
8. James MacGregor Burns, *The Vineyard of Liberty* (New York: Knopf, 1982), 598.
9. Joseph Schumpeter, *Capitalism, Socialism, and Democracy* (1942; reprint, New York: Harper and Row, 1947), 269.

10. Max Farrand, ed., *The Records of the Federal Convention of 1787*, vol. 1, rev. ed. (New Haven, Conn.: Yale Univ. Press, 1937), 48–49, 59.

11. Ibid., vol. 2, 88–93.

12. Ibid., 631–33.

13. Ibid., vol. 1, 20, 224–25, 242; vol. 2, 134, 137, 177, 193, 256.

14. Ibid., vol. 2, 465.

15. The source of the debates in the state ratifying conventions is Jonathan Elliot, *Debates*, 5 vols. (New York: Burt Franklin, 1965). For the Henry-Randolph exchange, see Elliot, *Debates*, vol. 3, Virginia, 22–23, 27–28, 36–37, 42ff. Rufus King, a member of the Philadelphia Convention, discussed the preamble briefly in the Massachusetts Convention. Elliot, *Debates*, vol. 2, 55. There was a spirited debate in the North Carolina Convention—23 July 1788, after eleven states had ratified the Constitution and it was in force, Elliot, *Debates*, vol. 4, 9–25.

16. McIlwain, *Constitutionalism*, 57, passim.

17. Arthur E. Sutherland, *Constitutionalism in America* (New York: Blaisdell Pub. Co., 1965), 198.

18. James MacGregor Burns, *The Power to Lead* (New York: Simon and Schuster, 1984), 104–5.

19. *Marbury v. Madison*, 1 Cranch 127 (1803); *Martin v. Hunter's Lessee*, 1 Wheat. 304 (1816); *McCulloch v. Maryland*, 4 Wheat. 316 (1819).

20. Forrest MacDonald, *We the People* (Chicago: Univ. of Chicago Press, 1958).

21. Ibid., 255.

22. Charles M. Hardin, *Presidential Power and Accountability* (Chicago: Univ. of Chicago Press, 1974). The quotation is from Richard Rovere and Arthur M. Schlesinger, Jr., *The General and the President* (New York: Farrar, Straus, and Young, 1951).

23. Ibid., 246.

24. Barnard Gwertzman, *New York Times*, 14 May 1984.

25. Steven J. Roberts, *New York Times*, 7 June 1984.

26. Arthur M. Schlesinger, Jr., *Political Economy and Constitutional Reform*, cited in n. 3, pt. 1, 228. See also the *Workbook*, cited in n. 1.

27. Farrand, *Convention of 1787*, vol. 1, 215.

28. B. F. Wright, Jr., "The *Federalist* on the Nature of Political Man," *Ethics* (Jan. 1949), Part 2.

29. Hardin, *Power and Accountability*, 148–52.

30. Schumpeter, *Capitalism, Socialism, and Democracy*, 260–61.

31. Burns, *Power to Lead*, 123.

32. *Workbook*, 368.

33. E. E. Schattschneider, *Party Government* (New York: Rinehart, 1942); Pendleton Herring, *The Politics of Democracy* (New York: Rinehart, 1940).

34. A. D. Lindsay, *The Modern Democratic State* (New York: Oxford Univ. Press, 1943).

35. Farrand, *Convention of 1787*, vol. 1, 421–22.

36. Kurt Riezler, "Political Decisions in Modern Society," *Ethics* 2 (Jan. 1954).

37. Burns, *Vineyard of Liberty*, 47.

Chapter 5

1. For a brief elaboration of McIlwain's views, see Chapter 4 above, "Thoughts on the Program of the Committee on the Constitutional System." See also Chapter 6 above, "The Constitution: That Delicate Balance Neglects the Separation of Powers,"—subsections "Charles H. McIlwain: *Jursdictio and Gubernaculum*" and "McIlwain's Attack on the Separation of Powers."

2. Richard E. Neustadt, "Politicians and Bureaucrats," David B. Truman, ed., in *The Congress and America's Future*, an American Assembly Book (Englewood Cliffs, N.J.: Prentice-Hall, 1965), 2.

3. Ibid., 113.

4. Ibid., 105.

5. Ibid., 119.

6. Ibid., 107, 117.

7. *Federalist* No. 10.

8. Charles M. Hardin, "The Tobacco Program: Exception or Portent?" *Journal of Farm Economics* (Autumn 1946).

9. References to farm price policy are based on Charles M. Hardin, *Food and Fiber in the Nation's Politics*, vol. 3, Technical Papers, National Advisory Commission on Food and Fiber, USGPO, August 1967. See especially 9–15, and 129–33. See also Charles M. Hardin, "Agricultural Price Policy: The Political Role of Bureaucracy," in Don F. Hadwiger, William P. Browne, and Richard Fraenkel, eds., "Symposium on Agricultural Policy," *Policy Studies* (Summer 1978).

10. Lest this seem to be ancient history, consider the continuity since the 1960s as expressed in Jeffrey Zaslow, "Life on the Land: Farm Recession Spurs Radical Restructuring of Agriculture in U.S."

"The sweeping changes of the 1980s have their roots, to a large extent, in events of the 1970s. Farmers went on a binge of equipment and land buying and piled up a mountain of debt, equal to nearly one-quarter the amount of all developing-nation debt. They were making a bet: that the value of their land and their crops would continue rising." *Wall Street Journal*, 9 Nov. 1984.

11. Charles M. Hardin, *Presidential Power and Accountability* (Chicago: Univ. of Chicago Press, 1974), 113. Chapter 4 set forth "The Problem of Bureaucracy," Chapter 5 examined the nature of the military bureaucracy and Chapter 6 probed its influence.

12. Theodore H. White, "Weinberger on the Ramparts," *New York Times Magazine*, 6 Feb. 1983.

13. Robert Scheer, *Los Angeles Times*,—see "McNamara Says U. S. Scared Soviets into Nuclear Arms Race," *Sacramento Bee*, 9 April 1982.

14. R. G. Collingwood, *The New Leviathan* (1942; reprint, Oxford: Oxford Univ. Press, 1947), 88–89.

15. Norman Malia, *New York Review of Books*, 29 Sept. 1983, 20.

16. Sam Bass, *Unlikely Heroes* (New York: Simon and Schuster, 1983). See also Anthony Lewis on the Sullivan decision in the *New Yorker*, 5 Nov. 1984.

17. Barbara Tuchman, *The March of Folly* (New York: Knopf, 1983).

Chapter 6

1. Fred W. Friendly and Martha J. H. Elliot, *The Constitution: That Delicate Balance* (New York: Random House, 1984), ix.

2. Ibid., vii, 281.

3. Ibid., ix.

4. Ibid., 277.

5. Ibid., 281.

6. Ibid., 1.

7. Ibid., 53.

8. Charles H. McIlwain, *Constitutionalism: Ancient and Modern* (1940; reprint, Ithaca, N.Y.: Cornell Univ. Press, 1958).

9. Ibid., 136.

10. Ibid.

11. Ibid., 137.

12. Ibid., 139.

13. Ibid. (italics added).

14. Ibid., 140.

15. Ibid., 141–42.

16. Ibid., 142.

17. Ibid., 142–43.

18. Ibid., 143.

19. Kenneth N. Waltz, review of *Our Own Worst Enemy*, by I. M. Destler, Leslie H. Gelb, and Anthony Lake, *New York Times Book Review*, 9 Sept. 1984.

20. For an elaboration of the argument using examples from agriculture, see Chapter 5, "Constitutionalism and Bureaucracy"—especially the subheading "Agricultural Price-Support, Production Control Policy."

21. Robert Manning, review of *The Right Hand of Power*, by U. Alexis Johnson, with Jef Olivarus McAllister, *New York Times Book Review*, 23 Sept. 1984.

22. Philip Geyelin, *Washington Post*, *Sacramento Bee*, 5 Dec. 1984.

23. *New York Times*, 3 March 1985.

24. Theodore H. White, "Weinberger on the Ramparts," *New York Times Magazine*, 6 Feb. 1983.

25. Strobe Talbott, *Deadly Gambits* (New York: Knopf, 1984), 206.

26. Theodore C. Sorenson, *Kennedy* (New York: Harper and Row, 1965), 3.

Chapter 7

1. Don K. Price, *America's Unwritten Constitution: Science, Religion, and Political Responsibility* (Baton Rouge: Louisiana State Univ. Press, 1983).

2. Ibid., 14.

3. Ibid., 135.

4. Ibid., 134.

5. Bernard Crick, *The Reform of Parliament* (New York: Doubleday/Anchor, 1965), 216.

6. Price, *America's Unwritten Constitution*, 134.

7. Ibid., 135.

8. Ibid., 136.

9. Ibid., 138, 139.

10. Ibid., 139.

11. Ibid., 140.
12. Ibid.
13. Ibid., 141.
14. Ibid., 140.
15. Ibid., 142.
16. Ibid.
17. Ibid., 143.
18. Ibid., 139, 144, and previously quoted material.
19. Ibid., 144.
20. Ibid.
21. Ibid., 145.
22. Ibid.
23. Ibid., 142.
24. Ibid., 132.
25. Ibid., 78, 80, 81, 87–88, 93, 94, 95, 170, 177. Price has made many derogatory references to the phenomenon.
26. Charles H. McIlwain, *Constitutionalism: Ancient and Modern* (1940; reprint, Ithaca, N.Y.: Cornell Univ. Press, 1958).
27. Ibid., 141–43.
28. Price, *America's Unwritten Constitution*, 132.
29. Richard E. Neustadt, "Politicians and Bureaucrats," in David B. Truman, ed., *The Congress and America's Future*, an American Assembly Book (Englewood Cliffs, N.J.: Prentice-Hall, 1965).
30. Price, *America's Unwritten Constitution*, 149.
31. Ibid., 133.
32. Ibid., 145.
33. Ibid., 23–24.
34. Ibid., 24, 144.
35. Samuel H. Beer, *Britain Against Itself: The Political Contradictions of Collectivism* (New York: Norton, 1982), 184; Beer cited Leon Epstein, *Political Parties in Western Democracies* (New York: Praeger, 1967), 167. See also Epstein, Chapter 1 for the party label and Chapter 8 for candidate selection.
36. Beer, *Britain Against Itself*, 185.
37. W. Ivor Jennings, *Party Politics*, vol. 1 of *Appeal to the People* (Cambridge, England: Cambridge Univ. Press, 1960), 111.
38. Ibid., 78.
39. James Q. Wilson, *American Government* (Lexington, Mass.: Heath, 1980), 610.
40. Price, *America's Unwritten Constitution*, 139.
41. David P. Calleo, review of *A Grand Strategy for the West*, by Helmut Schmidt, *New York Times Book Review*, 1 Dec. 1985.
42. Price, *America's Unwritten Constitution*, 139.
43. McIlwain, *Constitutionalism*, 143.
44. Ibid., 142–43.
45. Price, *America's Unwritten Constitution*, 141.
46. Ibid., 142.
47. Ibid., 1.
48. Ibid., 2–3.
49. Ibid., 72; Price quotes from Robert Green McClosskey, ed., *Works of James Wilson*, vol.1 (Cambridge, Mass.: Harvard Univ. Press, 1967), 77–81.
50. Price, *America's Unwritten Constitution*, 130.

Chapter 8

1. *Representative Mike Synar, et al. v. United States* 626 F. Supp. 1374 (7 Feb. 1986). Judge Antonin Scalia, later appointed a justice of the Supreme Court, wrote the decision according to Lincoln Caplan, *The Tenth Justice: The Solicitor General and the Rule of Law* (New York: Knopf, 1987), 247. References are also made to the *Congressional Quarterly*, 14 Dec. 1986, 2604ff.

Justice Scalia (Circuit Judge of the U. S. Court of Appeals), Justice Johnson, and Justice Gasch (respectively, District Judge and Senior District Judge of the U.S. District Court for the District of Columbia) participated in the decision.

The Supreme Court's majority echoed the three-judge court in *Bowsher v. Synar*, 106 S. S.Ct. 3181 (7 July 1986). Writing for the majority, Chief Justice Burger wrote: "To permit an officer controlled by Congress to execute the law would be, in essence, to permit a Congressional veto. By placing the responsibility for the execution of [the law] in the hands of an officer who is subject to removal only by itself, Congress in effect has retained control over the execution of the Act and has intruded into the executive function. The Constitution does not permit such an intrusion." Justices Brennan, Rehnquist, Powell, and O'Connor concurred. Justices Stevens and Marshal reached a similar conclusion but on different grounds. They discerned an unconstitutional delegation of power: Congress could not properly permit "a congressional agent to set policy that binds the nation." Burger, however, explicitly rejected the plaintiff's argument that the act was flawed because of an unconstitutional delegation of power.

Justices White and Blackmun dissented separately. White wrote that the majority had employed a "distressingly formalistic view of the separation of powers" to strike down "one of the most novel and far reaching responses to a national crisis since the New Deal." The unused provision of the 1921 Budget and Accounting Act that permitted Congress to discharge the comptroller general should be regarded as a triviality.

2. *Synar v. United States*, 626 F. Supp., 25.
3. Ibid., 48, 49.
4. Ibid., 48.
5. Ibid., 33.
6. Ibid., 13.
7. Ibid., 46.
8. Ibid., 43–44.
9. Ibid., 18.
10. Frederick C. Mosher, *The GAO: The Quest for Accountability in the American Government* (Boulder, Colo.: Westview, 1979).
11. *United States ex rel. Brookfield Construction Co., Inc. v. Stewart*, 234 F. Supp. 94 (D.D.C.) *affirmed* 119 App. Ct. D.C. (1964). This case is among those cited by the *Synar* decision as exceptions to the position that the GAO is an agency of the legislative branch, n. 29.
12. Mosher, *The GAO*, 243.
13. Ibid., 334–35.
14. Ibid., 345.
15. *Synar v. United States*, 626 F. Supp., 49–50.
16. Ibid., 40.
17. Mosher, The GAO, 361–62.
18. Ibid., 338–39, 361–63.

19. *Synar v. United States*, 626 F. Supp., 44.

20. Ibid., 46, 49–50.

21. McIlwain, *Constitutionalism*, 143.

22. Ibid.

Chapter 9

1. Strobe Talbott, *Deadly Gambits* (New York: Knopf, 1984), xi.

2. This paper was prompted by Talbott's book that seemed to provide abundant evidence for a considerably expanded application of the theory of the "triangles" heretofore used chiefly to illuminate pork barrel politics. I first developed a detailed interpretation of Talbott's book. Some long-suffering colleagues suggested that I should provide an introductory framework, including the theory that I was using and an adumbration of the findings. So they will have to share some of the onus for the existence of this effort if not for its contents.

3. Talbott, *Deadly Gambits*, 22.

4. Leslie H. Gelb, "U.S. Will Hold out for a Soviet Shift in Talks on Arms," *New York Times*, 2 June 1985.

5. Talbott, *Deadly Gambits*, 16.

6. Charles H. McIlwain, *Constitutionalism: Ancient and Modern* (1940; reprint, Ithaca, N.Y.: Cornell Univ. Press, 1958). See also Charles M. Hardin, "The Separation of Powers Needs Major Revision," in Robert Goldwin and Art Kaufman, eds., *Separation of Powers—Does It Still Work?* (Washington, D.C.: American Enterprise Institute, 1987); Hardin, "Constitutionalism and Bureaucracy: A Comment on Herman Belz's Article," in *News for Teachers of Political Science* (Autumn 1985); Chapter 6 above.

7. Richard E. Neustadt, "Politicians and Bureaucrats," in David B. Truman, ed., *The Congress and America's Future*, an American Assembly Book (Englewood Cliffs, N.J.: Prentice-Hall, 1965).

8. I anticipated the triangle theory in "The Tobacco Program: Exception or Portent?" *Journal of Farm Economics* (Autumn 1946) and in *The Politics of Agriculture* (Chicago: Free Press, 1952). I employed the theory explicitly in *Food and Fiber in the Nation's Politics*, vol. 3, Technical Papers, National Advisory Commission on Food and Fiber, USGPO, August 1967.

9. Arthur Maass, *Muddy Waters* (Cambridge, Mass.: Harvard Univ. Press, 1951); id., *Congress and the Common Good* (New York: Basic Books, 1984).

10. Maass, *Common Good*, 43–44.

11. Ibid., 34.

12. Karen Elliott House, "Selling of a Dam: Tie Between Congress, Engineers Corps Leads to Dubious Projects," *Wall Street Journal*, 17 July 1977; Grace Lichtenstein, "West's Water Fight Intensifies as Carter Plans Project Cuts," *New York Times*, 7 March 1977. Related discussions: Dorothy Gallagher, "The Collapse of the Great Teton Dam," *New York Times Magazine*, 19 Sept. 1976; Benjamin Zycher, "An Item Veto Won't Work," *Wall Street Journal*, 24 Oct. 1984.

13. Maass, *Common Good*, 5–6.

14. Ibid., 11, 26.

15. Ibid., 25, 44.

16. Ibid., 42.

17. Walter Dean Burnham, "A Continuing Political Gridlock," *Wall Street Journal*, 24 June 1985.

18. Hugh Heclo, "Issue Networks and the Executive Establishment," in Anthony King, ed., *The New American Political System*, (Washington, D.C.: American Enterprise Institute, 1978), 88.

19. Louis Fisher, *President and Congress* (New York: Free Press-Macmillan, 1972), 180.

20. Heclo, "Issue Networks," 102–5.

21. Quotations are from Richard F. Fenno, Jr., "U.S. House Members in Their Constituencies," *APSR* 71, no. 3 (Sept. 1977): 886, 914.

22. Talbott, *Deadly Gambits*, 3.

23. Philip Taubman, "The Schultz-Weinberger Feud," *New York Times Magazine*, 14 April 1985.

24. Talbott, *Deadly Gambits*, 17.

25. Ibid.

26. Ibid., 16, 236.

27. Ibid., 16, 218, 219.

28. Charles G. Dawes, quoted in Richard E. Neustadt, *Presidential Power* (New York: Wiley, 1960), 39.

29. John Newhouse, "The Diplomatic Round (Europe and Star Wars)," *New Yorker*, 22 July 1985.

30. Talbott, *Deadly Gambits*, 45–46.

31. Ibid., 209.

32. Ibid., 75–76.

Chapter 10

1. James Q. Wilson, "Does the Separation of Power Still Work?" *The Public Interest* (Winter 1987).

2. Ibid.; Lloyd N. Cutler, "To Form a Government," *Foreign Affairs* (Fall 1980).

3. Charles M. Hardin, "The Separation of Powers Needs Major Revision," in Robert Goldwin and Art Kaufman, eds., *Separation of Powers—Does It Still Work?* (Washington, D.C.: American Enterprise Institute, 1987).

Professor Wilson's article in the Goldwin-Kaufman volume also neglects McIlwain's thesis. Rather, Wilson examines popular and legislative voting behavior in the United States to find that the tendency to divide along party lines is too weak and variable to validate the arguments of constitutional reformers who virtually unanimously propose to strengthen party government (assuming considerable party discipline). Wilson ignores the influence that institutional changes might have on the voting behavior of both individuals and legislators. Thus Professor Frank E. Wilson discerned a tendency following the adoption of the Fifth Republic and the direct election of the president in France for parties and voters' behavior to change, so that what emerged was something more resembling the "British model of responsible governmental parties and . . . linkage between people and government." Vincent E. McHale and Sharon Showanski, eds., *Political Parties of Europe* (Westport, Conn.: Greenwood, 1983), 242–43.

In West Germany during the 1950s the new electoral law and the adoption of the constructive vote of confidence quickly and sharply reduced the number of parties that had at first proliferated as they had in Weimar Germany. Consider also the radical change in the organization and discipline of British political parties following extensions of the suffrage, particularly in 1867, and the emergence of the institutions of cabinet government described by Bagehot. In the United States, despite its fabled heterogeneity, only two political parties repeatedly duopolize the presidential vote—because the presidency looms large as a single prize that can be seriously contested only between two parties.

4. See Hardin, *Presidential Power and Accountability* (Chicago: Univ. of Chicago Press, 1974) and this book.

5. Theodore Lowi, *The End of Liberalism* (New York: Norton, 1969), 48, 55.

6. Grant McConnell, *Private Power and American Democracy* (New York: Knopf, 1966), 361, 363.

7. Richard E. Neustadt, "Politicians and Bureaucrats," in David B. Truman, ed., *The Congress and America's Future*, an American Assembly Book (Englewood Cliffs, N.J.: Prentice-Hall, 1965).

8. Max Farrand, ed., *The Records of the Federal Convention of 1787*, vol.1, (New Haven, Conn.: Yale Univ. Press, 1937), 465.

9. Ibid., vol. 2, 388; Madison had also urged providing in the Constitution for the proper training of the militia; left to themselves, he said, the States would ignore this as they had ignored the confederation's request for money, vol. 2, 386–87.

10. Ibid., vol. 2, 616–17. Gouverneur Morris opposed the motion as setting a dishonorable mark of distinction on the military classes of citizens. Nine states voted Nay; only Virginia and Georgia voted Aye. However, Mason's proposal was poignantly echoed in the second amendment to the Constitution, part of the bill of rights proposed by Congress on September 25, 1779, with ratification completed on December 15, 1791, that declares: "A well regulated Militia being necessary to the security of a free State, the right of the people to keep and bear Arms shall not be infringed."

11. Alfred Vagts, *History of Militarism* (New York: Norton, 1937).

12. For General McClellan, see Bruce Catton, *Mr. Lincoln's Army* (Garden City, N.Y.: Doubleday, 1951), 86–121, passim—I am indebted to Austin Ranney for this reference. For General Joe Hooker, see Carl Sandburg, *Abraham Lincoln, the Prairie Years and the War Years* (London: Cape, 1955), 356–57—I am indebted to Robert Hackney for this reference.

13. Joseph P. Nye, Jr., *New York Times Book Review*, 28 Sept. 1986.

14. Deborah Blum, "Scientists March to a Military Beat," *Sacramento Bee*, 12 July 1987.

15. Tim Carrington, *Wall Street Journal*, 28 May 1987.

16. Naomi S. Travers, *Wall Street Journal*, 3 June 1987.

17. *Sacramento Bee*, 22 Nov. 1985.

18. Theodore Draper, "American Hubris: From Truman to the Persian Gulf," *New York Book Review*, 16 July 1987.

19. Richard Halloran, *New York Times*, 24 June 1983.

20. James LeMoyne, *New York Times*, 19 April 1987.

21. Garry Wills, "The CIA From Beginning to End," *New York Review of Books* 27 Jan. 1976; Theodore Draper, Reagan's Junta, *New York Review of Books*, 29 Jan. 1987.

22. Draper, "Reagan's Junta," 5.

23. James Bamford, "Carlucci and the N.S.C.," *New York Times Magazine*, 18 Jan. 1987.

24. Draper, "Reagan's Junta," 10. See also Bamford, "Carlucci."

25. L. Gordon Crovitz, "Boland Laws May Be the Real 'Crime,'" *Wall Street Journal*, 4 June 1987.

26. *United States v. Curtiss Wright Export Corporation*, 299 U.S. 304 (1936).

27. E. S. Corwin, *The Constitution of the United States of America*, 82d Cong., 2d sess., Senate Doc. no. 170, 1952, 380. Compare Alton Frye, "North's Abuse of Precedents," *Wall Street Journal*, 24 July 1987.

28. Wills, *CIA*, 33.

29. *Sacramento Bee*, 16 May 1987.

30. Elizabeth Drew, "Letter from Washington," *New Yorker*, 22 June 1987, 76.

31. David Rogers, "North, Fascinated with War in Angola, Hoped Network Could Grow Beyond Iran-Contra Effort," *Wall Street Journal*, 11 June 1987. My attention was called to this remarkable article by Martin Smith, Political Editor, *Sacramento Bee*, whose column, "North's Military Junta," 16 June 1987, is a trenchant statement of the problem.

32. Karen Elliott House, Foreign Editor, "Gulf Risk's More Geopolitical than Military," *Wall Street Journal*, 25 June 1987.

33. Arthur Schlesinger, Jr., "Britain's Stiff-Upper-Lip Scandal," *Wall Street Journal*, 11 May 1987; *Manchester Guardian Weekly*, 3 May 1987, also stressed the contrast between the British treatment of the Wright allegations and the United States treatment of the Iran-Contra affair.

34. Sir James Callaghan, "Too Secret a Service," *Economist*, 9 May 1987.

Chapter 12

1. The Joint Economic Committee, 97th Cong., 2d sess., *Hearings on Political Economy and Constitutional Reform*, pt. 1, 16 (Cutler); 191 (Dillon); 221 (Fulbright); ix (Reuss).

2. Donald L. Robinson, ed., *Reforming American Government* (Boulder, Colo.: Westview, 1985); *Constitutional Reform and Effective Government* (Washington, D.C.: Brookings, 1985); *A Bicentennial Analysis of the American Political Structure: Report and Recommendations of the Committee on the Constitutional System* (Washington, D.C.: 1986). This essay grew out of my review of Sundquist's excellent book *Constitutional Reform and Effective Government*, in which I dissented from his advocacy of incrementalism, in favor of a comprehensive approach that would require a number of interrelated steps taken simultaneously or almost so. *American Political Science Review* (December 1986).

3. The constituent group comprises people ("not too few" and "in and out of government") who know a good deal about the Constitution and how it works. This concept is crucial to my argument. See Charles M. Hardin, *Presidential Power and Accountability* (Chicago: Univ. of Chicago Press, 1974), 183 and literature cited.

4. I sent my review of Sundquist to a number of prominent political scientists with a letter asking their response to the wisdom and timeliness of incorporating a serious discussion of constitutional alternatives in the political science curriculum. All twenty-eight respondents were strongly affirmative.

5. *Federalist* No. 51.

6. *Federalist* No. 47.

7. Frederick C. Mosher, letter to the author, 20 August 1986.

8. Fred W. Friendly and Martha J. H. Elliott, *The Constitution: That Deli-*

cate Balance (New York: Random House, 1984), 281; see Chapter 6 above.

9. Don K. Price, *America's Unwritten Constitution* (Baton Rouge: Louisiana State Univ. Press, 1983), 14; see Chapter 7 above.

10. Walter Lippmann, *Chicago Sun Times*, 14 Aug. 1958.

11. See Hardin, *Presidential Power and Accountability*, Chapters 3–5; Hardin, "The Separation of Powers Needs Major Revision," in Robert A. Goldwin and Art Kaufman, ed., *Separation of Powers—Does It Still Work?* (Washington, D.C.: American Enterprise Institute, 1986); Hardin, "Constitutionalism and Bureaucracy," *APSA News* (Summer 1985); Chapter 9 above; Richard E. Neustadt's seminal article, "Politicians and Bureaucrats," in David B. Truman, ed., *The Congress and America's Future*, an American Assembly Book (Englewood Cliffs, N. J.: Prentice-Hall, 1965). For Lowi's statement, see *The End of Liberalism* (New York: Norton, 1969), 112; McConnell, *Private Power and American Democracy* (New York: Knopf, 1966), esp. Chapter 7.

12. Michael Barone and Grant Ujifusa, *The Almanac of American Politics 1986* (Washington, D.C.: National Journal, 1986), 341.

13. See Joseph S. Nye, Jr., review of *The Defense Game*, by R. A. Stubbing and R. A. Mendell, *New York Times Book Review*, 28 Sept. 1986.

14. Arthur Maass, *Congress and the Common Good* (New York: Basic Books, 1984); Hardin, "Problems of the American Separation of Powers"; Hugh Heclo, *A Government of Strangers* (Washington, D.C.: Brookings, 1977), discusses iron triangles, e.g., 166–67, 224–25, reminding readers that individuals in the bureaucracy may strengthen themselves by linking with outsiders ("issues networks"). The analysis becomes more intricate as policies multiply and increase in complexity, spurred in considerable part by the explosion of congressional staffs that were designed to improve congressional grasp of policy and congressional influence within government, but often result in multiplying demands on the members who may then become hostages to their own staffs (information-providers on the rapidly rising number of complicated decisions members must make). The staff members' own career objectives further convolute the process. Michael J. Malbin, *Unelected Representative* (New York: Basic Books, 1980).

15. For elaboration and references, see my comment on Herman Belz's article, *APSA News* (Summer 1985).

16. Ibid.

17. The role of the public is one of the most crucial and controversial; see Hardin, *Presidential Power and Accountability*, Chapter 8 as well as Chapter 4 above.

18. The plebiscitary presidency is discussed at length, albeit with a somewhat different interpretation, in Theodore J. Lowi, *The Personal Presidency* (Ithaca, N.Y.: Cornell Univ. Press, 1985); for Missouri, see Steven V. Roberts, "Politicking Goes High-Tech," *New York Times Magazine*, 2 Nov. 1986.

19. Joseph Schumpeter, *Capitalism, Socialism, and Democracy*, (1942; reprint, New York: Harper and Row, 1950), 269.

20. Charles M. Hardin, "The Separation of Powers Needs Major Revision," in Robert Goldwin and Art Kaufman, eds., *Separation of Powers—Does It Still Work?* (Washington, D.C.: American Enterprise Institute, 1987).

21. Barnard Crick, *The Reform of Parliament* (New York: Doubleday / Anchor, 1965), 216.

22. W. Ivor Jennings, *The British Constitution* (Cambridge, England: Cambridge Univ. Press, 1942), 78.

23. Lindsay Rogers, *The Pollsters* (New York: Knopf, 1949), 89.

24. Roland Young, *This Is Congress* (New York: Knopf, 1943), x.

25. Barone and Ujifusa, *The Almanac of American Politics 1986*, xxxv.

26. The disparity is only partly caused by gerrymandering. In California, prior to the post-1980 reapportionment, the state's congressional delegation was split, Democrats 22, Republicans 21. After reapportionment, even though Republicans had 49.3 percent of the total vote for congressional candidates in 1984 against 48.4 percent for Democrats, twenty-seven Democratic congressmen were elected and only eighteen Republicans. Nevertheless, a cursory perusal of Barone and Ujifusa indicates that even if all votes for Congress were reflected proportionately in the partisan make-up of that body, the Republicans would still have been short. Part of the disparity may reflect the great advantage that incumbents enjoy. Some 90 percent of incumbents who seek reelection are successful. In that the Democrats now hold a considerable majority, inertia may benefit them considerably.

27. Martin P. Wattenberg, *The Decline of American Political Parties* (Cambridge: Harvard Univ. Press, 1984), 22.

28. Milton C. Cummings, *Congressmen and the Electorate* (New York: Free Press, 1966), 46–47.

29. Norman J. Ornstein et al., *Vital Statistics on Congress, 1984-1985* (Washington, D.C.: American Enterprise Institute), table 2.14, 56.

30. Xandra Kayden and Eddie Mahe, *The Party Goes On* (New York: Basic Books, 1985), 165–66.

31. Wattenberg, *The Decline of American Political Parties*, 115.

Index of Names

233

Subject Matter Index